D0207835

CORPORATE SOCIAL RESPONSIBILITY FAILURES IN THE OIL INDUSTRY

Edited by
Charles Woolfson and Matthias Beck

Work, Health and Environment Series
Series Editors: **Charles Levenstein and John Wooding**

Baywood Publishing Company, Inc.
AMITYVILLE, NEW YORK

Baywood Publishing Company, Inc.
26 Austin Avenue
Amityville, NY 11701
(800) 638-7819
E-mail: baywood@baywood.com
Web site: baywood.com

Library of Congress Catalog Number: 2003070850
ISBN: 0-89503-293-7 (cloth)

Library of Congress Cataloging-in-Publication Data

Corporate social responsibility failures in the oil industry / Charles Woolfson and Matthias Beck (editors).
    p. cm. -- (Work, health and environment series)
  Includes bibliographical references and index.
  ISBN 0-89503-293-7 (cloth)
    1. Petroleum industry and trade--Moral and ethical aspects. 2. Petroleum industry and trade--Environmental aspects. 3. Social responsibility of business. I. Woolfson, Charles, 1946- II. Beck, Matthias. III. Series.

  HD9560.5.C59 2004
  338.2'728--dc22

                                       2003070850

Table of Contents

Introduction:
Oil and the Contradictions
of Development

Charles Levenstein and John Wooding

Economists tell us about efficiency and the effective use of scarce resources. They don't tell us much about the common good. But there are minimal conditions that must be preserved in society: we do not ask the market to defend us against anthrax, we do not ask the market to make serious judgments about child labor, we do not even ask the market to make sure that food is safe to eat. As a moment's reflection will reveal, the priorities of society must come first, the efficiency of the market later.

But who has time for a moment of reflection in a market-driven society? We are paralyzed before the magic of the economists, and they are comfortable with their eternal truths. In the absence of a god, we are driven by the imperatives of Pareto optimality. The global flexible economy requires that we relinquish attachment to place and search for the new world, where interstate highways are paved with gold. But, as this volume illustrates, gold—black gold especially—comes at a huge price.

NORMAL ACCIDENTS, NORMAL INJURIES, NORMAL DISEASE

Charles Perrow's work on technological disasters suggests that industrial society developed increasingly complex and hazardous technologies but failed to develop the commensurate social arrangements [1]. Barry Commoner has observed that our social practices with respect to energy—not only technology,

v

but especially materials—are hopelessly inadequate [2]. This is nowhere more true than in that great driver of industrial production in the century that has passed, and in the century that is emerging in the midst of ever-new and ferocious carnage: oil.

Our exploitation of petroleum as a fuel and as a basis for entire petrochemical industries has enormous social, political, economic, and environmental implications: we have built an entire industry on the waste products from petroleum refining—petrochemicals have invaded every aspect of the lives of citizens of the industrial world—and have had perhaps even more dire consequences for citizens of the South. None of this was done with intention: we are simply living with the devastating unintended consequences of the pursuit of profit.

Some observers, such as Barry Castleman, have warned us particularly about the dangers of exporting hazardous materials and processes to developing countries where state regulation is less vigorous than in the North [3]. But we suspect that such warnings are linked to old ideas about imperialism. Capital moves about the world according to rules that are neither national nor patriotic. In the modern world, the normal injuries and diseases of economic development are presumed to be effectively contained in advanced industrial nations, while capital has sought "under-polluted" havens and cheap labor elsewhere. In the twenty-first century, there are no geographically defined safe zones: capital and development can make their particular brand of havoc at home and abroad.

Today, multinational corporations tell working people throughout the world to expect worse working conditions, less security, and lower wages because of the pressures of globalization. For most workers, the realities of this purported New World Order (or *dis*order) have already become everyday facts of life. The "export of hazard" is an integral part of this globalization process. Corporate hazard, however, occurs not only in benighted dictatorships in third-world environments, but also is prominent in the operations of multinationals in so-called democracies. Our story is about the "internalization of hazard" by multinationals operating in capitalist economies. It challenges the presupposition that corporate harm is exclusively the product of multinational companies operating in less developed nations.

We believe that the international oil industry is an exemplar of the rules of this new globalized empire. The work presented here illustrates only too graphically the depredations that the industry has visited on industrial countries. This book is not about ancient robber barons; it describes the current workings of an industry fundamental to the modern world. And it is not about Middle East politics or the bombing of Afghanistan (or of the World Trade Center)—or for that matter about the bombing of Iraq. This book is about the homely, everyday slaughter of workers in the oil industry. It documents—from Alaska to the fringes of the former Soviet empire (itself one of the world's largest oil producers)—the activities of a technologically sophisticated, mature (and global) industry, operating in industrial societies and sanctioned by democratically elected and "civilized" governments. That it also documents the death and injury of many workers and the devastating pollution of the environment should therefore come as a surprise. For this is not Somalia or Myanmar, but the United States and Canada and the former Soviet Union and the United Kingdom.

BLACK GOLD

Oil is a special case. In the United States and Europe we are utterly dependent on oil and gasoline. This dependency has created ridiculously vulnerable cities and production systems, while polluting air, water, and soil. The manufacture of corporate hazards by multinational oil companies, operating in advanced liberal democracies, is laid bare in this book. As the editors note, "The debate on corporate standards and behavior is being shaped by the interests of multinationals. . . . [N]o industry has been more prominent as a driving force of globalization or more vigorous in defending its own image and interests than the oil industry." Woolfson and Beck trace the path of an industry that uses all the tools of public relations to create images of itself as a corporate "good citizen." These corporations are the political agenda-setters and policy makers, "aiming for a public credibility sufficient to paralyze unwelcome monitoring through the media and sanctioning through the legal system." The book discusses not only a conflicted and authoritarian industry that is ultimately driven by cost concerns, but the all-too-often inadequate governmental and regulatory responses to the industry. "The industry's attempt to portray itself as leader in corporate responsibility," say Woolfson and Beck, "ultimately creates only a thin veil that badly disguises the real price of an industry that aggressively pursues the bottom line, irrespective of the costs to society, its workers, and the environment" [4].

Oil is everywhere and in everything. It is the consummate global product. It is essential that we find ways to control this addiction—or if that is not possible, to develop feasible social and technological alternatives.

REFERENCES

1. C. Perrow, *Normal Accidents: Living with High-Risk Technologies,* Basic Books, New York, 1984.
2. B. Commoner, *Making Peace with the Planet,* Pantheon Books, New York, 1990.
3. B. I. Castleman and V. Navarro, Industrial mobility of Hazardous Products, Industries and Waste, *Annual Review of Public Health, 8,* 1987.
4. C. Woolfson and M. Beck, Editorial, Big Oil, *New Solutions: A Journal of Environmental and Occupational Health Policy, 10,* Nos. 1-2, (2000):9.

CHAPTER 1

Corporate Social Responsibility in the International Oil Industry

Charles Woolfson and Matthias Beck

INTRODUCTION

The year 2003 marked the fifteenth anniversary of the Piper Alpha disaster, the world's worst offshore oil disaster. The Piper Alpha oil production platform, owned by Occidental Petroleum, was situated in the UK sector of the North Sea, off the coast of Northern Scotland, 110 miles northeast of Aberdeen. It began oil production in 1976, exporting oil to the onshore terminal at Flotta in the Orkney Islands, and gas to the St. Fergus terminal in Grampian. Its platform was linked to a number of other production platforms in the North Sea providing a key junction box for the onward export of hydrocarbons. On the night of July 6, 1988, Piper Alpha was consumed by a series of fires and explosions.

THE CAUSES OF THE PIPER ALPHA DISASTER

The immediate cause of the Piper Alpha disaster appears to have been the ignition of a low-lying cloud of gas condensate. The official investigation into the disaster identified as the immediate cause, a gas release following the removal of a key pump for maintenance purposes and its replacement by a blank flange. When a second pump tripped, the crew started what they thought was the alternative pump as the relief system, unaware that the previous shift had already removed it. In so doing, a chain of events was initiated that led to an uncontrolled gas emission, and, later on, to an initial explosion at 10:00 P.M. when the escaping gas found a source of ignition.

The initial explosion resulted in a large crude oil fire that engulfed the north end of the platform in dense black smoke. The fire was spread by oil leaking from the main oil pipeline to shore and from ruptured pipelines carrying oil and gas from the linked Claymore and Tartan platforms. Between 10:00 P.M. and 11:20 P.M. there were two further cataclysmic explosions caused by pipeline ruptures and, at this time, large sections of Piper Alpha's topsides began to disintegrate and fall into the sea. Despite the visible conflagration on Piper Alpha, the linked oil platforms continued to export oil and gas to Piper Alpha thus feeding the inferno, because, in the words of the official inquiry the responsible managers were "reluctant to take responsibility for shutting down oil production" [1]. Summarizing these events, a survivor is quoted, "The Piper did not burn us; it was the other rigs that burnt us."

From the very first moment of the disaster, all of the platform emergency systems proved to be inadequate. The initial explosion knocked out the control room and disabled power supplies and communications. Survivors spoke of an eerie silence that descended on the platform, as the familiar background noise of generators and plant abruptly ceased. The fire-water deluge system had been out of commission for several months and was inoperable. The parts of the system that did operate did so only with the remnants of water left in the system.

Most of the persons on board the installation were in the accommodation area, many in the cinema room. Others, who were on duty, made their way to the galley area in accordance with installation emergency procedures. However, the smoke and flames enveloping the accommodation area made the anticipated mode of evacuation by helicopter or lifeboat impossible. After ten minutes, the lighting in the galley area failed and panic began to set in. Within another fifteen minutes, dense smoke began to penetrate the galley area. Men were forced to crawl along the floor to escape the smoke, using wet towels to assist their breathing. Others were quickly overcome. According to one survivor, Ed Punchard, with the rupture of the gas-import riser from the Tartan at 10:20 P.M., "the conflagration was multiplied tenfold":

> Eleven and a half miles of eighteen-inch-diameter gas pipeline started to release hydrocarbon gas at a pressure of 1,800 p.s.i. The effects were devastating. A fireball shot out from below the centre of the jacket, enveloped the platform and rose to a height of some 700 feet. The roar was blood-curdling and it did not stop for the next four hours [2].

Eventually, some of the men decided individually, or as a group, to ignore the company advice to wait in the accommodation area for rescue. They realized that to remain on the platform was to face certain death. There was no systematic attempt to lead the men out. Those who survived did so either because of sheer luck or because of their familiarity with the platform layout. The entire 18-man catering crew, whose knowledge of the platform outside the accommodation area was minimal, perished, as did the 81 personnel who remained in the accommodation area. Of those who left the area, 28 survived. Among the total of 61 survivors, some had jumped into the sea from heights of 175 feet. Many of those who escaped were horribly burned on their hands and feet as the platform literally melted under them. For those who made it to the water their grim struggle for survival was by no means over. With the platform disintegrating above them, and the sea on fire around them, the only hope for survival was to be plucked from the water quickly.

As dawn broke on the morning of July 7, most of the superstructure of what had been Piper Alpha had been incinerated or had collapsed into the sea. What was left of the platform was a smouldering, tangled heap of metal and the still-burning remains of a gas flare. Of the 167 who died that night, 30 remained missing, presumed dead.

CORPORATE DENIAL
AND JUDICIAL ACCOUNTABILITY

Occidental's response to the disaster was a textbook case of corporate denial. While the offshore oil industry as a whole, represented by the United Kingdom Offshore Operators' Association (UKOOA), sought to salvage its own reputation, Occidental's management remained reluctant to acknowledge responsibility. Glen Shurtz, chairman of Occidental Petroleum (Caledonia) maintained, "We have always practised the management of safety. Offshore it's our number one priority." Shurtz had little else to say and steadfastly refused to take part in any public debate on the causes of the disaster or subsequent criticism of the company's safety management practices. Times, of course, have changed, and today, if faced with a "crisis event" on the scale of Piper Alpha, a corporation would in all likelihood call on the services of any number of "corporate reputational management consultants," a burgeoning industry that, in itself, reflects growing sensitivity to issues of accountability rather than the will of companies to act responsibly.

Occidental, even before the Piper Alpha disaster, was not a company with a pristine safety record. On the contrary, in 1984 it had narrowly escaped a near disaster that required a mass evacuation of its platform. In 1987, it experienced a fatal incident caused by key factors that were present in the later disaster. The company had failed to learn from its mistakes, even though it was fined on a number of occasions prior to the Piper Alpha explosion.

The issue of attitudes toward judicial accountability with respect to the crimes of oil companies is exemplified by the Piper Alpha disaster. After some deliberation, Peter Fraser, the Lord Advocate, then Scotland's chief legal officer (a Conservative political appointment), took the view that the public interest would not be served by a prosecution.

Fraser became minister of state at the Department of Trade and Industry, where he had responsibility for export trade promotion and overseas investment, with particular emphasis on the oil and gas industry, and was minister of energy until May 1997. Today, as Lord Fraser of Carmyllie QC, he is listed in the current Register of Lords' Interests under "Remunerated directorships" as 1) nonexecutive chairman, JKX Oil and Gas plc, an oil and gas exploration and production company with license interests in the Ukraine, the United States, Italy, and the Caspian Sea; and 2) nonexecutive chairman of "theoilsite.com," which specializes in e-tendering solutions for the oil and gas industry worldwide. This company is no mere "dot-com" bubble, however. It also has as its nonexecutive director, Pierre Godec. Godec is a key figure in the United Kingdom Offshore Operators' Association, and managing director of Elf Exploration UK plc, a subsidiary part of the successor company to Occidental in the Piper field. Peter Fraser is also listed as 3) nonexecutive director, International Petroleum Exchange, Europe's largest energy market, best known for its futures contracts in North Sea Brent crude oil and 4) nonexecutive director of Ram-energy Ltd, an independent exploration and production company which operates primarily in the United States. Lastly, Fraser is listed as 5) nonexecutive director of TotalFina Elf Upstream UK Ltd, one of the world's largest oil conglomerates [3].

The recruitment of former U.K. Ministers of Energy to the senior boardrooms of the oil multinationals stretches back to the 1980s [4]. Such linkages illustrate the power of the oil industry to create "revolving doors" at the highest level of the State, although there is no guarantee that former politicians will actively intervene on behalf of the industry at a higher level.

THE DELEGITIMATION OF CORPORATE POWER

The public at large increasingly viewed the legal system as a veil behind which corporate negligence would go unpunished. On the morning after the official report of the disaster was published, the Scottish tabloid the *Daily Record* ran a banner headline with two succinct words—"CHARGE THEM!" [5].

What happened on Piper Alpha, in many ways, could have happened on any of the platforms in the U.K. offshore sector. Piper Alpha was a disaster that many had predicted and yet their warnings had not been heeded. In this respect, the disaster had many features in common with other disasters that had occurred in the mid- to late 1980s. Those resulting in multiple fatalities in the United Kingdom included the sinking of the *Herald of Free Enterprise*, *The Marchioness* riverboat on the Thames, and the seemingly unending, series of rail disasters, beginning with Clapham Junction through to Ladbroke Grove, Hatfield and Potters Bar. Internationally, a seemingly endless list of disasters such as Bhopal, Westray, Exxon Valdez, and Chernobyl served to undermine public confidence in the ability of the state to regulate, and of corporations to conduct their activities in a manner that prevents harm to the public and consumers. In each of these disasters, management failure was subsequently identified as a crucial factor. Add to this the succession of financial governance scandals occurring over two decades, especially in the United Kingdom and the United States, and it is easy to see why public confidence in corporate behavior has severely eroded.

In the United Kingdom, these events led to backlash, which undermined public trust in the ability of corporations to act responsibly. The roots of current calls for reform of the law with respect to all forms of corporate governance and the demands for greater accountability spring from this period. However, as we write, the U.K. government is still equivocating over long-awaited plans to introduce corporate killing legislation that would criminalize companies for gross failures in safety management that result in deaths of employees. Announcing draft legislation, the responsible U.K. minister conceded:

> There is great public concern at the criminal law's lack of success in convicting companies of manslaughter where a death has occurred due to gross negligence by the organisation as a whole. . . . The law needs to be clear and effective in order to secure public confidence and must bite properly on large corporations whose failure to set or maintain standards causes a death [6].

Occidental, however, not only escaped prosecution but was given assistance by the U.K. government in the form of Petroleum Revenue tax relief, which resulted in the construction of a new £780 million platform, Piper Bravo, largely funded by taxpayers. Legal proceedings were initiated by Elf, as successor company to Occidental Petroleum, against the offshore contracting companies working on the platform at the time of the disaster. This was an attempt to recover losses inherited from Occidental associated with compensation payments to contractors' personnel. These proceedings resulted in the longest running court case in Scottish legal history. The result was a legal victory for the oil majors over the contractors in which the relatives of the victims had, yet again, to endure the raking over of the events of the disaster. Attempts to mount a private prosecution against Occidental for corporate homicide (manslaughter) foundered due to lack of finances. Occidental Petroleum was allowed to disengage from its operations in the U.K. sector with scarcely a whisper of official condemnation. In the memorable words of an offshore union leader, Occidental was allowed to "tiptoe away" from the North Sea, unmolested by the judicial authorities. History provides its own jolting ironic footnotes. In the Sunday Times Top 500 listed companies for 2001, Occidental Petroleum ranks 422nd. It continues as a major and profitable operator in the energy industry. Occidental Petroleum has now acquired, and is operating, some of the assets of the Enron Corporation.

CHAMPIONS OF "GOOD GOVERNANCE"

Nowadays most multinational companies attempt to portray themselves as champions of good governance. Meanwhile, where ethical, political, and social conflicts occur, they resort to the mantra of "globalization." Globalization, accordingly, imposes pressures that can be met only if individual national governments accommodate the multinationals' requirements. Frequently, then, the debate on corporate standards and behavior is being shaped by the interests of multinationals. Recognizing this, the Canadian corporate criminologist Harry Glasbeek describes the contemporary corporate social responsibility movement as "the latest in Maginot lines to save capitalism," the final but flawed line of defense against invasive demands for corporate accountability [7]. When World War I ended, the French generals swore never to let the Germans invade again. The Maginot Line was an impressive network of fortified barriers built for defense against a land invasion along the Franco-German border. It created a false sense of security, insofar as the German forces simply sent their divisions around the end of the line and invaded through neutral Belgium. Although notorious as a universal metaphor for bungling, a revisionist view holds that the defensive system in fact was not the blunder it has been made out to be, but rather a model of clever engineering and technological accomplishment. We suggest this makes the metaphor particularly apt. If that is so, then finding a way around the latest Maginot Line of corporate social responsibility is politically, socially, and ethically imperative.

PRINCIPLES OR PROFIT?
GOOD CORPORATE CITIZENSHIP

Oil multinationals are among the most aggressive players in the contemporary corporate social responsibility movement. In many respects these efforts can be traced to the special position that oil occupies in the political economy of multinational-state interactions.

Oil production necessitates the temporary or permanent cession of property rights by the state to the company. For the company, in turn, oil production requires extensive sunk investments, which encourage companies to obtain the most favorable fiscal and regulatory conditions possible. Ultimately, this relationship can lead to public accusations of an exceedingly favorable treatment of these companies by the state.

Throughout this relationship, the oil industry has been well aware of the reputational dangers this situation can pose. The industry has, therefore, pioneered efforts to manipulate political sentiment. A 1954 publication by the U.S. Oil Industry Information Committee, titled *Oil's Way of Winning Friends* and published at the height of the Cold War, linked the unrestricted operation of the industry, free from regulatory interference, directly to the welfare of society:

> . . . no one part of the oil industry can prosper unless the industry as a whole is free to serve the public in its own way—free from unnecessary restraints and regulations. . . . If misconceptions are allowed to persist, eventually

they will threaten the very existence of the oil industry, and the jobs of oil
men and women everywhere. And there is another, even greater threat hidden
in these mistaken ideas. If it were possible to destroy the public's confidence
in the oil and other businesses, it would be possible to destroy the public's
belief in the American competitive enterprise system itself [8].

Today, surprisingly little has changed in the oil industry's outlook on itself.
Although thematic priorities may appear to have shifted, the reality is that "Big
Oil" has remained a champion of unrestrained free enterprise and a vigorous
opponent of pro-regulatory forces.

Arguably, the collapse of the "evil empire" of communism has been accompanied by a shift in scrutiny toward the human rights and environmental record
of multinational corporations. This is not necessarily good news for oil corporations, which often find themselves operating in dubious regulatory and
political environments. As a consequence, recent years have seen a renewed and
growing self-absorption of large multinational oil companies with their image
as corporate "good citizens." Virtually all of the major oil companies today
claim not to put "profits before principles" and to be genuinely concerned with
environmental and human rights issues.

In the wake of the execution of Ken Saro-Wiwa in Nigeria, Shell International
attempted to persuade a concerned public of the need to "understand the dilemma
in which Shell Nigeria finds itself" [9]. Company spokepersons have suggested
that Shell "is trying to do an honest job under difficult conditions, and . . . is a
force for good in the country—probably doing more in direct help than any
other single organization." After these difficulties in Nigeria, and the debacle
over the pollution impacts of the disposal of the redundant Brent Spar installation, Shell International embarked on a public relations offensive that included
full-page color ads in the U.K. press and the production of its first glossy
"stakeholder" annual report [10]. The opening paragraph of the *Shell Report*—
tellingly entitled, "Profits and Principles—Does There Have to Be a Choice?"—
begins with a "debating expectations" section that represents a typical example of
corporate agenda setting:

> Multinationals have been criticized as being overly concerned with profit
> and failing to take their broader responsibilities seriously: to defend human
> rights, to protect the environment, to be good corporate citizens.

The brochure contained a prepaid "Tell Shell" reply card, inviting comments
(nowadays by e-mail) to "be taken into account and published on our Web site."
The *Shell Report* outlined a corporate code of conduct and its "Statement of
General Business Principles." Such codes are an increasingly prominent feature
of contemporary "socially responsible" corporations. Whatever the intentions
of corporate leaders, they bear only the remotest connection with realities that
are often brutal and inhumane.

SETTING THE AGENDA

Over three decades ago, the American political scientist Robert Engler argued in his *The Politics of Oil* that multinationals no longer respond to criticisms and are no longer measured against established yardsticks of human and trade union rights [8]. Equally, he suggested, they no longer seek to deflect the criticism they face from the political arena or political action groups. Rather, they center their strategy on becoming political agenda setters, trend setters, or policy makers aiming for a public credibility sufficient to paralyze unwelcome monitoring through the media and sanctioning through the legal system.

Proffering claims of self-constructed and self-regulated "corporate good citizenship" (or equivalent terms such as corporate social responsibility) today provides immunization against "misconceived" criticism, very much along the lines suggested by Engler in the 1960s, with oil companies dictating terms of a corporate social responsibility debate that only rarely deviates from the party line. John Browne, the group chief executive of BP, has been explicit about where he sees the current position of multinationals:

> Now there is a wider agenda, including the environment, employment and labor standards, distribution of income, and the behavior of governments, as well as business ethics. Companies are considered to be actors on the international stage in their own right, if *not the directors of the play*. Of course there are good reasons why people should think companies have that sort of power. More than 20 companies now have the turnover greater than the GDP of Hungary or Ireland or Venezuela [11] (emphasis added).

For corporate leaders like John Browne, the power of oil companies poses few, if any, dilemmas. Browne describes himself as "a great believer in short-term profit." Meanwhile he sees "no trade-off between the short-term and long-term . . . Open markets, the efficient production and use of natural resources in ways which pose no environmental threat, steady economic development and an open society are the conditions in which we can best pursue our business."

In the harmonious meld of corporate and public goals envisaged by Browne, concern over human rights and public welfare evolve naturally as part of a corporate, rather than a contested political agenda. BP has embraced the United Nations Declaration of Human Rights and now works closely with Amnesty International, implementing a liberal democratic vision of the future, where "true development and full human rights" are achieved through "freedom from poverty" and the "freedom to develop skills." Nongovernmental organizations (NGOs) such as Amnesty International now seem prepared to concede that there has been an awakening of the corporate conscience and that "there seems to be a genuine conviction that profit and principle can go together" [12].

Local conflicts also no longer pose problems to the self-proclaimed aims of the corporation, but rather offer an opportunity to further develop the oil industry's corporate recipe for world salvation. Says Browne:

Geology has not restricted the distribution of hydrocarbons to areas governed as open pluralistic democracies. The cutting edge of the issue of corporate responsibility comes from the fact that circumstances don't always make it easy for companies to operate as they would wish [11].

In the darker corners of the planet, collaboration between repressive regimes and oil multinationals has been documented only incompletely. These countries include Angola, Algeria, Burma, Cameroon, Chad, Colombia, Ecuador, Gabon, Iran, Iraq, Nigeria, Peru, and Venezuela. This is a list with no claim to completeness, if only because it is growing day by day. As a senior oil executive of a U.S. oil engineering group active in Algeria stated, for the oil industry "the big money is in countries whose names end with "ia" and "stan" . . . places other people don't want to go to." In many of these countries oil worker unions have played a key role in the wider fight for trade union and democratic rights. In Colombia, where both BP and Occidental are significant players, a particularly heavy price has been paid by oil workers, with an estimated 120 union leaders murdered in the past ten years. From January 2003, U.S. Special Forces began operating in Northern Colombia as advisers to the notorious 18th Brigade of the Colombian army. Their designated mission will be to protect Occidental's 500 mile pipeline from Leftist guerrillas, as part of the Bush administration's congressionally approved "global war on terrorism." Colombia supplies only 3% of U.S. oil, but as the United States embarked on its intervention in Iraq, in the words of the U.S. envoy to Colombia, "every percentage is important" [13].

In the oil provinces of advanced capitalist nations, we would not expect to find the "unfortunate excesses" that have accompanied the activities of major companies in less developed parts of the world. Here repression takes more subtle forms. It includes the cooption of the debate on corporate responsibility by the oil multinationals themselves, together with the deflection of questions about safety and trade union rights through a new "shared" agenda that views environmental issues and "sustainability" as preeminent [14].

Today's oil multinationals have developed a comprehensive "ethical tool kit" aimed at defusing threats to the industry's long-term as well as regional interests. Claims of social responsibility have become an integral and useful part of their business strategy. The Web pages of most oil companies proffer a "corporate social responsibility" link. The ChevronTexaco Web site, for instance, reads:

> At ChevronTexaco, we know that success demands the highest standards of responsible corporate citizenship in our operations worldwide. Our approach to this responsibility is rooted in our core values, known as the ChevronTexaco Way: "to conduct business in a socially responsible and ethical manner . . . support universal human rights . . . protect the environment, and the communities where we work . . . learn from and respect cultures in which we work" [15].

Even Occidental has its own "social responsibility" and "health, safety and environment" Web pages claiming that health and safety has been its number-one priority for the past 20 years. Occidental's Web site makes no mention of the Piper Alpha disaster [16]. At the first major international conference of the offshore oil industry, the Society of Petroeum Engineers at Stavanger, Norway, in 2000, which devoted a special session to the issue of corporate responsibility, an Occidental spokesman was one of the key panelists.

An attempt has been made to reinsulate the industry from all but the most sympathetic public gaze. Internationally, this has involved the oil companies in capturing the moral high ground in international forums such as the World Summit on Sustainable Development in Johannesburg, in September 2002. Here, U.K. Prime Minister Tony Blair used the occasion to announce the global "Extractive Industries Transparency Initiative," which is aimed at the establishment of a "broad coalition" committed to developing a framework to promote transparency of payments from oil and mining companies to host-country governments [17]. Among the high profile oil company signatories supporting this anticorruption initiative are BP and Shell, with others (TotalFinaElf, Talisman, and Statoil) expressing interest in getting involved. In spring 2003, the United Kingdom was set to host an international conference (involving government ministers, senior officials, industry, and NGO leaders) to take the Transparency initiative forward in the run-up to the G8 Summit of industrialized nations.

In the United Kingdom, the New Labour government and the *Financial Times* annually join forces to present Business in the Community Awards to a roster of socially aware corporations. Meanwhile, generous oil company sponsorship has been made available for studentships and even for research into aspects of risk and safety management at sympathetic institutions of higher education. In the words of Prime Minister Tony Blair at one awards ceremony, "business can marry competitiveness and social engagement" [18]. BP, now merged with Amoco, was especially commended recently for its socially aware annual report and its corporately responsible Web site. Shell, too, received honorable mention in dispatches [19].

As each new oil field is inaugurated, it has been celebrated with a snowstorm of publicity about its state-of-the-art safety features. A full-page advertisement appeared in the financial press featuring a picture of the "tow-out" of the giant Hibernia oil production platform to the Grand Banks of Newfoundland [20]. The oil industry's "Atlantic frontier," now bereft of codfish, was once the major source of livelihood of Newfoundland's inhabitants. The advertisement, sponsored by Mobil (now ExxonMobil), a key player in the Hibernia project, proclaims with unwitting irony— "In Newfoundland, going out to sea is still a good way to make a living." Readers are invited to visit Mobil's Web site [21]. A search under "Safety" revealed the following comforting message:

> Mobil also has won many awards for its efforts in protecting the environment
> and the health and safety of its workers, neighbours, vendors and others.

What Mobil's corporate site did not record are the safety and environmental penalties it has incurred as a result of its activities, including a £175,000 "record" fine imposed on Mobil North Sea following a fatality in the U.K. offshore sector. This fine, however, equaled precisely .009% of Mobil's global annual profits [22].

CONCLUSION

In order to promote the globalization of the world economy, the industrial nations and their less developed counterparts have endured sustained political "deregulation," the softening of the regulatory underbelly in order to promote neoliberal economic policies. Thus, the current administrations of the United States and United Kingdom have endorsed many of the assumptions of their predecessors with respect to the need to "free" business from what is described as "burdensome regulation." This places future prospects for corporate accountability in a troubling position. If the recognition of regulatory failure is now dependent on a) massive loss of life and b) sustained public reaction to this, then governments have essentially ceased to play the role of proactive policy makers. Vacillation toward introducing effective accountability through corporate governance and corporate homicide legislation would seem to confirm the continuing tension between the public desire for accountability and corporate resistance to external regulatory and judicial oversight. In this political vacuum, excesses of corporate self-promotion and self-delusion flourish.

There was a recent series of compelling U.K. television advertisements sponsored by Shell. One shows a misty-eyed environmentalist. He is liltingly described as an "impossible" dreamer: "Once, he would have been an oil company's worst nightmare" intones a Scottish actor's soft voiceover . . . "Today, he is their brightest hope." The advertisement fades out as the prow of a Shell oil exploration vessel cuts through pristine blue waters, unsullied by oil pollution. This comforting cameo aptly identifies the capacity of the industry to absorb its critics, to the point of imaginative self-parody. There is another parody of corporate social responsibility. It is the famous dictum of Marx—Groucho that is, not Karl—"Integrity and honesty are the foundations of success. . . . If you can fake those, you've got it made."

For Shell, as a champion of corporate social responsibility, this dictum has a bitter irony. In the Spring of 2004, its chairman Sir Philip Watts, followed by Walter van de Vijer, Shell's head of exploration and production, and latterly by Judy Boynton, Shell's director of finance, were forced to resign when it became clear that the company had consistently exaggerated the size of its potential oil production reserves in order to boost share values and "fool" the market. The incautious words of the hapless and frustrated Mr. van de Vijer, revealed in an e-mail to Sir Philip, summed up the growing crisis at senior management level: "I am becoming sick and tired about lying about the extent of our reserves issues and the downward revisions that need to be done because of far too aggressive/optimistic bookings" [23]. When staff had attempted to alert Mr. van de Vijer one month later to the impending gravity of the situation, pointing out that Shell had a legal obligation to disclose the true level of reserves, he responded in an e-mail, "This is absolute dynamite, not at all what I expected and needs to be destroyed" [23]. In the end, Shell had to make four downwards revisions of its reserves in order to satisfy U.S. market regulators, and in the process provoked a wave of class-action suits from outraged investors, while the key individuals responsible face possible criminal proceedings initiated by the U.S. Justice Department. Nevertheless, Shell's forecasted first quarter profits for 2004, riding high on the upwards spiral of record oil prices, were expected to reach $3 billion.

REFERENCES

1. Hon. Lord Cullen, *The Public Inquiry into the Piper Alpha Disaster*, Vols. 1 and 2 (London: HMSO, 1990), ch. 7, 49.
2. E. Punchard, *Piper Alpha: A Survivor's Story* (London: W. H. Allen), 130.
3. See www.publications.parliament.uk/pa/ld/ldreg/reg09.htm.
4. C. Woolfson, J. Foster, and M. Beck, *Paying for the Piper: Capital and Labour in Britain's Offshore Oil Industry* (London and New York: Mansell, 1997), 282.
5. *Daily Record*, 1992.
6. "Government to Tighten Laws on Corporate Killing," Home Office news release, May 20, 2003.
7. H. Glasbeek, "The Corporate Social Responsibility Movement: The Latest in Maginot Lines to Save Capitalism," *Dalhousie Law Journal* 11 (1988): 363-402.
8. Cited in R. Engler, *The Politics of Oil: A Study of Private Power and Democratic Directions* (Chicago: University of Chicago Press, 1967).
9. Shell International Petroleum Company, letter to Ms. S. Archer, Isle of Arran, November 22, 1995 (author's possession).
10. Shell International Petroleum Company, "Profits and Principles—Does There Have to Be a Choice?" *Shell Report* (London, 1998); J. G. Frynas, "Corporate and State Responses to Anti-Oil Protests in the Niger Delta," *African Affairs* 100, no. 398 (January 2001): 27-54; D. Wheeler, H. Fabig, and R. Boele, "Paradoxes and Dilemmas for Stakeholder Responsive Firms in the Extractive Sector: Lessons from the Case of Shell and the Ogoni," *Journal of Business Ethics* 39, no. 3 (September 2002): 297-318.
11. J. Browne, "A Presentation to the Council on Foreign Relations," New York, November 13, 1997; available at BP Website, Corporate Responsibility in an International Context: www.bpamoco.com/_nav/pressoffice/speech.htm?/speeches/sp_971113.htm.
12. *Financial Times*, Responsible Business Supplement, June 1999.
13. *Chicago Tribune,* November 12, 2002.
14. UKOOA (United Kingdom Offshore Operators' Association), "UK Oil and Gas Industry Publishes First Report on Progress Towards Sustainability," News Release, London, July 23, 2002.
15. ChevronTexaco Social Responsibility Web site at: www.chevrontexaco.com/social_responsibility.

16. See: www.oogc.com/hes/hes_frameset.htm.
17. See: www.dfid.gov.uk.
18. *Financial Times,* July 16, 1999.
19. *Financial Times,* May 19, 2002.
20. *Financial Times,* April 6, 1999.
21. See: www.mobil.com.
22. *Aberdeen Press and Journal,* March 3, 1998.
23. *The Economist,* "Sick and tired about lying." 371, Issue 8372, April 22, 2004: 63.

CHAPTER 2

The Piper Alpha Disaster and Industrial Relations in Britain's Offshore Oil Industry

Charles Woolfson, Matthias Beck,
and John Foster

INTRODUCTION

In July 1988, the fire and explosions on Occidental's Piper Alpha platform, 120 miles northeast of Aberdeen, resulted in the world's worst offshore oil disaster, claiming 167 lives. The occurrence of this event was not circumstantial. Rather, it was the outcome of an intrinsically flawed regulatory safety regime and an employer-dominated labor-relations regime. Both are testament to the power of multinational capital to secure, at state level, a congenial regulatory and industrial environment for the exploration and recovery of offshore hydrocarbons. The cumulation of power in the hands of a few multinational oil companies, as experienced in Britain, contains important pointers to possible developments in other oil provinces. This applies in particular to the interconnection of safety and industrial relations, which is often denied by the industry but nonetheless painfully obvious in disasters such as the Piper Alpha explosion.

Since the Piper Alpha disaster, the regulatory system of the British offshore oil industry has been modified in line with the report of the public inquiry into the disaster conducted by the Scottish High Court judge, Lord Cullen. The Cullen report has since been held up as a safety blueprint for the global oil industry. At the same time, there have been industry claims of a profound accompanying change in employer attitudes toward labor relations practices in the offshore oil industry. As the fifteenth anniversary of the disaster passes, it is important to assess whether these changes are as far-reaching as their proponents would claim.

This chapter explores the issue of powerful multinationals that dominate safety agendas and dictate working conditions, in the following order. First, we explore the evolution of the U.K. oil industry's political economy and regulatory regime. Second, we briefly examine the Piper Alpha disaster as a key event in the evolution of U.K. offshore regulation, alongside Lord Cullen's recommendations aimed at preventing a similar disaster. Third, we scrutinize the industry's response to the Cullen report, which is characterized by latent resistance to new regulatory requirements and the industry's continuing prioritization of concerns over costs and expenditures. The fourth part of the chapter provides a quantitative and qualitative analysis of safety indicators that throws doubt on industry claims to radical safety improvements since Piper Alpha. We conclude by analyzing the development of labor relations in the U.K. offshore oil industry as the underlying context for the existing safety regime.

THE POLITICAL ECONOMY OF U.K. OFFSHORE OIL AND "REGULATORY CAPTURE"

The discovery of oil on the U.K. Continental Shelf in the 1960s was preceded by roughly 50 years of close cooperation between the oil industry and the British state. Before World War I, the importance of oil was strategic and military, rather than economic. Oil provided fuel for the British Navy's warships which policed the empire. For this reason, Anglo-Persian (later BP) became, in 1913, the first major British firm in which the state took a controlling interest. At this time oil made up only 1.4% of the value of U.K. imports and only 1.6% of reexports [1], with energy resources coming mainly from coal.

Although oil prices tended to fluctuate markedly pre-World War II, the size of the oil companies and their cartellized organization enabled them to survive and operate strategically in this uncertain environment. When necessary, British oil companies called on the power of the state to sustain their dominance in markets and exploration territories. By the mid-1930s, Anglo-Persian and Shell had already become crucial to the U.K. balance of payments and the value of the pound sterling. On a global scale, these companies matched the largest U.S. companies, a position that was eroded, but not destroyed, by World War II, when Britain's dependence on American economic support during the war entailed conceding key oil bearing territories in the Middle East to U.S. dominance.

It was only after World War II that the direct use of oil as a weapon in international diplomacy emerged. Oil became crucial for use as industrial energy. U.S. control of cheap Saudi oil underwrote the fast European and Japanese postwar economic reconstruction. Within the Middle East, U.K. and U.S. oil companies played a key role in brokering deals to preserve regimes under threat from left-wing and nationalist forces. Between the United States and Britain, however, oil brought rivalries because each saw oil as central to their economies and currencies; an issue that became explicit during the Suez crisis. By 1953, the profits of the oil companies constituted 14% of the total profit income of all U.K. industrial companies. The two big U.K. oil companies, Shell and BP, were now closely interlocked at directorship level with leading city merchant banks.

By the late 1950s, political problems arose within oil producing nations as a result of a fall in oil prices to about one-third. At the time, U.S. control over client regimes in Latin America, North Africa, and, above all, in the Middle East, no longer looked certain. In 1960, the Organization of Petroleum Exporting Countries (OPEC) was formed as a producers' cartel. At the time, the Arab-Israeli conflict called into question the continuity of supplies. At the same time, Germany, France, and Japan, as industrial rivals of the United States, sought freedom from U.S.- and U.K.-controlled energy supplies. These developments triggered a radical shift in the corporate policies of multinationals. Henceforth, oil exploration was to focus on politically stable areas, so that in the longer-term future the oil majors could draw a significant part of their supply from outside OPEC.

It was at this point that oil exploration began in Canada, Alaska, Australia, and the North Sea. The oil multinationals knew that oil in these locations was likely to be more expensive to recover, but its principal value was now seen as a bargaining counter. Exploration in these provinces could give the oil companies long-term leverage. The discovery of North Sea oil in 1969 became part of a strategic response to the changing geopolitical requirements of the time. Ultimately, however, North Sea oil extraction became economically feasible only after the leap in oil prices in the early 1970s, when the high costs involved in exploiting the deep waters of the North Sea no longer appeared prohibitive.

At the time, the scale of investment required, calculated at one-fifth of all industrial investment for a decade, was beyond the resources of the British government or the city of London. Moreover, the technology necessary to recover the hydrocarbons did not exist in the United Kingdom. North Sea oil exploration therefore required a strategic alliance with U.S. capital, which, inevitably, as part of the implicit pact with U.S. multinationals, was accompanied by the importation of a U.S.-style production regime. Britain's oil was to be extracted at the fastest rate possible, with limited state control and under conditions of close commercial partnership between American oil companies and banks. In the absence of any serious concerns over the long-term sustainability of the North Sea as an oil province, W. G. Carson was to call state complicity in the unfettered exploitation of North Sea oil, "the political economy of speed" [2].

In the context of this agenda, safety concerns were early on placed behind economic considerations. In his pathbreaking 1982 work, *The Other Price of Britain's Oil,* Carson analyzed the slow response of U.K. regulatory agencies to safety problems in the offshore industry [2]. Although, in 1965 a jack-up rig, the Sea Gem, collapsed resulting in the loss of thirteen lives, it was a full six years before the Mineral Workings (Offshore Installations) Act (MWA) of 1971 was to be put on the statute book. The MWA empowered the Secretary of State for Energy to require that installations be certified as fit-for-purpose and made procedures for safety regulations. Further regulations were also slow to emerge. It was not until 1973 that the reporting of casualties was formalized and it took another three years for occupational health and safety regulations to be introduced. The MWA itself, being highly prescriptive in nature, invited compliance with the letter of the law rather than its spirit. More important, it was never rigorously enforced, which led Carson to describe the offshore regulatory regime as the "institutionalized tolerance of non-compliance" [2].

"Regulatory capture" has been identified as a process whereby a regulatory agency comes to wholly identify the public good with the interests of the industry it regulates. If we apply this definition to the U.K. offshore industry, then "capture" was nearly complete. The Department of Energy repeatedly lined up with the industry to prevent the encroachment of other agencies onto its territory. This was evident at the end of the 1970s, when a Labour government inquiry into offshore safety under J. M. Burgoyne recommended continuation of the current arrangements despite the industry's worsening safety record [3].

Following the Robens report *Safety and Health at Work,* safety regulation in the United Kingdom moved away from prescriptive rules toward a goal-setting regime [4]. Onshore, the Health and Safety at Work Act of 1974 encouraged the systematic assessment of risk, and a shift from externally policed regulation toward industry "self-regulation." The development of goal-setting regulation was overseen by a single unified independent agency, the Health and Safety Commission/Executive (HSC/E). Although the Robens report had envisaged that, in time, the offshore industry would come under the accompanying Health and Safety at Work Act (HSWA) of 1974, this was not to be. The Department of Energy jealously guarded its "special relationship" with the oil industry; a relationship cemented by frequent interchanges of personnel and the recruitment of senior officials and even government ministers by the industry in a system that sometimes involved elements of "deferred bribery" [5]. At the time, supporters of the Department of Energy argued that the department alone had the necessary specialist expertise to respond to the rapidly changing needs of this technologically frontier industry.

While the HSWA was formally extended offshore in 1977, the operation of an "agency agreement" between the Department of Energy and the HSC prevented the effective supervision of offshore safety and allowed the Department of Energy to keep the development of future regulations within its remit. This led to the maintenance of a sympathetic regulatory regime for the industry, and strengthened the industry's ability to resist the offshore application of key sets of regulations, including those dealing with hazardous substances and, crucially, those permitting organized trade unions to appoint workplace safety representatives. In this context, requirements for trade union safety representatives became particularly anathema to the oil industry. Due to their access to the levers of state power, the oil industry was able to create a virtual "zone of exclusion" offshore in which it could conduct their activities largely unmolested by regulatory interference. As a consequence, offshore safety regulation in the United Kingdom was placed in a paradoxical context. The sponsoring ministry, the Department of Energy, charged with ensuring the rapid development of offshore oil, was also the body responsible for ensuring the safety and health of those who worked in the industry. This contradiction pervaded U.K. offshore regulation until the flaws of this regulatory regime became painfully obvious in the Piper Alpha disaster.

PIPER ALPHA AND THE CULLEN REPORT

In his report on the Piper Alpha disaster, Lord Cullen concentrated on the causes of the disaster and what steps could be taken to prevent a similar recurrence [6]. His criticisms of the operators of Piper Alpha, Armand Hammer's Occidental Petroleum, were scathing, particularly concerning their failure to operate a safe system of work, despite a number of previous incidents on the platform. Offshore workers pointed to the cutbacks in maintenance following the oil price downturn in the mid-1980s, which had led to postponed maintenance work and production taking place simultaneously. They noted that what happened on Piper Alpha could have happened on any platform. Lord Cullen's criticisms extended to the regulatory regime administered by the Department of Energy. He noted that only five inspectors were responsible for policing the entire North Sea, and that, as a rule, an installation would be visited perhaps once every two years. The inspection of Piper Alpha in the weeks before the disaster was described by Cullen as "superficial to the point of being of little use as a test of safety" [6, ch. 15.48]. He further noted that the approach of the Department of Energy in general was marked by "overconservatism, insularity and a lack of ability to look at the regime and themselves in a critical way" [6, ch. 22.20]. Little had been learned from the more modern onshore approach to hazard, characteristic of the U.K. Health and Safety at Work Act, or from the more forward-looking regime in Norway [6, ch. 22.20].

At the core of these approaches stood the notion that safety risks had to be assessed in a comprehensive framework. The concept of "Formal Safety Assessment" (FSA), highlighted by Lord Cullen, involved "the identification and assessment of hazards over the whole life cycle of a project" through all its stages of development, to final decommissioning and abandonment. Included in the concept of FSA were certain analytical techniques of risk assessment. Formal Safety Assessment was to lead to a "Safety Case," a systematic documented review of all potential hazards existing on an installation, and the safety management systems put in place to deal with them.

The notion of the Safety Case was derived from onshore experience, particularly following the Seveso disaster and the subsequent European Directive, and, within the United Kingdom, the explosion at the Flixborough petrochemical plant that resulted in a complete reappraisal of major hazard regulations. Central to the Safety Case, was the demonstration that an installation possessed a "temporary safe refuge" (TSR), an area with specified durability in the event of a major incident in which employees could shelter for sufficient time to permit their safe evacuation.

Lord Cullen saw Quantitative Risk Assessment (QRA) as an important tool in this respect, its purpose was "to assess the risks, to identify and assess potential safety improvements, and to ensure that the TSR meets the standard set" [6, ch. 17.61]. But he did not concur with the industry's view that FSA and the Safety Case were sufficient in themselves as a system of safety management. In Cullen's view, FSA and the Safety Case required the complement of a system of goal-setting regulations "setting intermediate goals [that] would give the regime a solidity it might otherwise lack," for example, in construction, fire and explosion protection, evacuation, escape, and rescue [6, ch. 17.63]. This transition to a new offshore regime would not "take place overnight" [6, ch. 17.67].

Lord Cullen's proposal to assign a central role to FSA and the Safety Case led him to consider what would be the appropriate body to evaluate the operator's Safety Case. The choice was between a continuation of safety regulation under the Department of Energy (DEn) and the Health and Safety Executive (HSE), which had experience in administering a goal-setting regime onshore. At the Piper Alpha inquiry the oil operators claimed to be "agnostic" in this matter: a position that stood in marked contrast to their previous hostility to the HSE. Based on the view that the offshore management of safety under the DEn lagged "a number of years behind the approach onshore" [6, ch. 22.21], Cullen formally recommended a transfer of responsibility for offshore safety from the DEn to the HSE, and suggested that a new division of the HSE be formed to accomplish the task of reconstructing offshore safety [6, Vol. 2, Recommendation 25]. This was to become the Offshore Safety Division, which came into existence in the spring of 1991.

In the end, a total of 106 recommendations were made in Lord Cullen's report, which the government accepted in full. Ultimately, the success of these recommendations depended on factors other than formal government approval. For the new safety regime to be effective two major ingredients were required. First, it required industry approval and support, and second, it required effective workforce involvement in safety matters. On both counts, the result proved to be, at best, ambiguous.

OFFSHORE SAFETY RECONSTRUCTION— THE INDUSTRY RESPONSE

In the aftermath of the disaster, the U.K. Offshore Operators Association (UKOOA), the body in which the major oil companies in the North Sea were grouped, was anxious to show that the industry was "proactively" reforming itself. In advocating such concepts as Formal Safety Assessment, the industry claimed it had already anticipated the main thrust of Cullen's recommendations. Behind the facade of compliance with the future regulatory regime, however, lay a different agenda. This agenda was driven by two goals: the avoidance of costly specific regulations through exploitation of the notions of "flexibility" and "goal setting," and the avoidance of mandatory union and workforce involvement in safety matters.

The Cullen inquiry had sent several delegations to Norway to examine the Norwegian Petroleum Directorate (NPD). The NPD had a much more prominent regulatory profile in the industry than the DEn. The essence of the Norwegian system is what is described as "internal control." The operators are responsible for organizing the safety of their installations within the general goal-setting framework laid down by the NPD, rather than through a mass of externally policed detailed prescriptive regulations. The UKOOA now seized upon the Norwegian system because it allowed maximum latitude to retain control over all aspects of installation safety. A Safety Case-based "goal-setting" regime, said the UKOOA, was entirely in line with Robens's rejection of detailed regulations, going back to "first principles" of safety management. The UKOOA's advocacy of Formal Safety Assessment and the Safety Case at the Cullen inquiry was based on the flexibility such an approach would offer to the oil operators. This was spelled out in the UKOOA's internal briefing document, which was prepared to present the best possible face for the industry to the media, following the publication of the Cullen report. A paper entitled "Offshore Safety—The Way Forward" noted that FSA has "many advantages" in that it is "flexible" and can take account of the different types of installations in the U.K. offshore environment. For the industry, FSA had the advantage in that it "does not *dictate* to the operator *how* safety should be achieved" [7]. The UKOOA's expectations of the benefits of the new regime were far-reaching. Once the FSA had been completed, the industry expected that existing formal regulations should no longer be applied. It is important that this position had been explicitly rejected by Cullen as going too far too quickly.

The UKOOA's "strategy" in dealing with media on the publication of the report was outlined in the same briefing document:

> We should use the media opportunities presented to us to state UKOOA's aims and objectives and where possible show how they have been advocated by Lord Cullen. . . . The advantages of FSA can be used to answer any detailed question. . . . Using this strategy we should be able to avoid being dragged into detailed argument about specific proposals. If Lord Cullen makes a specific recommendation, which is counter to the actions already under way in the industry, we should embrace it objectively, and agree that it seems sensible and promise to look at it [8].

Among the "useful phrases" that the UKOOA had ready for media sound bites were statements such as: "Safety Is Our Number 1 Priority" and, "A Safe Platform Is a Profitable One." The UKOOA claimed that in the two years since Piper Alpha, the operators had spent £750 million on safety improvements, roughly

£1 million a day. A total of £230 million of this expenditure was on the fitting or relocation of topside emergency shutdown valves on risers at the interface with the platforms. These were required by the Emergency Pipe-line Valve Regulations, passed in July 1989 in the wake of Piper Alpha. Another £230 million was spent on subsea isolation systems, and an additional £300 million on other safety measures. In any event, up to 80% of this total expenditure could be offset against petroleum revenue tax.

Although difficult to quantify, probably the greatest bulk of this expenditure was occasioned by the postponed maintenance work that was left over from the oil price downturn of 1986. In cost terms, enhanced safety work was almost impossible to separate out from essential maintenance. Nevertheless, the UKOOA's huge safety expenditure figures went largely uncontested.

The industry's response to the new safety regime, however, soon moved from public relations gimmicks to open hostility to the new requirements imposed by the new regulatory authority, the Offshore Safety Division (OSD) of the HSE. The Safety Case, by requiring the systematic analysis of all hazards and the assessment of related risk, sought to reduce hazards and guard against the escalation of accidents into a major disaster. A central plank of the Safety Case was the provision on each installation of a temporary safe refuge that would provide employees with a safe haven in the event of a major incident, and an enhanced means of escape and survival. Cullen recommended that every installation have a temporary safe refuge, or safe haven of specified durability, to enhance the survival of installation personnel in the event of major incidents such as a fire or explosion and systems failure [6, ch. 17.38]. The first draft of the Safety Case regulations was published in December 1991: In March 1992, it was published as a consultative document [9]. The HSE had indicated, in response to representations from the UKOOA, that the TSR requirements might be modified where *a satisfactory alternative* could be demonstrated. It was conceded that TSR requirements might be relaxed with respect to certain installations that are not normally manned or mobile drilling rigs. Nevertheless, this concession did not go far enough for the UKOOA. At a major conference, industry spokesman Harold Hughes (director general of the UKOOA) issued a challenge to the new regulatory authority:

> Although the HSE have already signaled that exemptions will be available for such cases, it is a fact that over half of current UK installations are likely under this proposed legislation to be the subject of applications for exemptions. . . . It does not seem to us, to put it mildly, to be good law that demands, *ab initio,* the exemption of over half the installations to which that law is supposed to apply [10].

The cost of each TSR was expected to amount to about half the total costs of the installation Safety Case. The HSE estimated the outlay on TSRs alone as between £1.3 billion and £1.7 billion for the industry as a whole [9, p. 8]. Viewed from this angle, the UKOOA's sensitivity to what it regarded as "prescriptivity" was perhaps understandable.

Following the March 1992 publication of the consultative document on the draft Safety Case regulations and the accompanying guide to the Safety Case [11], the HSE met with the UKOOA on a regular basis. It also met with the International Association of Drilling Contractors (IADC) and the British Rig Owners Association (BROA), which represents the major drilling rig owners. During the course of the consultation concerning TSRs, the very concept of a TSR was successively redefined by the substitution of the term "temporary refuge" for temporary safe refuge, stressing the functional rather than structural dimension of survivability [12]. As the HSE guide to the Safety Case regulations described this:

> . . . measures to protect the workforce should include arrangements for temporary refuge from fire, explosion and associated hazards during the period for which they may need to remain on an installation following an uncontrolled incident, and for enabling their evacuation, escape and rescue [11, p. vii].

It was argued by industry, simplistic notions of a refuge in terms of a "protected box" or physical entity, normally the accommodation block, needed to be replaced by a more "sophisticated" concept of a processual "flow." Personnel could be removed from the hazard source in a series of protected access or escape routes to evacuation points.

In this context, it was even suggested that in certain circumstances a lifeboat could fulfill the function of a temporary refuge. In terms of safety engineering, it was argued, this had much to commend. It offered flexibility in adapting to different installation requirements. However, as with the concept of "goal-setting" itself, such flexibility also created space within which the operators could redefine safety parameters more freely and interpret regulatory objectives with discretion. Effectively, the UKOOA was seeking to create a zone of containment within which recourse to the notion of flexibility provided a useful counterstrategy to potentially costly regulatory requirements.

Evidence for a systematic reinterpretation of goal setting can be found in several industry publications, including a paper by Harold Hughes to an HSE-sponsored conference on offshore safety [10]. Here, the UKOOA adopted a three-pronged attack against prescriptive elements within the new draft Safety Case. The UKOOA argued first, that most mobile installations differed from Piper Alpha (a northern waters fixed installation), and asserted that the draft regulations assumed there was uniformity. Second, it criticized the requirement for each installation to have a temporary safe refuge as overly "prescriptive." Last, the UKOOA opposed the requirement that the new regulatory authority, the Offshore Safety Division, would have to formally "accept" the installation's Safety Case, a requirement that it felt went beyond the existing onshore Control of Industrial Major Accident Hazard (CIMAH) regulations. Hughes pointed out on behalf of the UKOOA that the cost and time-scale for the preparation of Safety Cases would itself be a considerable burden on the industry. He stated the crux of his argument as follows:

> The concept of acceptance places a great deal of power and discretion in the hands of the HSE without any of the safeguards often brought into such legislation to cover instances where real issues of difference arise between the regulatory body and industry [10, p. 4].

In addition to these specific representations, the UKOOA applied a multitude of arguments in its attempt to undermine the regulatory stringency of the new regime. These ranged from "concerns" that the Department of Employment, to which the HSE and OSD at that time ultimately reported, was "nontechnical" and therefore not well equipped to judge "quite arcane technical issues," to repeated references to the industry's own superior expertise [10, p. 5].

Interventions by the UKOOA designed to contain Lord Cullen's recommendations, if anything, intensified as the third and ongoing phase of post-Cullen safety legislation was launched. The first phase had involved the passing of the Offshore Safety Act, while the second phase involved the introduction of Safety Case regulations. In the third phase, existing offshore health and safety legislation was to be revised to a less prescriptive style that would complement the new Safety Case regime. Specifically, offshore-specific regulations on evacuation, escape, and rescue, fire and explosion protection, on design and construction, and on management and administration were to be overhauled. Meanwhile, certain key existing onshore regulations under the HSWA, such as the Control of Substances Hazardous to Health (COSHH) Regulations (1988), were also to be extended offshore. In addition to implementing European Union health and safety directives, the HSE proposed new across-the-board safety regulations.

Offshore-specific regulations, goal setting rather than prescriptive in nature, were typified by the Offshore Installations (Prevention of Fire, Explosion, and Emergency Response [PFEER] Regulations and Approved Code of Practice (ACOP) [13]. These PFEER Regulations were implemented in the latest phase of regulatory reconstruction [14]. At their core, these regulations were meant to simplify, rationalize, and replace existing prescriptive regulation governing the prevention of fire and explosions, as well as emergency response on offshore installations. Related to these regulations, Lord Cullen had emphasized the need for a degree of regulatory "solidity" in the Safety Case goal-setting regime:

> The regime should not rely solely on the Safety Case . . . the regulation requiring the Safety Case should be complemented by other regulations dealing with specific features. . . . These regulations would complement the Safety Case by setting intermediate goals and would give the regime a solidity which it might otherwise lack [6, ch. 17.63].

Offshore Safety Division officials conceded early on that "PFEER does contain more detailed and more specific primary duties with which duty holders need to comply" [15]. In responding to such intermediate regulations, the UKOOA tried to establish a false opposition between goal setting and prescription. In a speech to the Offshore Engineering Society in Aberdeen, Harold Hughes stated that the UKOOA "wants to ensure that all elements of prescription are done away with." The UKOOA seemed content to embrace a goal-setting regime, but only insofar as it was denuded of any regulatory demands or controls of a more specific nature.

This attitude extended to the industry's position on the legal status of other regulatory instruments, such as Approved Codes of Practice. Approved Codes of Practice prescribe the particular means of compliance with the general legal requirements of the regulations, which, if not followed, oblige the operator to demonstrate that an equally effective system of safeguards has been devised. The normal burden of proof is then reversed and it is up to the "duty holder" (the employer) to satisfy the default requirement in any legal proceedings.

Predictably, the UKOOA suggested that all Approved Codes of Practice be reshaped as more general nonmandatory "Guidance Notes," arguing that the Approved Codes of Practice were "too prescriptive," because they carried potential "legal implications." Said the UKOOA:

> By supporting goal-setting Regulations with ACOPs rather than non-mandatory Guidance, the flexibility provided by goal-setting Regulations is greatly reduced [16].

This was the reiteration of a line of argument seeking to minimize regulatory oversight that the operators had put forward since the Burgoyne report in the early 1980s [3, Cmnd 7866, 134, para. E]. Similar conflicts about the more or less binding nature of new safety requirements arose over the matter of standby vessels. Again, economic considerations dictated much of the UKOOA's approach to this issue. This was noted by one serving standby vessel ship's officer who stated that:

> It appears that the whole industry is trying to paper over the cracks with the cheapest possible options, and hope that another large-scale disaster does not happen [17].

Lord Cullen had urged that the standard of the existing standby vessel fleet be improved "with dispatch" [6, ch. 20.41]. The code covering such vessels had first been proposed in 1974, its "binding force . . . based on a voluntary agreement whereby members of UKOOA undertook to abide by the standards set out in the code" [6, ch. 20.37]. The Department of Transport felt that the voluntary agreement had been honored. Lord Cullen, however, expressed his concern about the length of time taken to update the voluntary code for standby vessels. The third edition of the code had first been proposed in 1986 but was not published in draft form until 1989. It had still not been completed by 1990 when Cullen's report was released. Eventually it come into effect in July 1991.

In the mid-1990s, the industry's attempt to minimize its safety obligations found a new target: the Certifying Authorities. This gave rise to concerns among Certifying Authorities such as Det Norske Veritas. One of the officials of this company noted with regard to the UKOOA's activities that:

> more and more, the larger operators emphasize the *challenging* of all standards and in particular non-mandatory guidances. . . . This challenging is not always as the purist would have it, namely by virtue of improving the level of safety. Rather it is usually a challenge to find a cheaper alternative or equivalent solution, and not to set goals from that solution. Current experience with regard to this challenging shows that it extends to critical features related to availability of equipment during an emergency [18, emphasis added].

Such candid appraisals were not welcomed by the industry, and unsurprisingly the UKOOA questioned the HSE's list of Certifying Authorities endorsed as competent to approve design and construction fitness-for-purpose. In its submissions on the draft Design and Construction Regulations for offshore installations, the UKOOA claimed that the specified list of six Certifying Authorities secured "those bodies as providing such services with a largely captive market" [19]. The UKOOA further argued that:

> proof of fitness-for-purpose should be a duty of the operator under his Safety Case and that scope for appointment of a suitable authority should be much wider, *extending for instance to another expert branch of his own organisation* provided he could show to HSE's satisfaction its competence and that independence of judgment was still being achieved [19, pp. 4-5, emphasis added].

Another key arena of continuing regulatory resistance by the offshore industry concerns European legislation. While the Social Charter in itself creates no enforceable rights, the resulting Social Action Program and the Directives on worker protection that flow from it have the potential to do so. Under the Single European Act (1986), which introduced Article 118A into the Treaty of Rome, the European Commission was given the authority to adopt Directives laying down "minimum requirements." The European Framework Directive (89/391/EEC) of 1989, which sought to encourage improvements in the safety and health of workers, and the various "daughter" Directives that have been promulgated, therefore affect British domestic legislation [20].

For the offshore industry one of the least desirable pieces of European legislation was and is the European Working Time Directive, which, applied fully, would outlaw many current shift systems. In a remarkably frank newspaper article, Chris Ryan, the external affairs director of the UKOOA, spelled out the trepidation with which the oil operators' association viewed the "increasing deluge of European legislation . . . threatening to swamp U.K. industry, including firms involved in the North Sea offshore oil and gas industry" [21]. In the industry's analysis, the proposed "Directive Concerning Certain Aspects of the Organization of Working Time," or the "Working Time Directive" limiting the maximum working week to forty-eight hours, presented a major threat [22]. When the Directive was adopted on November 23, 1993, its provisions were to be implemented by member states within three years. The United Kingdom secured an additional seven year opt-out period during which employees could work longer than forty-eight hours a week on a voluntary basis. In 1996, the U.K. government, with the operators' support, sought to challenge the legal basis of this Directive in the European Court of Justice. It did so on the grounds of the alleged lack of evidence of a link between working hours and accidents, arguing additionally that because the proposal related to working conditions and employment matters, it thus required unanimous approval of the Member States before it could be adopted [23]. The European Court decided against the U.K. government.

As part of a strategy of resistance, the UKOOA launched a campaign to oppose limitations on offshore working hours when it appeared that the European Commission was about to reclassify oil and gas production as a "continuous industrial process." This would have subjected the industry to the same regulations setting the maximum working hours per shift, or over the course of a week, as onshore. In 1993, however, the industry, in collaboration with the Department of Trade and Industry (DTI), had launched a major cost-reduction exercise, the Cost Reduction Initiative for the New Era (CRINE) [24], which led to alterations in shift patterns to three-week tours offshore (from the previous two-on, two-off pattern), thus increasing total working hours. The new shift rotations, as Eric Brandie of Chevron candidly revealed, saved his company £20 million per annum in helicopter charges alone [25].

In mid-1994, the UKOOA learned that the exclusion, which had been granted from the Working Time Directive for "Work at Sea," was to be reviewed and that a special review group had been established. Renewed representations were made by the UKOOA's Employment Practices Committee to the European Commissioner for Social Affairs, Padraig Flynn. The chairman of Esso warned the U.K. government that if the directive was implemented "energy-intensive industries . . . will simply migrate to other, less foolish parts of the world" [26]. Prior to the 1996 European intergovernmental conference, Esso spoke for the industry, noting, "efforts to restore competitiveness will be the touchstone for change and policy priorities rather than more chapters, charters, regulations and directives."

One characteristic of the post-Cullen reconstruction, therefore, is that a containment of regulatory interference has occurred, despite an outward emphasis on regulatory renewal. In past years, this containment has taken on new targets. Far from offshore safety legislation being "ring fenced," industry resistance to new regulatory interference is now being replicated by the UKOOA's deregulatory initiatives at both the European and domestic levels. In the post-Cullen debate, the industry no longer confronts critical arguments directly. Rather it delivers its message in a coded form, focusing on issues such as the alleged "dilution" of the Safety Case regime through new tranches of safety regulation; the attempt to substitute industry's own guidelines for official regulatory codes of practice; and finally, the attempt to squeeze out external audit by the Certifying Authorities in favor of in-house certification. In the arena of European politics, the industry, meanwhile, continues to focus on the Working Time Directive.

Like many similar attempts to reform regulatory systems in relation to a hostile industry, the post-Cullen reconstruction is likely to have resulted in a "gradual erosion scenario" [27]. The gradual erosion scenario describes a situation where a legislative agenda, which clearly mandates a behavior change, gradually deteriorates as it faces a host of "veto points." These veto points emerge when concrete regulations are negotiated. In our context, the negotiation of these regulations allowed the UKOOA, after an initial spell of seeming acquiescence, to reaffirm its opposition to regulatory interference, both at the national and European levels. Along these veto points, resistance to legislative proposals such as Safety Case "acceptance" by the regulator, the requirement for temporary safe refuges, the PFEER regulations and Approved Codes of Practice, and the removal of the requirement for dedicated standby vessels, allowed the operators to gradually reassert their hegemony.

Industry resistance immediately followed the publication of Lord Cullen's report and the establishment of the OSD. With the end of Lord Cullen's inquiry, the enforcement of a new offshore regime had become the responsibility of the HSE. Initially, HSE staff involved in this effort were perhaps enthusiastic. However, this commitment wore off as more managerial staff, anxious to reduce conflict, were added. Meanwhile, the agency's supporting constituency, the media, and in part the offshore workers, has largely withered away, while the opposition, organized under the UKOOA, has become increasingly demanding and vociferous. This weakening of the regulator, in turn, has encouraged the regulated business to make less effort in complying with the newly established rules; thereby further reducing the credibility of the regulator.

The ultimate question of policy import, however, is whether or not significant improvements in industry safety performance since the Piper Alpha disaster can be identified. The regulatory regime is one aspect of the issue. However, its effectiveness is predicated not just on industry compliance, but on the support of its actors, key among whom are the members of the offshore workforce. Before examining their role in the post-Piper Alpha safety regime in the next section, we analyze the available evidence on offshore safety performance.

OFFSHORE SAFETY TODAY: QUANTITATIVE AND QUALITATIVE EVIDENCE

The UKOOA has repeatedly suggested that the injury rates of those employed in oil and gas extraction are generally in the low range, falling well below other so-called dangerous industries. The reality, unfortunately, has been much more bleak. Once data were stripped of distortions arising from the inclusion of onshore employees and the inclusion of minor injuries, which were chronically under-reported offshore, the offshore industry, post Piper Alpha turned out to be the third most dangerous industry, ranking only behind (1) open cast coal workings, (2) coal mines, and (3) forestry. This rank order of 'third most dangerous industry' was not merely a contingent feature of the most recent available statistics, it applied to a series of years (see Table 1). That the offshore industry was, and is the most dangerous sector is also confirmed by the "hardest" figure of all, namely workplace fatalities (see Table 2).

Perhaps more important to the debate on offshore safety than the comparative position relative to other industries, is the industry's record over time. Here it can be observed that the past two decades have brought no major improvements in the industry's accident record (see Table 3). Rather, there is evidence of the incident rates fluctuating with upturn and downturn in the industry. This is particularly pronounced for the periods from 1985 to 1990 when the industry faced a major profit crunch, first on account of the falling oil price, and then on account of the costs associated with Cullen's post-Piper Alpha safety regime. A similar pattern is observable again, albeit less pronounced, for the period, from 1993 to 1995 and 1997/98 when there was a renewed fall in the oil price.

Evidence of a more qualitative nature moreover points toward a systematic underreporting of offshore incidents. Scott has identified what he terms a "hidden transcript" developed by the disempowered in socially oppressive situations [28]. Offshore, most attempts to develop a "safety culture" based on open and shared communication fail if only because existing managerial agendas have given no place to genuine workforce participation [29]. At the same time, the notion of safety is being used as a weapon to reestablish managerial control and legiti-macy. In most cases this agenda reproduces the "common values" of Human Resource Management. These values themselves are difficult to accept in an industry whose management practices appear to be more concerned with manu-facturing "improvements" than with uncovering genuine workplace problems.

The hidden transcripts of worker testimonies that we have collected are often all too obvious. The following testimony, which we have altered to protect the identity of the worker concerned, illustrates management practices of suppressing the reporting of accidents that run counter to the industry's self-proclaimed commitment to an offshore safety culture:

My accident happened on the "A" installation and resulted in my having . . .
to wear a surgical collar. On the "A" (2 days later) the company phoned me

Table 1. Ranking of Industries by Injury Rates per 100,000 Employees, Using Combined Incident Rates (Fatalities and Serious Injuries) 1990/91, 1991/92, 1992/93, and Average

	1990/91	1991/92	1992/93	Average 1990/93
1. Open cast coal mining	—	729.2	952.4	840.8
2. Coal mines	651.7	709.3	646.8	669.3
3. Offshore extraction of mineral oil and natural gas	370.0	318.5	329.4	339.3
4. Forestry	291.7	307.7	324.7	308.0
5. Coke ovens	200.0	428.6	285.7	304.8
6. Construction	289.3	247.3	247.3	261.3
7. Railways	245.9	224.6	224.8	231.8
8. Metal manufacturing	231.2	222.5	224.3	226.0
9. Repair of consumer goods and products	206.7	193.2	221.4	207.1
10. Food, drink, tobacco manufacturing	227.5	204.6	218.5	216.9
11. Production of man-made fibers	269.8	112.9	218.2	200.3
12. Supporting services to transport	160.0	172.6	193.2	175.3
13. Manufacture of metal goods not elsewhere specified	208.1	221.1	191.1	206.8
14. Manufacture of non-metallic mineral products	209.5	214.5	190.9	205.0
15. Timber and wooden furniture industries	200.5	190.1	187.9	192.8
16. Processing of rubber and plastics	182.4	178.0	171.5	177.3
17. Non-energy mineral extraction	199.2	179.7	171.3	183.4
18. Water supply industries	145.6	126.4	135.4	135.8
19. Manufacture of other transport equipment	130.8	138.0	126.9	131.9
20. Manufacture of motor vehicle and parts	142.2	114.7	125.7	127.6
21. Production and distribution of energy	135.6	113.2	109.3	119.4
22. Postal services and telecommunications	118.7	89.3	105.2	104.4

Source: HSC Annual report, various years, HSE/OSD Offshore accident and incident statistics report, various years.

up asking if I would come into the office when I was due to go offshore which I was due to . . . (1 week later), and do some light duties. The company obviously tried to avoid a Lost Time Injury. I refused. A few days later X suggested to me about getting some letters and forms sent over to the house and to do some paper work with the help of my wife. Once again avoiding a Lost Time Injury. I agreed but only after speaking to Y first as we both said

Table 2. Average Fatality Rate 1986/87 to 1993/94

	Average rate per 100,000 employees
Extraction of minerals/ores other than coal, oil, and gas	25
Forestry	21
Extraction of mineral oil and natural gas	15[a]
Coal extraction	15
Railways	10

[a]This excludes the 167 fatalities in the Piper Alpha disaster. The average with these deaths would have been 64 per 100,000 employees.
Source: HSC Health and Safety statistics 1994/95:8.

> I'd get my full money and not the usual 80% sick pay. Although I don't agree with this I do have to consider my family.

This testimony is by no means unique[1]. The following worker's testimony involved a Lost Time Incident that the company "reclassified" as an occupational injury:

> While working for X Group Engineering an incident occurred whilst working night shift. Myself and a pipe fitter were trying to split two flanges which had not been opened since the 1970s. Because of the rust we had to use wedges and a sledgehammer. I worked approximately twelve hours on this project, resulting in a severely inflamed elbow. I saw the doctor on the accommodation barge, who bandaged it and gave me medication and ordered the next two shifts off to rest it. It was not better and the X Group manager suggested light duties. But the Doctor gave me a letter for my GP and insisted I went onshore. I was prescribed anti-inflammatories. After my two weeks shore leave, the company arranged for me to see another doctor. This doctor would not pass me as fit as my elbow was still swollen. I reported to the company office and was found office duties for the next two weeks, instead of returning for offshore duties or signing off on sick leave. When I eventually went back offshore, I was told this incident was being classed as an occupational injury and not as a Lost Time incident, even though I was sent off before my shift had ended.

This testimony closely matches the experiences reported in BBC television's *Frontline Scotland* by a Wood Group employee [30]. This employee recounted being put up by the company in an expensive Aberdeen hotel, the Royal, being "treated like a king" and being assigned light office duties in order to prevent

---

[1]The above and subsequent testimony evidence are in the authors' possession.

Table 3. Combined Incidents (Fatalities and Serious Injuries),
Combined Incident Rate, 1980/81 to 2000/2001 and
Three-Year Moving Average

Reporting year April/May	Combined incidents raw data	Combined incident rate (per 100,000 employees)	Three-year moving average
1980/81	49	224	254
1981/82	65	259	220
1982/83	52	227	251
1983/84	56	204	218
1984/85	72	279	308
1985/86	111	460	396
1986/87	104	571	519
1987/88	65	275	351
1988/89	80	345	336
1989/90	89	377	379
1990/91	97	382	349
1991/92	118	319	333
1992/93	116	329	295
1993/94	88	257	365
1994/95	69	254	321
1995/96	72	248	296
1996/97	46	171	314
1997/98	77	334	279
1998/99	75	294	243
1999/2000	55	289	205*
2000/2001	53*	227*	

Data exclude the 167 fatalities of the Piper Alpha disaster. *Data for the most recent period are provisional with likely increases of around 20 %.
Source: Woolfson, Foster, and Beck (1997), *Paying for the Piper:* 399 and HSE, Hazardous Installations Directorate, Offshore Injury and Incident Statistics 2000/2001, http://www.hse.gov.uk/hid/osd/hsr1001/annex1-1htm.

a Lost Time Injury being recorded that would allegedly have threatened the company's bonus of a quarter of a million pounds. To date there has been no response or denial from the company.

The next testimony shows just how much of the oil industry's safety policies are window dressing, with potential perverse effects. The testimony is by a safety representative who resigned from his duties "in disgust" over his company's conduct. These statements describe a situation where nonreporting was an official and explicit company policy:

> One major concern of many of the workforce and especially myself was not only the amount of incidents occurring, but the actual reporting and categorizing of the incident, especially the dreaded Lost Time Injury (LTI), which the oil industry uses as a measurement of safety.
>
> On this contract men suffering an LTI were given "light duty" in offices or classed as restricted work-case injuries in order to prevent the incident being reported as an LTI, and to reach the magical figure of one million man hours without an LTI. During the "new initiatives" senior management and safety advisers admitted to me that incident statistics had been doctored. They suggested that the practice would stop forthwith, and so it did for a certain period of time. However, shortly after, certain management were transferred from the project and the practice resurfaced and still flourishes today. I believe that statistics are doctored for financial gain, i.e. bonuses paid for a good safety performance and penalty clause payments imposed for poor safety performance. Therefore, I believe the oil industry's methods of measuring safety by the use of LTIs are severely flawed and open to abuse. If the oil companies and the contracting companies insist on this method of measurement then they should stick to the rules and not move the goalposts when it suits them. Lessons could then be learnt, thus helping to prevent similar incidents in the future. Of course every man and his dog knew that the statistics had been fiddled. From that moment on, the safety meetings went down hill. Arguments broke out as to why an accident was not classed as an LTI or why this incident had not been reported. It was getting so bad that the safety department was nicknamed the Bluff Department by a large number of regulars.

Strategies aimed at suppressing incident reporting are not limited to individual accidents. Nonreporting also encompasses potentially safety-critical events and even near misses. The following testimony is from an offshore worker who recounts a potentially dangerous hydrocarbon release:

> I was personally involved in an oil mist release in one of the separator modules. I actually raised the alarm. Believe you me it was pretty scary. After questioning by the then offshore installation manager (OIM) I was praised for my prompt actions and rewarded with a £50 gift voucher.
>
> The very next trip at the safety meeting the usual statistics were read out by the safety officer. To my surprise no mention of the oil mist release was made. I raised this point with the safety officer as to why no incident report had been made. The safety officer denied all knowledge of the incident. He replied that the OIM had been fully briefed and he felt there was no need to report the incident as there had been similar incidents in the past and there was nothing to gain by raising a report.

The current system of accident reporting in the words of this former safety rep "has been proved to be wide open to abuse time and time again." The testimony continues with a case of scaffolders who were pressured into doing unsafe tasks:

> An example of safety being compromised was the case of scaffolders being pressured by Z's supervision, to work "over the side" in hours of darkness. In fact the scaffolders concerned were threatened with final warnings and dismissal if they failed to comply. It must be pointed out, that the dozen or so "scaffs" with years of experience behind them, had never worked or been asked to work under these conditions in the past.
>
> Myself and a "scaff" safety rep immediately approached the OIM and complained at the treatment and threats directed at the men. The OIM thought that this practice was a reasonable request. No one would be forced to work under such circumstances. However, he reserved the right to implement this practice if required. It should be noted that the "scaffs" had a test run prior to the meeting with the OIM in artificial light, and concluded this practice was deemed to be unsafe due to blind spots.

Today the United Kingdom Offshore Operators' Association, continues to proclaim its accomplishments in lowering offshore incidents [31]. While it is difficult to assess how widespread the manipulation of accident data is, anecdotal evidence would suggest that these claims of "improvements" by the industry should be viewed very critically. In the past the self-congratulatory attitude of oil operator spokespersons has undermined a critical debate on offshore safety. Today's industry leaders may be somewhat more self-critical.

STEP CHANGE—A STEP BACKWARDS?

A cornerstone of Lord Cullen's recommendations for the new offshore safety regime was the involvement of the workforce in the safety process [6, Vol. 2, Recommendation 27]:

> It is essential that the whole workforce is committed to and involved in safe operations. The first-line supervisors are a key link in achieving that, as each is personally responsible for ensuring that all employees, whether the company's own or contractors, are trained to and do work safely and that they not only know how to perform their jobs safely but are convinced that they have a responsibility to do so. Possibly the most visible instrument for the involvement of the workforce in safety is a safety committee system [6, ch. 18.48].

While the operators were determined to resist regulatory requirements that would have involved the trade unions in achieving this via collective power, it was necessary that the alternative system of safety committees be regarded as a credible vehicle for workforce safety concerns. Evidence from a study by Aberdeen University for the HSE, from a Market and Opinion Research International (MORI) opinion survey and from internal company studies, however, pointed to continuing problems in the "safety climate" and workforce communication on safety matters [32]. The results of the MORI survey specifically noted as an issue of workforce concern "You have anxieties about speaking out" [32]. These problems were aggravated by the fact that the new technocratic language of the Safety Case regime could be matched with equal authority by the voice of the workforce. In September 1997 a new initiative, "Step Change," was launched by the industry in tacit recognition that the area of workforce involvement in safety at the platform level was a continuing weakness. This initiative brought together three major sectors of the industry, the operators as represented by the UKOOA, the exploration side as represented by the North Sea Chapter of the IADC, and the contracting companies grouped together in the Offshore Contractors' Association (OCA).

Step Change had three aims. First, to "deliver a 50% improvement in the whole industry's safety performance over three years." Second, through "safety performance contracts," Step Change would "demonstrate visibly our personal concern for safety as an equal to business performance." Third, the industry would "work together to improve sharing of safety information and good practice across the whole industry, through the act of involvement of employees, service companies, operator, trade unions, regulators and representative bodies" [33].

For perhaps the first time the trade unions (or at least those acceptable to the operators) were to be invited to play a limited role in safety offshore as "social partners," albeit at strategy level, rather than through representatives speaking directly for the workforce on the offshore installations. There was also much talk of "changing the culture" of the industry and of "empowering" employees. Attempts were to be made to raise safety awareness through safety packs, common induction programs, posters, the wearing of green hardhats for "newstarts," and even a safety video featuring a "Terminator lookalike." Where they are contradicted by "day-to-day experience at the point of production," such initiatives are likely to make "workers skeptical of the propaganda" [34].

When Step Change commenced, there was indeed evidence of pronounced workforce skepticism with respect to the program. One important source of doubt was the attempt to deliver the "50% improvement" in the safety performance of the industry over the next three years. Even the manifesto of the Step Change initiative conceded that the industry's annual improvement in safety performance as measured by the all injury rate frequency, had slowed in the past two years [35].

But Step Change hit upon a much more ingenious way of achieving its 50% improvement target. The "traditional" accident and injury statistics were supplemented "with some more proactive measures of safety activity, often referred to as 'leading indicators'." Visits by senior management to worksites "to carry out safety audits and to lead workforce discussions," as well as safety training "as measured by program days and spending," were designated as leading indicators. With inverted logic, Step Change proposed that "measuring increased 'input' activity will be just as important as measuring 'output'" [35]. One highly committed safety representative commented:

> You say you want workforce involvement in "Step Change," but you have already set up the whole basis of the scheme. There is simply no mechanism for achieving involvement at a fundamental level. What you really want is workforce compliance, compliance with decisions already arrived at. What you want are people who will nod in agreement with these edicts you hand down to them. You want "Nodders." And as P.G. Wodehouse, who could always put these things better than almost anyone else, said of Nodders: "A Nodder is something like a Yes-man, only lower down the social scale" [36].

Ultimately the Step Change program failed to ignite the imagination of the offshore workforce. This was evidenced by the low level of participation in the initiative, even by elected safety representatives [37]. Recognition of this fundamental flaw led to the introduction of a "workforce involvement trial" on the Brent Charlie [38]. The dedicated presence of workforce representation was "now seen as an essential element in making the STEP change a success." This involved a member of the platform crew being seconded onshore for six months to take part in Step Change team meetings. The workforce on the Brent Charlie was duly invited to put their names forward as volunteers. Platform management selected the lucky individual, not from the ranks of elected safety representatives one of the most vocal of whom happened to be onshore on leave, but from six names drawn out of a hat.

Understandable skepticism was also expressed in the minutes of Shell's internal quarterly safety representatives meetings. These confirmed how safety initiatives were framed by the workforce in terms of their own preoccupations. For the contract workforce, these revolved around their basic insecurity of employment. The representatives at the Step Change meetings were quite clear as to the workforce priorities:

> The consensus was that a marked apathy has developed within the workforce with regard to "Step Change." The program is generally viewed as, "yet another management initiative on health and safety with no direct impact on the day-to-day life of the employee." A major part of the current level of "apathy" and the general unsettled feelings . . . derives from the insecurity and the conflicting messages which are being received. This, in particular, related to changes to contract without any formal notification being received before its implementation. Also assurances of no imminent redun-dancies immediately followed within a week by this being applied to two long-term . . . employees [39].

A lack of feedback and information on actions or progress on the Step Change initiatives, within the stated policy of active employee involvement, made identifi-cation with the initiative difficult. Indeed, after the initial "star-spangled" launch, the program appeared to have faltered requiring "rejuvenation" in late 2002. A more quantitative approach using a three-year "rolling" average of fatal and major injury rates (per 100,000 workers), the only really "robust" measure, over the years following the implementation of the Cullen Report recommendations, suggests a long-term upwards trend in offshore incident rates. For the years of the Step Change program, since its launch in 1997, incident rates appear to have reached a plateau showing no significant safety improvements, following an initial increase in rates during the first years of Step Change, which may be a "reporting effect." In sum, by this measure, Step Change did not reach its initial projected target, i.e., to deliver a 50% improvement in the whole industry's safety performance over three years. Indeed, combined incident rates, at best, show marginal improvements only in most recent years (see Table 4).

Table 4. 3 Year Rolling Average of Injury Rates (per 100,000 workers)
April 1992-March 2003(p)

	1993-96	1994-97	1995-98	1996-99	1997-00	1998-01	1999-02	2000-03(p)
Average workforce	30,134	27,685	26,285	25,118	22,500	22,610	21,845	22,933
Combined fatalities and major injuries	156.0	162.5	216.9	262.8	**306.7**	**274.2**	**247.2**	**248.6**

Note: (p) = provisional. **Source:** HSE Hazardous Installations Directorate Offshore Division. Offshore Injury and Incident Statistics 2002/2003 (provisional data). Available at http://www.hse.gov.uk/offshore/statistics/hsr1003/annex1pt1.htm

As one safety representative put it:

> Improved safety was a goal they all agreed with and would like to achieve. It was however difficult to relate to this while worries over their personal future was so much in the forefront of their minds [39].

Like so many of the concerns around safety and health, workers when asked will point to the seemingly obvious but routinely ignored truth that the under-lying context of industrial relations ultimately determines the efficacy of a safety program, no matter how sincere the intentions of its proponents might be. In the final part of this chapter we analyze this industrial relations context, which has its own complex history in the unfolding trajectory of tragedy that led to Piper Alpha, and remains unresolved to the present day.

UNION AVOIDANCE IN THE OIL INDUSTRY

The industrial relations regime that the U.S. companies had brought to the North Sea was uncongenial to most U.K. workers. Louisiana and Texas oilmen of the early 1970s had brought with them an individualistic, macho, "kick-ass," antiunion culture that was embraced by home-grown "plastic Yanks." Women were not welcome in this male-dominated world and only rarely were allowed to work offshore. The companies exercised absolute power over who could and could not stay on the rigs. A worker could be ordered back to shore on the next helicopter, simply because the foreman didn't like the look on his face, didn't like long hair, and, in one legendary case, didn't like any Frenchmen on the rig. Diaries compiled by offshore workers graphically record that for many Americans, the Scots were little more than "tartan coolies." Attitudes to safety and occupational welfare of employees were casual, as were general views on existing U.K. regulations on safety. In the early phase of North Sea development, priority was given to getting the oil out of the seabed. Money was no object, and the drilling companies' and operators' men made the workforce "jump to it" to get the job done. Safety considerations were very often secondary. In the words of one U.S. toolpusher (drilling supervisor), "There's only two can'ts—if you can't do it, you can't stay."

With men working in the industry drawn from every known walk of life, offshore work, nonetheless, acquired the mystique of a "frontier" existence. The reality was far more brutal. Accidents and injuries were frequent. Management practices were capricious and authoritarian, utilizing bullying and victimization tactics. Any worker identified by the operator or client as a "troublemaker," perhaps someone who had raised a safety concern or a union activist, was likely to be immediately "run off" the platform. The institutionalized victimization was known throughout the industry by the initials "NRB," designating a worker as "Not Required Back" on that platform. Legal protection for victimized workers, meanwhile, was nonexistent, and organized trade unionism had yet to establish any kind of foothold offshore.

Many obstacles had to be overcome in organizing the offshore workforce. An internal 1976 union analysis noted that oil companies, virtually without exception, employed a host of strategies to obstruct unionization. These included:

> The insistence on full ballots, not only for collective bargaining rights but also for simple representational rights; company initiated anti-union propaganda being spread in the run up to the ballot; prolonged delays in holding ballots, and delays in affording rights where the ballot has been successful; the setting up of staff consultative machinery to undermine the activities of *bona fide* trade unions . . . more favorable conditions of service to non-unionized areas and asking prospective employees their attitudes to trade unions [40].

These observations applied to U.S. and U.K. companies alike. In fact, the document stressed the particular difficulties experienced with Esso (Exxon) as well as with BP and Shell. From the 1970s to the early 1990s, Britain's offshore oil workers experienced a continuous line of disempowerment, blacklisting, and victimization, whenever they posed a challenge to the nonunion structure of industrial relations. Not surprisingly, actual levels of union membership remained low.

However, retrospectively, not all of the obstacles to offshore unionization can be attributed to the oil companies. The unions themselves, despite early attempts to develop a unified approach to this new industry, pursued a path of competitive, sectional rivalry, in which each saw the advancement of their own position as occurring at the expense of rivals. This rivalry was aggravated by the lack of clarity over occupational boundaries and legitimate "spheres of influence" between the half dozen or so unions with an interest in recruiting offshore. Thus mechanics, motormen, and rig technicians were organized by the engineering union, the Amalgamted Union of Engineering Workers, the electricians by the Electrical, Electronic, Telecommunications and Plumbing Union (EETPU), and the welders by the Amalgamated Society of Boilermarkers, which joined with the general workers' union, the National Union of General and Municipal Workers (to become the GMB). Divers and catering crew were organized by the seafarers' union, the National Union Seamen, although the transport workers' union, the Transport and General Workers Union (TGWU), also had an interest from its onshore activities in this latter area. The TGWU, with existing interests in crews working on trawling vessels and waterways, sought to recruit the lower grades of drill crews, from roustabouts up to derrickmen, who could be otherwise classed as general laborers. The technicians' union, the Association of Scientific Technical and Managerial Staffs (ASTMS) (later to become Manufacturing Science Finance [MSF]) instructed its local officer to prioritize recruitment in the North Sea on production platforms, particularly among the technicians who were direct employees of the operator companies such as Shell. The ASTMS also had ambitions that went beyond the direct employees. Seeing itself as *the* offshore union, it aimed to organize the offshore workforce comprehensively.

When an interunion committee of local officials, the Inter Union Offshore Oil Committee (IUOOC) was formed in Aberdeen, it met only quarterly and lacked the resources and strategy to match the employers. Nevertheless, with a Labour government in power in the mid-1970s and a sympathetic minister, Secretary of State Tony Benn at the Department of Energy, some pressure was put on the oil companies to accommodate union demands for access to offshore installations. In response, the oil companies raised the bogey of "demarcation disputes" interrupting the flow of production if unions were allowed offshore. Eventually, some oil companies conceded that the IUOOC could act on behalf of its constituent unions in matters of access and of recognition agreements. The new "Memorandum of Understanding," however, proved largely ineffectual in advancing the scope of unionism offshore. Thus, minutes of the IUOOC record continual frustration at what was seen as a consistent delay by the companies in consenting to reasonable requests for access by union officials to offshore installations.

By the 1980s, with the arrival of a Conservative government, the oil operators reconsidered even limited concessions. Union officials wishing to go offshore for recruitment purposes now found that they had to wait between four and nine months to arrange visits with certain operators. Opportunities for officials to speak to the workforce as a collective body, once on the installation, were also dramatically restricted. As a consequence, union officials had to approach the men as best they could, at meal breaks or in their cabins. Frequently, no prior notice would be given of an official's arrival. Sometimes the union official would be placed in a cramped cabin next door to the office of the offshore installation manager (OIM). Many men feared that to express open interest in trade unions might damage their career prospects; a not unreasonable feeling in view of the recent history of the industry.

As an integral part of a union-avoidance strategy, the companies put in place a series of "consultative committees" to address employees' concerns, without union involvement. The establishment of such consultative committees had traditionally served as a union-avoidance strategy in the United States, especially in the post–World War II period. Kochan, Katz, and McKersie note that U.S. oil and chemical multinationals had fostered consultative committees as an alternative to the involvement of "third parties" since the 1950s [41]. The philosophy of one large U.S. oil company is reported as follows: "The company does not feel that a third party bargaining unit is necessary and will deal with employees directly pursuant to the (our) human relations philosophy" [41].

By the 1980s, U.S. management had gathered extensive experience in creating surrogate forms of employee representation "in response to the threat of, or as a direct substitute for, unionization" [42]. Brody describes this tradition of "unitarist" management as follows:

> Workers did not need a "third party" such as a broad-based trade union and would naturally benefit from . . . management-created structures because, as one observer contended in 1929, "modern business acted on the 'sincere belief that the interests of the employer and employee are mutual and at bottom identical'" [43, cited in 42].

Even at the early stages of offshore exploration, U.K. trade unions had already voiced dissatisfaction with management-dominated consultative committees, which they perceived as "a device of employers to inhibit the development of trade unionism offshore." The employers, meanwhile, asserted that such consultative committees were "a normal medium for communication between the company and its employees." An unpublished doctoral dissertation cites an industry handbook that defined "consultation" as "a process for communication between staff and management to enable the views of staff to be expressed, discussed and taken into account before management makes a decision on a matter" [44, p. 102]. The handbook states that the consultative committee is not "a forum for negotiating terms and conditions" [44, p. 102]. While this dissertation suggests some minor variations in the scope of such committees, their common function, was to act as a "safety valve." Indeed, one instance is reported when employees persisted in talking about negotiating terms and conditions, which led to the collapse of consultative arrangements. In this instance management had made it clear that such issues were not open to discussion and removed them from the arena [44, p. 102].

Where unionization threatened, management consultants were on hand to provide employers with supportive advice, which in one instance depicted the desire for collective representation as a form of neurotic response. A report, by Robert de Board of Henley Management College, found that the workers on the platform were suffering from "acute anxiety." The workers were "looking for the feminine mothering side of human nature which is being deliberately excluded in the macho management style." The consultant concluded that the wish for union representation was "a cry for help, 'come and look after us'."

The use of management consultants was particularly important for companies such as Mobil, which delayed a request for a visit by IUOOC representatives to the Beryl Alpha for over three months. Ostensibly, Mobil's grounds were that there had already been one such visit and that two visits per year were "reasonable." Industrial relations problems that summer had led Mobil to bring in Henley Management College consultants. Mobil denied that this was part of a "union-avoidance" strategy. The Mobil employee relations manager noted:

> Sensitive discussions were taking place with our employees to resolve the difficulties identified earlier. As we informed you, a union visit during these discussions would endanger proper focus on the actual problem at hand, and jeopardize our immediate objective to resolve the issues through direct consultation with our employees [45].

If the presence of a "third party" union official could be avoided until after management consultants had sorted out the problems and a consultative system was securely in place, so much the better. As Mobil declared:

> It remains our aim to institute an employee relations environment offshore, which is second to none. Our employees have been fully involved in the review of future needs, and in-depth consultation with them will continue. An increasing number has indicated trade union representation is not wanted and expressed the desire to see formal internal consultative machinery established. The feeling is that further union visits should be suspended until our discussions are completed [45].

Consultative committees remained a continuing feature of oil company union-avoidance strategy into the 1980s. At that time, however, there was growing trade union and political pressure to concede traditional forms of collective bargaining arrangements. The challenge facing the operators was to prevent union pressure from undermining the anomalous industrial relations regime they were seeking to implement offshore.

At this point two fundamentally different sets of expectations clashed. On a national level, unions expected an extension of collective bargaining to all sectors of the economy. On the oil multinational side, there was an expectation that unionization could be radically circumscribed, if not avoided altogether, in the long run. Many operators believed that business could be conducted offshore in the absence of comprehensive collective bargaining, without creating conflicts with the contemporary British political economy. The strategy adopted, therefore, was not always one of explicit challenge to unionization but rather one of delaying tactics and prevarication.

"USEFUL" BARGAINING

The production regime established by the oil majors in the North Sea relied heavily on a dependent layer of specialized subcontractors who followed the industry globally. Only a quarter to a third of the total workforce were direct employees of the oil companies, the clients. The majority were employed by contractors. The contract labor force, particularly that drawn from the onshore engineering and construction industry, pushed for, and eventually achieved, limited collective bargaining rights. But here, as elsewhere in the offshore oil industry, the exception proved the rule. Temporary and limited union recognition that did exist, was granted by the contracting employers only with the tacit approval of the oil company clients, and only insofar as it directly served their interests.

This pattern of a "useful" bargaining agreement was exemplified by the Offshore Construction Agreement, the so-called Hook-up agreement. The precondition for "first oil" was to "hook up" the complex system of pipes and attendant plant. Any unanticipated labor stoppage, even though involving small groups of workers, could be highly disruptive. Prior to the completion of the hook-up phase, construction workers could inflict hugely expensive delays on the operators by engaging in official, or, more often, unofficial, action. In economic theories this represented a classical case of hold-up, that is, a situation where technical circumstances permitted a small group of workers to exert temporary and "disproportionate" pressure on a firm that could not reap any return on its investments unless the respective groups of workers contributed their part [46].

In the early and mid-1970s, it was in the interests of the operators to bring their platforms into production as quickly as possible. This desire was rooted in two factors: first, government pressure to accelerate oil production for wider economic imperatives; and second, the wish of the oil companies to recoup their considerable outlays. Under these circumstances, there were important advantages in having a trade union agreement, whereby procedures for resolving industrial relations problems without the threat of work stoppages were first in place. As the construction workforce brought with them their onshore unionized identities, as well as their tradition of unofficial action, the offshore contractor companies, and, more critically, their clients, were resigned to some degree of union penetration in this sector. The key challenge was to contain the overall level of unionization and to prevent any outbreak of uncontrolled local-level bargaining.

The Hook-up agreement served this purpose by providing an orderly framework of collective bargaining from the mid-1970s onward. Indeed, when challenged by unofficial strike action in 1978, union officials lined up with the employers to protect the agreement. At the time, union officials ordered a return to work, which created a lasting legacy of bitterness and suspicion between themselves and the workforce. The real limitations of the agreement, however, rested not so much in its failure to provide for improved pay or work shift rotations for hook-up workers, but rather in the inability of unions to extend the terms of the agreement into periods of "post-construction" work or ongoing maintenance. With the commencement of "first oil" the Hook-up agreement and, along with it, union recognition would lapse. As a consequence, workers who were employed in maintenance work on the same platforms, experienced derecognition and a drop in their levels of pay. Successive attempts to widen the sphere of collective bargaining were met with consistent resistance by the oil major clients and their dependent contractors. Contractors wishing to concede to union demands risked subsequent exclusion by the oil majors in the system of competitive contract bidding. This then, was the background of industrial relations which provided the context for the Piper Alpha disaster.

PIPER ALPHA AND THE SUMMERS OF DISCONTENT

Survivors' transcripts submitted to Lord Cullen's public inquiry into the Piper Alpha disaster reveal the total breakdown of emergency procedures during that cataclysmic event. Communications were knocked out, sprinkler deluge systems failed to operate and support vessels could not perform rescue functions adequately. Management, both on the platform and on pipeline-linked platforms, failed to shut down and continued to feed the fires on Piper. Those responsible for emergency action were totally unprepared for a major emergency of this sort. For the workforce as a whole, there was the collective guilt that by their enforced disempowerment, they too were implicated in the circumstances that made such a catastrophe possible. As one oil worker commented to the authors:

> We heard what was happening on the radio on a platform a few miles away
> with horror and a degree of shame too, because we knew that by our silence
> we had contributed to that tragedy.

In the wake of the disaster, trade union activists began to organize onshore mass meetings. These mass meetings called for union recognition, the broadening of collective agreements, and a new role for trade unions in safety offshore. First in the summer of 1989, and then on a much larger scale in the summer of 1990, a wave of occupations of offshore installations by striking contract workers took place. These occupations challenged the legitimacy of offshore management. The actions were led by the Offshore Industry Liaison Committee (OILC), an unofficial union activist committee drawn from different installations and different trades among the contractor workforce across the North Sea. The OILC's planned industrial action was designed to hit the oil operators at their most vulnerable point, when the platforms were shut down for summer maintenance work and could not be started up again without the cooperation of the contractor workforce. It was hoped that this pressure would drive the oil companies into conceding a comprehensive industry agreement for contractor employees. The rigorous legal requirements of Conservative employment legislation and the scattered nature of the offshore workforce, working a system of two-week shifts with replacement crews, made the organization of official, legally balloted, industrial action very difficult. Unofficial industrial action, therefore, was a much more potent weapon with which to confront the oil operators in the aftermath of Piper Alpha. Such "surrogate" action was intended to persuade the contracting companies of the desirability of conceding formal recognition to the official trade union bodies.

While the contract workforce was on the point of succeeding in this objective during the first "summer of discontent," pressure from the client oil companies on the contractors prevented them from conceding bargaining rights to the unions. The second "summer of discontent," which involved a protracted overtime ban followed by an intensified wave of rig occupations, ended in a stalemate [47]. In response to these strikes offshore contractor companies employed a combination of stick and carrot. One the one hand, some contractors offered pay rises amounting to as much as 40%. On the other hand, court action to expel the occupying workforce from the offshore installations, together with mass dismissals of up to 1,000 strikers, served to quench the anger and militancy of the post–Piper Alpha workforce insurrection.

THE ANATOMY OF OFFSHORE
INDUSTRIAL ACTION

Perhaps the most remarkable feature of the oil workers' occupations of 1989 and 1990 is that they occurred at all. They took place in an industry where union members were a relatively small minority, where most employers had long refused union recognition, and where there was no tradition of collective bargaining. They occurred at a time when the level of strike activity within the United Kingdom as a whole was at a historic low, and in the face of some of the most oppressive antitrade union legislation in the Western world.

The offshore strikes took a form that evaded the legal ban on solidarity action or the requirement for ballots. The strikes relied on workplace organization that had to be created very quickly and demanded the active mobilization of the workforce for a specific end. These were not strikes in the classical sense. The workers remained on the platforms, but progressively withdrew from the jurisdiction of their employers, first through an overtime ban, and then through sit-ins. In doing so, the workforce developed its own alternative command structure. Intransigent managers were left humiliated. Those who sought to negotiate were drawn into tacit complicity.

As a form of industrial action, the tactic of sit-in, however, had inherent weaknesses. It was limited in time: It could not have been prolonged much beyond a month. It relied on the commitment of a relatively small core of activists who were very vulnerable to exclusion and victimization. It involved isolated groups of workers separated by hundreds of miles of sea and with no sure method of communication—and depended on securing sufficient unity across the U.K. Continental Shelf to be able to disrupt the operators at just that moment when they were required to undertake their maintenance operations. Because of the physical interconnection of the pipeline infrastructure, industrial action could inflict very heavy losses running into tens of millions of pounds. Stopping the oil, as U.S. consul Funkhouser noted in the mid-1970s, gave organized labor an immensely powerful lever [48]. The very capital intensity of the oil industry could put its relatively small workforce, once organized, in a commanding position.

The occupations of 1989 and 1990 occurred in an industry where there were no comprehensive structures of collective bargaining. In this respect, the offshore oil industry was similar to many other areas of the economy that had dispensed with trade unions in the 1980s [49]. Offshore managerial authority crumbled very quickly once it was challenged. Because of the lack of established negotiating structures, managers had restricted options for limiting conflict. Moreover, the demand for collective bargaining and participation in safety proved a powerful one that was not easily denied without further undermining managerial authority.

Interestingly, this challenge had not emerged wholly spontaneously from the rank and file. Nor had it been the result of a top-down initiative by the leadership of one union. Rather, it stemmed from the emergence of a common perspective among union activists at the local level, which drew upon a reservoir of previous experience. It was this perspective that initially served to unite both union officers and lay members across a number of different unions. Without this alliance it would not have been possible to access the organizational resources of the existing trade union structures or to unite the loyalties of a diversity of union members within the industry. It was in the aftermath of industrial action that Lord Cullen's long-awaited report into the disaster was published.

THE CULLEN REPORT
AND TRADE UNION RESPONSE

Although in his report Lord Cullen had been keen to address the issue of "workforce involvement" in the safety process, he had little to say about offshore industrial relations or the merits of union recognition. In the context of safety, however, Lord Cullen opened up the possibility of formal trade union partici-pation. He suggested that, where the trade unions could demonstrate that they had achieved substantial recognition and membership on a given installation, there might be a case for union-appointed safety representatives. Cullen noted that "union involvement in the safety representation process could be of some benefit . . . mainly through the credibility and resistance to pressures which trade union backing would provide" [6, ch. 21.84]. Moreover, he suggested that the issue of victimization needed to be addressed and recommended that legal protection be made available to offshore safety representatives.

The problem was that, given the existing low levels of union density and of penetration by individual unions, no single union was likely on its own to be able to cross the threshold of "substantial" numbers for recognition. In leading the unofficial industrial actions offshore, the OILC had broken down existing sectional divisions in the workforce. It had succeeded in forging a new more homogeneous identity for the workforce, which was in part, based on common grievances and, in part, upon shared experiences of danger. It was a logical next step to match this growing unity by establishing a formal trade union structure. If the existing unions with offshore interests were to collectively pool their indi-vidual memberships in a new Offshore Federation, then Cullen's threshold for membership and recognition would become attainable.

The OILC policy document, *Striking Out: New Directions for Offshore Workers,* provided a detailed manifesto of change [50]. Having already achieved an unprecedented measure of unity during the "summers of discontent," the established unions had agreed that existing fragmentary bargaining arrange-ments, such as the Hook-up agreement, should be suspended for the duration of the industrial action. In place of fragmented bargaining agreements such as the Hook-up agreement, the trade unions made demands for "single-table bargaining"; an agreement that would cover the entire offshore workforce, pro-viding comprehensive recognition and safety rights.

As the unofficial industrial action played itself out, many unions found that a reinstatement of previous sectional arrangements with the employers presented a more "realistic" fall-back position. With individual unions being unwilling to contemplate surrendering their offshore membership to the proposed new Offshore Federation, the national trade leaderships could not be persuaded to broker a radical departure from existing structures. More important, the estab-lished unions in the engineering and electrical trades were now intent upon amalgamation in pursuit of "super-union" status. Proposals for an Offshore Federation ran counter to aspirations of super-unionism, which ultimately rested on a "business-friendly" stance of union leaderships toward the employers encap-sulated in notions of "social partnership."

In the fierce internecine struggles that followed, incomprehensible to many within the broader movement, the OILC underwent a metamorphosis from an unofficial lay member activist committee into an independent trade union in its own right. The OILC's claim to "industrial unionism" rested, in the first instance, on its status as the only trade union body specifically dedicated to offshore oil workers. Its "personality" was based on a common understanding of the nature of power relations in the offshore environment, which had been advanced through the experience of industrial struggle. For many offshore workers, the OILC had become a "class bargainer" in Kerr's sense, with a broad set of demands and an equally broad perspective of union combativeness seeking to establish a counterweight to the dominant employers [51].

TRADE UNION AND EMPLOYER RESISTANCE TO THE OILC

The emergence of the OILC as an independent trade union in the aftermath of the Piper Alpha disaster and the offshore labor struggles that followed it, was welcomed by neither the employers nor the established trade unions. Shirley Lerner's now classic study of union "breakaways" has shown how established unions attempt to combat their breakaway rivals [52]. Unsurprisingly, the announcement in 1991 that the OILC was to seek status as an independent trade union was also met with hostility from the established trade union movement, including the United Kingdom's Trades Union Congress and the Scottish TUC.

Most "breakaway" unions remain small organizations that never develop the industrial muscle of the dominant established unions. In the case of the OILC, this has certainly been so, if its membership is compared nationally to that of the giant engineering and electrical union, the AEEU. However, when specific offshore memberships are assessed, it is clear that the OILC is, numerically at least, equal to the established unions, especially in the Northern Sector of the North Sea. While accurate figures for offshore trade union membership are very hard to ascertain, at a TUC meeting in mid-1999, trade union membership in the North Sea was estimated at 25-30% of the workforce, including OILC membership. Engineering union officials placed their membership at around 1,000 offshore. For the smaller boilermakers' union, the GMB, a generous estimate would be between 500 and 1000 members offshore. Reported (October 2002) OILC membership is approximately 1,500 (see Table 5). To date 5,424 offshore workers have joined the OILC over the ten years since December 1, 1992, when the trade union received its certificate of independence. Of this total, only 90 could potentially be described as having had membership in another or rival trade union. The OILC has succeeded, in both its official and its previous unofficial incarnation, in creating and mobilizing collective power in a "difficult" industry for purposes of union recruitment. Outside its core engineering and construction membership, the OILC has also made inroads in recruiting catering and drilling employees. However, its numbers remain small and the shifting pattern

Table 5. OILC Membership

OILC membership Brent Field	OILC membership (incl. Brent Field)
Wood Group employees 134	Engineering 980
Other engineering 51	Catering 170
Catering 8	Drilling 346
Drilling 53	Total 1,496

Source: OILC 2002

of recruitment in this highly mobile industry is reflected in the significant turnover of union membership.

Lerner's study referred to above, suggests that employers prefer to deal with established trade unions which are usually more "moderate" than breakaway rival unions. This has been the case in the North Sea for the past decade, and successive attempts by the OILC, as a fully certificated independent trade union to represent employees in the offshore oil industry, have been consistently rebuffed by the employers.

In 1995, members of the OILC were instrumental in organizing ballots on key platforms in the Northern Basin (the Brent Charlie and Brent Delta) among employees of the major contractor, Wood Group. Employees were asked two questions: "Do you want trade union representation on your terms and conditions? "Do you want trade union representation on your terms and conditions? If 'Yes,' which trade union?" Of 219 ballot papers issued on the Brent Charlie platform, 213 were returned, and of these, 212 favored union recognition. On the Brent Delta, 145 papers were issued and 136 returned, with 134 indicating that union representation was favored. Of the total of 346 papers returned from the two platforms indicating a desire for union representation, 292 chose the OILC as their preferred union, 25 the AEEU, 10 the GMB, and 4 various other choices, while 15 indicated no preference. Wood Group's response to the OILC's claim for recognition, contained in a letter to the trade union, was as follows:

> We have for many years had regular dialogue with Trade Unions registered with the TUC. This association has worked well and given a high degree of comfort in our dealings on industrial relations matters. We would not wish to see this disturbed and our Terms and Conditions of Employment reflect this [53].

Another successful ballot was held on the drilling rig Divy Stena in the autumn of 1995. Again the workforce voted overwhelmingly for trade union recognition (73 for and 1 against), and of these, 64 favored representation by the OILC.

In this instance, the employer forestalled further OILC claims by arriving at a representation agreement with another trade union. On the whole, these experiences mirror Lerner's observation that "the argument that employers use breakaway trade unions as catspaws against the established unions has little validity in Great Britain today. Employers' associations oppose break-away trade union and new unions almost as strongly as do established unions" [52, p. 195].

The challenge to existing structures of accommodation between the established unions and employers, created by the presence of the OILC as an offshore trade union, prompted new initiatives. These included greater interunion cooperation among established trade unions, and between these trade unions and employer groups, especially on the contractor side of the industry. The previous TUC-based Inter Union Offshore Oil Committee, comprising local officials meeting quarterly in Aberdeen, was augmented by the successive creation of a number of interunion bodies that attempted to develop a single-table bargaining approach in the offshore industry. However, these attempts were largely undermined by the reluctance of the most significant union player to participate, the AEEU (a "super-union" created by the merger of the engineering union with the electrical union, the EETPU). The AEEU sought to be the dominating force both in onshore and offshore engineering construction. As such, it was signatory to controversial single-union agreements such as that at the Derbyshire Toyota car manufacturing company in 1992, and to the single-union agreement to replace the previous joint-union agreement at the Mobil refinery in Stanford Le Hope, Essex, and at Esso's refinery in Mosmorran in Fife.

Paralleling the reluctance of the AEEU to become a participant in new inter-union structures that might compromise its preeminent bargaining role was its enthusiasm for a new form of direct accommodation with employer groups. Thus, largely prompted by the AEEU, a new "Trade Union Consultative Committee" had been created that involved the offshore contractor companies and two of the key signatories to the previous Hook-up agreement, the AEEU in collaboration with the GMB union. However, other previous Hook-up agreement signatory unions, such as the technicians' MSF, found themselves excluded from this forum, hailed by the AEEU as "a significant movement by negotiation towards union recognition for offshore post-construction work" [54]. Despite these assertions, this new partnership forum did not achieve the hoped-for advances in the sphere of bargaining between contractor companies and trade unions offshore. Rather, it served as a vehicle for the employers to consult with trade unions in order to gain their cooperation for further cost-cutting measures within the industry as renewed economic stringency was necessitated by a further downturn in oil prices. Thereafter, at various points throughout the 1990s, major contractor employers such as Wood Group, first attempted to initiate, and then abandoned, employee "consultative forums," as it became clear that they were likely to serve as vehicles for workforce discontent. Seen from the employers' standpoint, such discontent was orchestrated by OILC activists on the platforms offshore.

EMPLOYMENT RELATIONS ACT 1999

In terms of the extension of collective bargaining in the offshore oil and gas industry, the 1990s may be effectively written off as a decade during which no significant progress had been achieved by trade unions. With the election of a New Labour government in the latter part of the 1990s came the first shift in the legislative procedures concerning trade union recognition for nearly two decades. This opened renewed prospects for collective bargaining in the offshore oil industry. However, New Labour's business-friendly measures on employment law represented only a partial break with the previous Conservative administration's approach [55]. Thus many policies remained predicated on individualist and deregulation assumptions [56]. While individual employment rights at work were legislatively strengthened by the arrival of New Labour, many hoped-for improvements have been undercut by the explicit exclusion of restoring the colletive bargaining power of trade unions that the previous Conservative administration had done so much to erode.

New Labour repeatedly sought to preserve an "arms-length" approach to the trade unions, arguing that there could be "no return to the bad old days of industrial conflict" that had undermined the position of the previous Labour administration of the late 1970s, and paved the way for the Thatcher governments. Instead, New Labour promoted enterprise-based "partnership" arrangements guaranteeing social peace and industrial cooperation [57]. The term "partnership" has been integral to New Labour's approach to employment issues. This was encapsulated first in the White Paper, *Fairness at Work* [58], and, subsequently, in New Labour's Employment Relations Act. In this context, "partnership" implies a trade-off, between enhanced rights to union recognition and the expectation that trade unions would view the granting of recognition as an implicit agreement to avoid industrial militancy [59].

In the autumn of 1999, the impending passage of the new Employment Relations Act was sufficient to prompt the oil companies, in the form of the United Kingdom Offshore Operators Association, to endorse a "memorandum of understanding" with the long-standing Inter Union Offshore Oil Committee. This memorandum, according to the director general of the UKOOA, was intended to signal "a new spirit of co-operation" by the industry [60]. It was signed on behalf of the trade unions by no less a person than John Monks, then general secretary of the U.K. TUC. His presence signaled which was to be the preferred partner union organization of the oil operators. The new memorandum was also a necessary prelude to a rapprochement between the dependent offshore contractor companies and oil company "approved" trade unions.

Such voluntary accommodations with the established trades unions, under the threat of legislatively imposed recognition procedures, nonetheless, did not prevent companies such as Shell from continuing to resist trade union recognition offshore. When the MSF white-collar and technical union requested that Shell cooperate in an offshore ballot for union representation of direct employees in technician and medical/administrative grades, Shell restated its implacable opposition to trade unionism in a briefing issued to offshore installation managers. This briefing, for use in answering questions from employees considering the ballot, echoed traditional oil company unitarist views on recognition:

> we do not wish a third party to be part of the relationship [we] have with yourselves. We believe it will get in the way of progressing that relationship for all sorts of reasons, which we will make plain over the next few weeks and months. We play to win and intend to fight for your votes because this is so important to us [61].

In a climate dominated by fear of job losses, the prospect of supportive union recognition legislation was not necessarily a sufficient counterweight to vigorous company initiatives to deter unionization, especially where these were conducted over a period of weeks or even months. In the event, Shell won the "fight for votes" and employees rejected the union. Gall and McKay's observation is apposite:

> Despite the realpolitik of employer organisations accepting the inevitability of the introduction of statutory UR [union recognition] provisions from a previous position of wholesale opposition, there are still many employers who are minded to frustrate and oppose union attempts to use the climate and machinery of the provisions [62].

The failed attempt by MSF to achieve union recognition with Shell highlights the limits of the "memorandum of understanding" as a vehicle to progress union recognition claims. Similar reservations, with essentially similar outcomes, may also apply to various forms of "voluntary" agreements reached with trade unions "in the shadow" of the Employment Relations Act. In the longer term, as the offshore oil industry illustrates, these latter agreements may pose the greater threat to the future of organized trade unionism.

The "memorandum of understanding" between the IUOOC and the U.K. offshore operators association was duly followed by the signing of a Partnership Agreement between the two major hook-up unions, the AEEU and the GMB, and the body representing the contracting companies in the North Sea, the Offshore Contractors Association [63]. The Partnership Agreement (excluding the third signatory union, MSF) was signed just two weeks before the June 2000 date at which the new Employment Relations Act came into force. It inaugurated "consultation arrangements," including regular meetings with local trade union officials "to enable an effective exchange of views; promote a better understanding of the challenges facing the offshore industry; diffuse potential areas of conflict and collaborate in finding solutions" [63, para. 4.1]. As an appendix, the Partnership Agreement incorporated a previous "agreement" between the signatories, dated November 1998. This included a promise by the trade unions of a "total non-disruption factor" [63, Appendix iv A1.4].

The Partnership Agreement has meant that the OILC prospects of using the terms of the Employment Relations Act 1999 (ERA) to secure recognition for their offshore members have become remote. The issue of the workforce being free to choose which union they wish to be represented by is foreclosed. Under the Employment Relations Act, if a voluntary agreement on recognition has been entered into *prior* to the legislation coming into force, a ballot on *which* union the employees might wish to be represented by is not required [64]. Nor can a future ballot take place upon the issue of "substitution" of the incumbent union by the workforce's preferred alternative union choice. Even the very complex procedures for de-recognition under the Employment Relations Act, stretching over three years, are now rendered unavailable. In response to contractor workforce representations on the absence of a ballot on union choice, the spokesperson for Wood Group Engineering, a key company in the Offshore Contractors' Association, pointed out the perceived advantages of the Partnership Agreement. The new arrangements, it was claimed, consolidated the "long and constructive working relationship" that the Offshore Contractors' Association (OCA) had had with both the AEEU and the GMB. The future bargaining agent and the bargaining unit of the Partnership Agreement were similarly defined by the Wood Group (WGE):

> WGE in common with the other main contractors serving the industry has formally delegated authority for all collective bargaining with its offshore staff employed in the UK territorial waters and the United Kingdom Continental Shelf to the OCA [65].

By relinquishing bargaining authority to the contractors' industry-wide body, the Offshore Contractors' Association, individual contractor companies like Wood Group Engineering could now avoid bargaining directly with their own workforces or, more specifically, with those "disfavoured" union representatives with whom they would rather not deal. In relinquishing bargaining matters to an industry body (the OCA), a reversal of the previous industry-wide "Model Terms and Conditions" was completed. The "Model Terms and Conditions" had provided a loose industry-wide framework of terms and conditions implemented at company level. In reality such terms and conditions in individual contracting companies were imposed by employers, rather than being the outcome of a genuine bargaining process. Now the bargaining agent had been redefined in a way that worked to the employers' advantage by shifting the locus away from company level to an industry-wide body. The scope of the bargaining unit, always a crucial bone of contention in recognition claims, could also be redefined in a manner that suited the partnership trade unions in their attempt to secure the exclusion of potential rivals. Hence, the bargaining unit would now be "offshore staff employed in the U.K. territorial waters and the UKCS," rather than in specific fields or installations. Thus, the OILC's "strength in depth," for example in the Brent Field, where the majority of Wood Group Engineering employees were OILC members, could now be ruled out as insufficiently comprehensive by established trade unions, with claims to speak for the entire continental shelf.

The reaction of trade union officers of the signatory TUC partner trade unions to the new partnership set-up was unsurprisingly enthusiastic. Local officials were sent offshore to propound the benefits of the Partnership Agreement to the offshore workforce. However, in areas where the OILC had significant support, especially on the Brent platforms, they met with a mixed reception.

In the summer of 2000, the AEEU also arrived at a similar "partnership agreement" with the offshore drilling contractors in the newly formed United Kingdom Drilling Contractors Association (UKDCA) [66]. This agreement came into being on June 4, 2000, and again without reference to the freedom of choice of the affected workforce of some 4,000 to 5,000 employees. It was patently a single-union deal with the AEEU, introduced just forty-eight hours before the Employment Relations Act came into force. This second partnership agreement, however, was insufficiently strong to prevent one of the key drilling employers, Global Marine, from withdrawing within a short space of time. With unconscious irony, the company rationale offered was that the withdrawal was at the behest of their employees who "did not want to be represented by a Trade Union." The real purpose appeared to be Global Marine's desire to exploit the advantages of "cheaper" East European labor, in direct contradiction to the terms of their agreement with the AEEU. Danny Carrigan, the national officer of the AEEU enthused over what he termed:

> (the) two landmark deals with the offshore contractors including the biggest recognition deal in 30 years for the union. Not only do these deals end the exploitation of the offshore workers, but they also allow us to have a direct input into the future of the industry [67].

Such hastily contrived arrangements and "agreements," imposing specific trade unions on nonconsulted employees, although not unique to the oil industry were a disturbing feature of the introduction of the Employment Relations Act [57]. Proponents of the Act would argue that "responsible" trade unions were merely being brought "in from the cold" by erstwhile recalcitrant employers, and that, therefore, such agreements represented an advance for collective bargaining. Other less sanguine views argued that there were issues of basic democracy and even human rights at work (conformity with International Labour Organization "core standards" on freedom of choice) that remained to be addressed [68]. The signing of the partnership agreement, for instance, met with considerable anger on the Brent Field platforms. On the eve of the Employment Relations Act coming into force, three-quarters (76%) of Wood Group employees voted for recognition by the OILC in a workforce-organized ballot, compared to 5% for the AEEU and GMB combined. A simultaneous ballot of AMEC employees in Shell's Northern Field (Eider, North Cormorant, Tern, Dunlin, and Cormorant Alpha platforms) yielded 68% for the OILC, as against 18% for the AEEU and GMB union combined [69]. This was to be the only opportunity for "democratic choice" presented to the workforce.

In May 2003, the OILC made application to the Central Arbitration Committee (CAC) for a hearing to determine the merits of its claim to be the recognized trade union in the Northern Shetland Basin with Wood Group Engineering, following Wood Group's rejection of a formal request for recognition [70]. In the event, the application for recognition with Wood Group was initially deemed inadmissible in a "provisional determination" by the CAC in July 2003 [71]. The device of provisional determination is one that allows a trade union to withdraw an application that is unlikely to succeed, thereby avoiding the "formal notification" process. The formal decision takes the form of letters to each side setting out the justification for the decision. This decision is also posted on the CAC Web site (/www.cac.gov.uk/) as in all such formal determinations. Most unions take advantage of the provisional determination and withdraw their application to avoid "negative" publicity.

The initial view of the CAC was that the OILC was effectively seeking to substitute another trade union as the recognized representative body, and remove a trade union with whom the employers have already reached a voluntary recognition agreement. Under Paragraph 35(1) of Schedule A1 of the Trade Union and Labour Relations Act (TULRA) which is incorporated in the Employment Relations Act 1999:

> An application . . . is not admissible if the CAC is satisfied that there is already in force a collective agreement under which a union is (or unions are) recognised as entitled to conduct collective bargaining on behalf of any workers falling within the relevant bargaining unit [71].

Accordingly, such competing claims should be a matter for resolution by the TUC Disputes Committee, rather than the CAC. Determinations of the CAC are made by panels of three committee members appointed by the chairman of the committee and consisting of either the chairman himself or a deputy chairman, one member whose experience is as a representative of employers, and one member whose experience is as a representative of workers. The list of twenty-two panel members described as "members with experience of representing workers" is overwhelmingly comprised of representatives of the TUC-affiliated trade unions [72]. However, the threat of judicial review forced a reconsideration by the CAC, and a hearing date was set for August 2003. For judicial review to have succeeded, it needed to be shown that "the CAC has either acted irrationally or made an error of law" [73]. Arguably, the provisional determination could not be faulted on either count, since the remit of the CAC expressly charges it with the mission:

> to adjudicate on applications relating to the statutory recognition and derecognition of trade unions for collective bargaining purposes, where such recognition or derecognition cannot be agreed voluntarily [74].

The CAC sees its task as commencing at the point at which voluntarism has failed, not in scrutinizing the character of that voluntarism. It would appear that when recognition has already been agreed between employers and a trade union on a voluntary basis, claims to recognition by different union bodies are deemed beyond the purview of the CAC. It is assumed that such voluntary agreements will be entered into by union bodies that are genuinely representative of the workforce. Ironically, while the ERA, as currently framed, offers employers procedures by which to test claims to representativeness of a trade union among those in the workforce, it does not offer the same opportunity to other trade unions. Whether this conforms to principles of natural justice is debatable.

At a hearing of the CAC in Glasgow on August 18, 2003, the OILC maintained that the union easily passed the two tests for admissibility of its claim under the Act: the requisite 10% level of membership in the bargaining unit, and the likelihood that the majority of workers in the bargaining unit would favor recognition of the OILC as their bargaining agent (Schedule A1 of TULRA paragraphs 36 (1)a and 36 (1)b) [71]. The core of the OILC's submission was the issue of whether or not the Partnership Agreement between the AEEU and GMB and the Offshore Contractors' Association constituted a genuine collective bargaining agreement covering Wood Group core employees [70]. Under TULRA, a collective agreement is defined by section 178 of the Act as any agreement or arrangement made by or on behalf of a trade union and an employer relating to matters such as terms and conditions of employment and the machinery of negotiation [75, para. 6].

At best, it was conceded, the Partnership Agreement with the AEEU and GMB set hourly minimum rates and terms, constituting a baseline agreement at industry level, below the value of which any imposed package of remuneration would not fall. This, however, bore no determinative relation to the terms and conditions of the annually paid Wood Group core contractor employees whom the OILC sought to represent in the Brent Field [75, para. 87]. Their pay could be anything above the minimum rates. With regard to hours, it was held that the Partnership Agreement was equally "undeterminative," as the work cycle and the number of hours were set by the individual employer [75, para. 9]. Similar arguments applied to holiday entitlements. Not only did OCA hourly rates bear no relation to the annual pay of the core workers, but the whole system of allowances set out in the Partnership Agreement covering matters such as night shift allowance, overtime, and Christmas working did not apply to the Brent core workers. In short, "there was in fact no or very little correlation between OCA rates and the salaries of the Brent core workers' [75, paras. 10-11]. Moreover, in the Terms and Conditions of Employment of the core workers and the acceptance statement, there was no reference to the Partnership Agreement, nor to any collective agreement. Nor were any local negotiations conducted beyond the OCA forum to determine the terms and conditions of Wood Group employees. Pay increases were simply imposed by the company based on agreed increases in hourly pay and converted into an annualized figure [75, paras. 14-15]. As such, this unilateral exercise could not be regarded as collective bargaining as implied by Paragraph 35(1) of Schedule A1 of TULRA.

For the company, Wood Group argued that the Partnership Agreement with the AEEU and GMB was a collective agreement as defined under Section 178 of TULRA and that it had issued a formal instruction to negotiate on its behalf to the OCA confirming:

> That the provisions of the [Partnership] Agreement relating to remuneration, working hours and holiday entitlement shall be implemented in respect of those employees engaged by (Wood Group Engineering) who fall within the scope of the Agreement [75, para. 17].

The company maintained that the rates of pay for all Wood Group offshore workers, including those working on the Brent Field, had been directly linked with the minimum rates negotiated between the OCA and the AEEU and GMB, producing the conversion calculations for the years 2002 and 2003. Wood Group also maintained that it conducted "complementary collective bargaining" with the recognized trade unions. It had responded to a request from the regional officer of the AEEU in June 2003 for a meeting to discuss a review of the basic rate of pay and the implementation of a consultative forum. The meeting had in fact taken place one month before the hearing, at a date by which it would, of course, have been well aware of the OILC's intention to seek a hearing with the CAC [75, para. 18]. For Wood Group, the existing arrangements for collective bargaining "constituted a settled and effective bargaining practice" and the partner unions also viewed the arrangements as a "robust and a satisfactory means of collective consultation" [75, para. 25].

For its part, the CAC Panel was persuaded that the Partnership Agreement was a collective agreement as defined in Section 178 of TULRA, that the agreement was in force, and that meaningful negotiations on terms and conditions of employment took place on an annual basis. The membership of Wood Group of the OCA satisfied the panel that collective bargaining between the parties to the agreement had taken place. The panel accepted the company's contention that the pay of the Wood Group core employees on the Brent Field was raised in line with any increase in nationally negotiated minimum rates by the application of a conversion factor known to the unions. Thus, the panel also accepted that the AEEU and GMB bargained on behalf of the core workers employed by Wood Group and that these unions were also involved in disciplinary and grievance procedures taken from the

Partnership Agreement, while officials of both unions were entitled to visit the core workers in the Brent Field to explain changes in terms. The panel concluded:

> These are all forms of employer/union interaction which are recognised as matters constituting collective bargaining in the Trade Union and Labour Relations (Consolidation) Act 192, s 178 [75, para. 31].

Accordingly, Paragraph 35 of Schedule 1A of TULRA applied; a collective agreement existed under which a union is entitled to conduct collective bargaining on behalf of workers within the proposed bargaining unit. The application of the OILC was therefore "inadmissable" [75, para. 32].

Reactions in the industry to the failure of OILC's bid for formal recognition were largely muted. Privately, the employers, especially in the OCA, may have breathed a sigh of relief that a severe irritant in their relationship with the established trade unions had at last been removed. Officially, however, there was no triumphalist press statement from either UKOOA or OCA. A disappointed Jake Molloy, General Secretary of OILC, was quoted in the aftermath as saying:

> We are trying to illustrate to the partnership unions . . . the shortcomings of the current arrangements between them and offshore employers. We are trying to convince these unions of the need to develop union partnerships as opposed to partnerships determined by employers . . . we will go back to the partnership unions in an attempt to convince them that there is a better way ahead which will truly involve and empower workers in the decision-making process of their lives offshore [*Aberdeen Press and Journal,* 2003].

CONCLUSION

The issue of recognition in the offshore oil industry was one of the direct stimulants for the Employment Relations Act 1999. The OILC, arguably the authentic workforce representative body, had an outstanding claim of seeking recognition for purposes of collective bargaining as an independent trade union for a decade. It could not strictly be said to be a "new" trade union, at least no more so than any other trade union offshore. Nor could it be regarded as a "breakaway" union, simply because it was a non-TUC trade union. Trade union presence in the unorganized offshore oil industry had always been vestigial at best. Hitherto, a hostile legal context and the nexus of employer resistance and competitive strategies between established trade unions prevented the OILC from realizing its objective as a legitimate bargaining agent. It seems likely that an objective test of workforce opinion in the Brent Field, certainly among employees in constructional and maintenance work, would confirm previous overwhelming ballots in favor of representation by the OILC, as against other trade union bodies. Such a test, at least in terms of the ERA procedures as presently interpreted by the CAC, is unlikely to take place.

A deep paradox remains. In the "shadow" of a statutory legislative framework, the ERA appears to have had at least limited success in promoting voluntary forms of trade union recognition. Employers in the offshore oil industry, as elsewhere, appear to have modified their previous unyielding antiunion stance [76]. Yet this appearance of willingness to embark upon collective bargaining is largely illusory in the offshore oil industry. In this context, the main purpose of the ERA, which was intended to further voluntary trade union recognition based on democratic employee choice, has hitherto been undermined by privileging recognition claims of employer-friendly trade unions aligned to the TUC. The absence of a ballot as to *which* trade union employees would wish to be represented by, effectively disenfranchises a significant prounion sector of the offshore workforce. Thus the current legislation has encouraged, at best, a weak form of recognition in the offshore industry, based on preemptive partnership arrangements of doubtful legitimacy in the eyes of the workforce. In promoting voluntary arrangements over statutory procedures, while failing to provide the means to test the legitimacy of voluntary arrangements, it appears that the ERA, from the very outset, has offered employees in the offshore oil industry little prospect of genuine employee choice in union representation.

As a trade union, the OILC has committed itself to the ongoing pursuit of a better framework of health and safety offshore, providing the possibility of enhancing the safety representative system put in place since 1989. It would also enhance the capacities for workforce involvement at the installation level as envisaged by Lord Cullen. Moreover, the OILC has its roots in the adversarial climate that prevailed in the industry in the years following Piper Alpha. However, since its official registration as an independent trade union, it has adhered strictly to current employment legislation. In the course of this, the OILC has sought to establish responsible working relationships with employers in the course of individual representation of workers' grievances at industrial tribunals and in other forums. There is at least an arguable case that recognition of the OILC as a trade union for collective bargaining purposes would be conducive to the further development of good industrial relations within the offshore oil and gas industry.

Despite hostility to the OILC at various times during the past decade, the AEEU and other trade unions with offshore interests have made overtures to amalgamate with the OILC, thereby bringing the trade union within the mainstream of TUC organization. In each case, these negotiations have failed to produce an acceptable formula that would guarantee the specific "offshore" personality of the OILC within the proposed structures of amalgamation. Today, the OILC remains outside the established structures of the TUC as an industrial union. Its uniqueness derives from its efforts to place the safety agenda at the forefront of offshore trade union concerns. This has been reflected in a series of submissions and interventions to various bodies on health and safety matters, as well as its financial support for legal representation at several major fatal accident inquiries. In terms of its representational role, the OILC, meanwhile, has at least "tacit" relations with some contractor employers, especially in representing individual workforce grievances, although not for purposes of collective bargaining. In addition, it has fought a number of high profile industrial tribunal cases on behalf of individual employees.

Yet the legacy of antiunionism in the offshore oil industry and the inability to overcome continuing interunion tensions make the successful reconstruction of offshore health and safety problematical. The now fading memory of Piper Alpha, punctuated only by occasional disasters of a "lesser" scale, brings with it the danger of complacency. In many respects the offshore industry has been, and remains, a dangerous working environment. Ongoing individual fatalities point to the still incomplete "safety culture" offshore. Again, multifatality incidents, such as the crash of a Sikorsky helicopter on a routine flight in clear weather in June 2002 in which eleven North Sea oilmen died, serve to underline the continuing inherent risks that the workforce is asked to endure. The likelihood of another disaster on the scale of Piper Alpha may have been mitigated to some extent, but such a scenario cannot be ruled out altogether. A new regulatory regime has been put in place. However, its foundations, as Lord Cullen has recognized, are only as secure as the strength of involvement of those who are the chief risk-bearers in the industry. While the full armory of human resource management has been deployed by the offshore companies, the real collective empowerment of the offshore workforce has yet to occur. In its absence, the industry and its workers will continue to face an uncertain future.

ENDNOTES

1. B. R. Mitchell, *British Historical Statistics* (Cambridge: Cambridge University Press, 1962), 301.
2. W. G. Carson, *The Other Price of Britain's Oil* (Oxford: Martin Robinson, 1982).
3. Burgoyne Report, *Offshore Safety,* Cmnd 7866 (London: HMSO, 1980).
4. Hon. Lord Robens, *Safety and Health at Work,* Report of the Committee 1970-72, Cmnd 5034 (London: HMSO, 1972).
5. T. Spiller, "Politicians, Interest Groups and Regulators: A Multiple-Principles Agency Theory, or 'Let Them Be Bribed,'" *Law and Economics 33* (1990): 65-101.
6. Hon. Lord Cullen, *The Public Inquiry into the Piper Alpha Disaster,* Vols. 1 and 2 (London: HMSO, 1990).
7. B. G. S. Taylor, (1991) "The UK Offshore Operators Response to Piper Alpha and Lord Cullen's Report." Paper presented at the Society of Petroleum Engineers, First International Conference on Health, Safety and Environment, the Hague, November 10-14, 1991, 349–356: 6, emphasis added.
8. UKOOA (United Kingdom Offshore Operators Association), Internal Briefing Documents on the Release of the Cullen Report (1990).
9. HSE (Health and Safety Executive), *Draft Offshore Installation (Safety Case) Regulations 199* (London: HMSO, 1992).

10. H. Hughes, "Towards a Goal-Setting Regime—Plans and Issues—the Operators' View," in HSE, *Health and Safety in the Offshore Oil and Gas Industries*, Proceedings of Conference, Aberdeen, April 6-7, 1992.

11. HSE, *A Guide to the Offshore Installations (Safety Case) Regulations 1992: Guidance on Regulations L30* (London: HMSO, 1992).

12. R. Pape, "Risk Assessment in UK Offshore Installation Safety Cases." Paper presented at the Risk Assessment: International Conference, 1992.

13. HSE, *Draft Offshore Installations (Prevention of Fire and Explosion, and Emergency Response)* Regulations 199 and Approved Code of Practice, Consultative Document (London: HSE, 1993).

14. HSE, "Prevention of Fire and Explosion, and Emergency Response on Offshore Installations," *Offshore Installations (Prevention of Fire and Explosion, and Emergency Response) Regulations 1995 and Appended Code of Practice* (London: HMSO, 1995).

15. Robert Patterson, "Offshore Safety—the New Regime: Part 2 Implementation." Paper presented at the Leith International Conference, Aberdeen, October 24, 1995, 9.

16. B. Hughes, "The Operators' Response." Paper presented at the conference on Offshore Safety Case Management, reprinted in Safety Management 10, no.6 (1994): 49.

17. Letter to *Telegraph,* journal of NUMAST, November 1995.

18. Det Norske Veritas, Submission to HSE on *Draft Prevention of Fire . . . Regulations,* November 13, 1993.

19. H. Hughes, "Developments of Safety, Health and Environmental Standards and Regulation Systems in North-West Europe." Paper presented at the Offshore Northern Seas Conference, Stavanger, Norway, 1994.

20. DTI (Department of Trade and Industry), *Review of the Implementation and Enforcement of EC Law in the UK* (London: Crown Copyright, 1993).

21. *Aberdeen Press and Journal,* February 25, 1991.

22. European Commission, Council Directive No 93/104/EC of 23 November 1993 concerning certain aspects of the organisation of working time.

23. B. Bercusson, *Working Time in Britain: Towards a European Model, Part 1: The European Directive* (London: Institute of Employment Rights, 1994).

24. DTI, Report of Working Group on Competitiveness in the UKCS, February 1993. CRINE Secretariat, Cost Reduction Initiative for the New Era Report, St. Paul's Press, November 1993.

25. E. Brandie, "Achieving the Balance Between Safety and Cost Reduction," in OFS/OILC, *Offshore Safety in a Cost Conscious Environment: From British and Norwegian Perspectives,* proceedings of a conference, Stavanger, Norway, November 15-16, 1994 (Aberdeen: Offshore Information Centre, 1995).

26. *Scotsman,* January 13, 1996.

27. A. Wildavsky, *Speaking Truth to Power: The Art and Craft of Policy Analysis* (Boston: Little, Brown, 1979).

28. J. C. Scott, *Domination and the Arts of Resistance: Hidden Transcripts* (New Haven and London: Yale University Press, 1990).

29. S. Tombs, "Piper Alpha and the Cullen Inquiry—Beyond 'Distorted Communication'?" in *Offshore Safety and Reliability,* ed. R.F. Cox and M.H. Walter (London and New York: Elsevier 1991), 28-41.

30. BBC Scotland Television, *Frontline Scotland,* "Paying for the Piper," May 1997.

31. See United Kingdom Offshore Operators Association, Frequently Asked Questions, Health and Safety in the UK Oil and Gas Industry; available at http://www.ukooa.co.uk/issues/health/faq.htm
32. See M. Spaven et al., *The Effectiveness of Offshore Safety Representatives and Safety Committees: A Report to the Health and Safety Executive. Vol. 1: Survey, Analysis, Conclusions and Recommendations* (Aberdeen: Offshore Study Group, 1993); Spaven and Wright (1993) "The Effectiveness of Offshore Safety Representatives and Safety Committees: A Response to Vulliamy," in *Workforce Involvement and Health and Safety Offshore: Power, Language and Information Technology,* eds. J. Foster and C. Woolfson, Proceedings of International Conference (Glasgow: STUC, 1993); Expro Results Summary, MORI, May 1997; Shell Expro Workforce Survey: Results for Northern Business Unit (unpublished report).
33. See "Step Change" homepage; available at http://step.steel-sci.org/
34. T. Nichols, *The Sociology of Industrial Injury* (Mansell: London, 1997), 54.
35. A Step Change in Safety: A Cross-Industry Commitment to Improve Our Safety Performance, UKOOA, IADC, OCA, September 1997, 5.
36. Speech given by Dave Stephenson at Shell Expro H,S&E Conference, March 20, 1998, reprinted in *Blowout* no. 54 (April/May 1998): 8.
37. Shell Platform Safety Minutes, North Cormorant, April 19, 1998, and various Step Change e-mails, April/May 1998 (authors' possession).
38. Shell Expro, Step Change—Workforce Involvement. Brent Charlie Trial, June 10, 1998.
39. Quarterly Safety Representatives H,S&E meeting, Ardoe House Hotel, May 7, 1998.
40. ASTMS (Association of Scientific Technical and Managerial Staffs), "Industrial Relations in the Oil Companies: An ASTMS View" (unpublished document, 1976).
41. T. Kochan, H. Katz, and R. McKersie, *The Transformation of American Industrial Relations* (New York: Basic Books, 1986).
42. F. A. Greenfield and R.J. Pleasure, "Representatives of Their Own Choosing: Finding Workers' Voice in the Legitimacy and Power of Their Unions," in *Employee Representation: Alternatives and Future Directions,* ed. B.E. Kaufman and M. Kleiner (Madison, WI: Industrial Relations Research Organization, 1993), 169–96: 184.
43. Brody (1980) cited in [42], "Representatives of Their Own Choosing," 184.
44. A. Thom, "Managing Labour Under Extreme Risk: Collective Bargaining in the North Sea Oil Industry," Ph.D. dissertation, RGIT, Aberdeen, 1989, 101.
45. Mobil, letter from T. Boston, employee relations manager, Mobil North Sea Limited, to Campbell Reid, secretary of the IUOOC, July 26, 1982. (Correspondence in authors' possession.)
46. B. Klein, "Contract Costs and Administered Prices: An Economic Theory of Rigid Wages," *American Economic Review 74* (1984): 332.
47. C. J. Woolfson, J. Foster, and M. Beck, *Paying for the Piper: Capital and Labour in Britain's Offshore Oil Industry* (London: Mansell, 1997).
48. Cited in C. Harvey, Fool's Gold: The Story of North Sea Oil (Harmondsworth: Penguin, 1994).
49. I. McLoughlin and S. Gourlay, *Enterprise Without Unions: Industrial Relations in the Non-Union Firm* (Buckingham: Open University Press, 1994).

50. OILC (Offshore Industry Liaison Committee), *Striking Out: New Directions for Offshore Workers and Their Unions* (Aberdeen: OILC, 1991).
51. C. Kerr, (1959) "The Impacts of Unions on the Level of Wages," in *Wages, Prices, Profits and Productivity,* ed. Charles A. Myers (New York: The American Assembly, Columbia University, 1959).
52. S. W. Lerner, *Breakaway Unions and the Small Trade Union* (London: Allen and Unwin, 1961).
53. Wood Group, letter from J. A. Lee, director, Contract Support Services, Wood Group Engineering to R. McDonald (OILC), May 16, 1995. (Correspondence in authors' possession.)
54. AEEU, Offshore Bulletin (November 1992), 5.
55. G. S. Norris, "The Employment Relations Act 1999 and Collective Labour Standards," *International Journal of Comparative Labour Law and Industrial Relations* 17, no. 1 (2001): 63-77.
56. M. Beck and C. Woolfson, "The Regulation of Health and Safety in Britain: From Old Labour to New Labour," *Industrial Relations Journal* 31, no. 1 (2000): 35-50.
57. P. Smith and G. Morton, "New Labour's Reform of Britain's Employment Law: The Devil Is Not Only in the Detail But in the Values and Policy Too," *British Journal of Industrial Relations* 39, no. 1 (2001): 119-138.
58. DTI, *Fairness at Work,* (CM, 3968) (London: HMSO, 1998).
59. S. Wood and J. Godard, "The Statutory Recognition Procedure in the Employment Relations Bill: A Comparative Analysis," *British Journal of Industrial Relations* 37, no. 2 (June 1999): 203-229.
60. "A New Era of Understanding!" *Blowout* no. 58 (October 1999), 9.
61. "In, Out, In, Out, Shake It All About . . ." *Blowout* no. 62 (December 2001), 11.
62. G. Gall and S. McKay, "Facing 'Fairness at Work': Union Perception of Employer Opposition and Response to Union Recognition," *Industrial Relations Journal* 32, no. 2 (2001): 94-113.
63. OCA (Offshore Contractors' Association), Partnership Agreement between the Offshore Contractors' Association and the AEEU and GMB (2000).
64. W. Brown, S. Deakin, M. Hudson, and C. Pratten, "The Limits of Statutory Trade Union Recognition," *Industrial Relations Journal* 32, no. 3 (2001): 180-194.
65. WGE (Wood Group Engineering), memo from John Stewart, managing director, Integrated Services to Brent Workforce Employees, May 12, 2000.
66. "Sold Down the River!" *Blowout* no. 61 (July 2000): 4-5.
67. AEEU, *Offshore News* (Summer 2000).
68. T. Novitz, "International Promises and Domestic Pragmatism: To What Extent Will the Employment Relations Act 1999 Implement International Labour Standards Relating to Freedom of Association?" *Modern Law Review* 63, no. 3 (May 2000): 379-393.
69. "Ballots or Buy Out?" *Blowout* no. 60 (March 2000).
70. OILC, Application for Recognition by OILC, under Schedule A1 to the Trade Union and Labour Relations (Consolidation) Act 1992, in respect of Wood Group Engineering (North Sea) Ltd. (2003).
71. CAC, CAC Statutory Duties, Part I of Schedule A1 of the Trade Union and Labour Relations (Consolidation) Act 1992 (TULR(C)A) (2003), as inserted by Section 1

of the Employment Relations Act 1999 provides for tests of admissibility of applications; available at: www.cac.gov.uk/cac_statutory_duties/cac_statutory.htm.

72. CAC, List of Members with Experience in Representing Workers (2003); available at: www.cac.gov.uk/members/members.htm.

73. CAC, Judicial Review (2003), The Queen on the Application of *Kwik-Fit Limited v. Central Arbitration Committee,* March 18, 2002; available at: www.cac.gov.uk/recent_decisions/Decision_texts/KwikFit_judicialreview.htm.

74. CAC, "What Is the CAC?" (2003); available at: www.cac.gov.uk/what_is_cac/what-is.htm.

75. CAC, Central Arbitration Committee, Trade Union and Labour Relations (Consolidation) Act 1992, Schedule A1—Collective Bargaining: Recognition, Decision on Whether Paragraph 35 of the Schedule Applies to the Application, The Parties: Offshore Industry Liaison Committee (OILC) and Wood Group Engineering (North Sea) Limited, Case Number: TUR1/282/(2003), August 27, 2003; available at: www.cac.gov.uk/recent_decisions/Decisions_texts/282%20FINALPara35decision 22August2003.htm.

76. S. Wood, S. Moore, and P. Willman, "Third Time Lucky of Statutory Union Recognition in the UK?" *Industrial Relations Journal* 33, no. 3 (2002): 215-233.

CHAPTER 3

Safety and Industrial Relations in the Newfoundland Offshore Oil Industry Since the Ocean Ranger Disaster in 1982

Susan M. Hart

INTRODUCTION

Worldwide, between 1970 and 1995, over 1,200 workers were killed in offshore accidents. During this time, 162 offshore installation units were recorded as total losses, 900 units were severely or significantly damaged, and there were 850 fires and 300 blowouts [1]. More recent figures show that from January 1995 until March 2001, 35 people were killed in the industry as a result of fires or explosions [2]. The inherently hazardous nature of petroleum exploration and production is compounded by health and safety risks arising from helicopter transportation to and from remote worksites in potentially hostile conditions, shiftwork, extended working hours, work and family tensions arising from separation, and the consequences of living in a closed, captive work environment [3].

Oil was discovered off the coast of Newfoundland during seismic tests in 1965, which showed large oil deposits in the Grand Banks, an area southeast of the province. In 1979, Chevron Canada struck oil in the Hibernia field. In 1977, the provincial government had claimed ownership of the oil offshore in legislation outlining petroleum development, but in 1981, the federal government legislated a national energy policy that clearly stated its ownership of offshore resources. Both the federal and Newfoundland provincial governments referred the dispute to the Supreme Court of Canada, who ruled in 1984 that subsea resources off the coast of Newfoundland and Labrador belonged to the government of Canada.

Exploration drilling continued until the mid-eighties. After a gap in oil activity due to falling oil prices, the Hibernia oilfield was the first to be granted a production license in 1990, for twenty-five years. Estimations are that it contains 666 million barrels of recoverable crude oil, 28.7 billion cubic meters of natural gas, and 111 million barrels of natural gas liquids. In 1988, the Hibernia Management and Development Company (HMDC) was established as operator, made up of Mobil Oil Canada Ltd. (28.1%), Chevron Canada Resources Ltd. (21.8%), Petro-Canada (20.0%), Canada Hibernia Holdings Co. Ltd. (8.5%), Murphy Atlantic Offshore Oil Company Ltd. (5.0%), Mobil Canada Hibernia Holding Co. Ltd. (5.0%), and Norsk Hydro Canada (5.0%) [4]. Construction of the Hibernia gravity base platform was completed in November 1996 and it was towed out to the field in June 1997. First oil was in October 1997.

Terra Nova was the second oilfield developed, located about 35 kilometers away from the Hibernia field and with an estimated 406 million barrels of recoverable crude oil. The Terra Nova Alliance is the operator, consisting of Petro-Canada (34.2%), Mobil Oil Canada (20.7%), Husky Oil Operations Ltd. (15.8%), Norsk Hydro (15%), Murphy Oil Co. Ltd. (10.7%), and Mosbacher Operating Ltd. (3.6%) [5]. Oil began flowing from the floating production storage and offloading (FPSO) in January 2002. A third project, White Rose, was announced as going ahead in March 2002. Husky Energy is the operator with a share of 72.5% and Petro-Canada owns the remaining 27.5%. Estimated yield is 200-250 barrels of oil with anticipated first oil by the end of 2005 [6]. The development of a further field, Hebron/ Ben Nevis, was shelved by Chevron Canada Resources and its partners in February 2002 [7].

The politics, power, and vision of, economic growth through offshore oil development in Newfoundland largely reflect the plight of a peripheral economy with more than double the national level of unemployment since confederation in 1949 [8]. From about 1990 onward, provincial governments have adopted market-driven policies, including privatization, deregulation, and cuts in social programs.

This study will examine the safety problems that emerged from investigation into the Ocean Ranger disaster off the coast of Newfoundland in 1982 and assess whether subsequent government action established an adequate regulatory framework for safety in the offshore oil industry. During the course of this assessment, the safety record of the offshore oil industry since the Ocean Ranger is discussed. Because active workforce involvement is seen as crucial to safety, a review of industrial relations in the industry is also included.

THE LOSS OF THE OCEAN RANGER

As in the United Kingdom and the Norwegian sectors, it was the activities connected to exploration drilling that claimed the earliest fatalities. In the early morning hours of February 15, 1982, the semisubmersible drilling rig the Ocean Ranger capsized and sank in a severe winter storm 166 miles east of St. John's, Newfoundland, with the loss of eighty-four lives. There were no survivors. Of the sixty-nine Canadian crew members aboard, fifty-six were residents of Newfoundland. As the report of the subsequent inquiry commented:

> . . . the shock wave created by the loss was felt particularly throughout that province. In that tightly knit maritime community there were few who did not discover a link, direct or indirect, to one of those lost in the tragedy [9].

The federal and provincial government established a joint Commission of Inquiry in March 1982 with Chief Justice Hickman as chair. There were three basic questions: Why did the Ocean Ranger capsize and sink? Why was none of the crew saved? How can other similar disasters be avoided? The commission published two reports. Report One attempted to answer the first two questions and was released in August 1984 with sixty-six recommendations; Report Two attempted to answer the last question and was released in June 1985 with sixty-nine recommendations. The commissioners acknowledged that their primary purpose was to identify practical means of enhancing human safety in exploratory drilling off the coast of Eastern Canada but looked to the future development and production of oil and gas, and commented:

> . . . many activities in the exploration and production stages are common, as are the principles governing the safety of operations and the risks to be encountered [10].

In examining Report Two, apart from the chapter devoted to design and construction specific to mobile offshore drilling units, the others on safety, environmental factors, management, training, health, escape and survival, rescue and regulatory regime are clearly pertinent to the production phase offshore.

At the time the Ocean Ranger sank it was the largest semisubmersible drilling unit in the world and it was designed to withstand 115 mile-per-hour winds and 110 foot seas [11]. The cause of the Ocean Ranger's capsize, together with the complete loss of its crew, was multifaceted, and the commission pointed to a number of factors, including those that indirectly increased the probability of a serious accident. There is a sense in the report of an accident waiting to happen. Local folklore has it that the rig was called by many of the workers from here the "Ocean Danger," a sobering thought in hindsight, and one that raises the question of adequate workforce involvement in safety.

Reminiscent of chaos theory, the start of the chain of events leading to the loss of the rig was an apparently small thing—a broken porthole in the ballast control room. The night in question was very stormy with large seas. Seawater entering through the broken porthole damaged the equipment in the control room, including the ballast control panel, the public address system, and the gas detection panel. Evidence indicates that the power to the control room panel was immediately switched off, probably for maintenance purposes. At some later stage it was restored, at which time short circuiting opened at random a number of remotely controlled valves in the ballast control system, and the initial list occurred. In the ensuing confusion, attempts to manually operate the ballast system resulted in a rapid worsening of the list to an estimated 12-15 degrees, causing the downflooding of the chain lockers, then the accommodation stairwell together with damaged and open ventilators on the upper deck, which precipitated the actual capsize and sinking of the rig [11, pp. 87-100].

ODECO Drilling of Canada Ltd. were owners of the rig and contracted by the operator, Mobil Oil Canada Ltd. (Mobil), to drill in the Hibernia field. Under this contract, ODECO was responsible for the rig and the crew, and Mobil was responsible for the well. The commission criticised ODECO for a number of design failures that contributed toward the disaster, because in combination they undermined the inherent stability of the rig. These problems included the location of the ballast control room in a rig column below the lower deck; inadequately strengthened glass in the control room porthole, considering its proximity to sea level; the ineffectiveness of the pumping system; the complicated layout of the ballast control panel and its inadequate protection from seawater damage; and the lack of a remote draft reading system, which necessitated the deadlight to be left open as a routine matter in order to view the draft marks on the adjacent rig column [11, pp. 100, 139-140]. In terms of upper deck design, the commission found that the downflooding angles had been calculated assuming flat sea states, which led to an underestimation of the risk of flooding the chain lockers in stormy seas, compounded by their lack of weather protection and drainage. Furthermore, there was no watertight protection for stairwells and ventilators when storm conditions prevailed [11, Figures 7-8, pp. 99, 141-142].

Referring to ballast control and the general stability of the rig, the commission pointed out that in any complex technologies, like nuclear power, aerospace, and chemical processing:

> . . . it is customary to protect against failure in critical systems by having back-up or redundant means of control, and to instrument the operations so that the fact of failure is made transparently evident to those responsible for intervening. While the offshore oil industry has appropriated the latest technology in seismic exploration, drilling and the structural design of drilling units, it is by no means clear that it has done so to an equivalent level in the instrumentation and redundant control of critical systems [10, p.15].

As to why all crew members were lost, the commission criticized the poor design features in the methods of evacuation. The ten life rafts relied on launching by throwing them overboard combined with scramble nets. This was seen as problematic in stormy conditions in frigid waters, given the tendency of life rafts to capsize in rough seas, the onset of hypothermia preventing boarding, and the tendency of the rafts to float back toward the rig or right away from it, jeopardizing boarding and rescue. Moreover, technical tests revealed age deterioration in some of the rafts [11, Appendix F, Item F-6]. Indications were that no life rafts were used in the disaster.

Only eight months before the disaster, the then Canadian regulator, Canada Oil and Gas Lands Administration (COGLA), sent a telex to all offshore operators recommending survival suits be provided for crew members in view of the loss of the Arctic Explorer and thirteen of its crew off northern Newfoundland. Despite this alert, little progress had been made in carrying out this recommendation by February 1982 [11, p. 25].

There were four davit-launched lifeboats on the Ocean Ranger, with one of those not in place on a launching platform and still stored on deck. From the evidence we can only be certain that one lifeboat was launched with survivors because one lifeboat pulled alongside the Seaforth Highlander, the supply/standby vessel. This lifeboat was damaged and flooded and very soon it capsized, throwing out its occupants into the water. Tragically, none of these men was able to transfer to the rescue ship. Technical evidence concluded the damage to the lifeboat at that time could have occurred during launch or afterward. Later recovery attempts showed that thirty-one or more people had been aboard this lifeboat and all of them had eventually died. Another lifeboat from the launching platform on the list side of the rig was found floating without survivors, showing severe damage consistent with the boat being torn off the winching mechanism due to extreme wave action made worse by the severe list. Evidence as to whether this lifeboat had ever been launched or occupied was inconclusive. The stored lifeboat was found, but can be discounted in terms of escape from the rig. No trace was found of the fourth lifeboat [11, Appendix E, Item F-6].

Echoing its comments on the critical systems for safety on a rig, the commission criticized the offshore petroleum industry for its lack of commitment to evacuation systems:

> . . . [the industry] has faced and overcome the problems associated with exploring for and producing oil and gas under major environmental constraints because, without these solutions, exploration and production could not take place. Thus when a rig is being built, such equipment as telescoping risers, drill-string motion compensators, and in some cases dynamic-positioning equipment are deemed essential to the rig's mission and therefore worthy of the latest innovations that technology has to offer. The evacuation system does not meet that same criterion of being essential nor does it elicit the same response [10, p. 104].

Furthermore, Mobil was criticized in the report for not ensuring the design of purpose-built rescue and recovery standby vessels: In fact, the hull shape of the supply vessels used as standby support prevented a group of survivors from boarding the Seaforth Highlander, especially important insofar as they were not wearing exposure suits and were suffering from hypothermia [11, pp. 111, 125]. Design failures both on the rig and in evacuation methods were aggravated by poor management systems. These were listed by the commission as including a lack of operational manuals and technical information relating to the ballast control console and lack of adequate training for key personnel both industrial and marine, together with a lack of proper procedures and training for emergencies in both the contractor and operator companies [11, pp. 32-34, 43-51].

Although there were gaps in the operations manual regarding the manual operation of the ballast control panel, the Booklet of Operating Conditions identified specific tasks for the ballast control operators. According to the report of the inquiry, these monitoring and logging activities were not followed and daily stability calculations were conducted in a nonmathematical and irregular manner [11, p. 47]. Overall, evidence revealed a lack of supervisory responsibility regarding the crucial function of ballast, exemplified perhaps by the occurrence of a six-degree list on February 6, only days before the loss of the rig. The commission noted that this incident, not reported to the Mobil office or the regulatory authorities, showed the master of the rig was not trained in the operation of the ballast system, and that the toolpusher was fully aware of this fact [11, p. 51]. Indeed, the commission viewed the appointment of a master without ensuring up-to-date training in all his responsibilities, and the lack of action regarding his role in the February 6 list ". . . [as] reinforcing the impression that the master was only on Board in order to comply with U.S. Coast Guard regulations" [11, p. 50]. Clearly, this incident should have alerted ODECO to the importance of the marine dimension of the rig's operations, and to the failure of both the ballast control and management systems. But apparently it did not.

The commission found huge gaps in training leading up to the disaster. Ballast control room operator training was primarily "on the job," did not follow ODECO's stated training policy, and provided no understanding of the electrical and mechanical operations of ballast control [11, pp. 32-34]. Furthermore, operators were not trained in how to manually operate the control panel with the brass rods provided, a tragic omission in the event, because evidence indicates that when the operators thought they were closing ballast tank valves they were in fact doing the opposite and opening valves, dramatically increasing the list and precipitating the capsizing [11, pp. 97-98].

With regard to training in emergency preparedness, there was a lack of a marine crew and of marine training, reflecting a general marginalization of marine safety. At the time of the loss, the Ocean Ranger was undermanned by a minimum of three certified lifeboatmen and two able-bodied seamen. Only one employee had marine certification, despite the requirements of the U.S. Coast Guard [11, p. 38]. The toolpusher was in charge of one lifeboat and the commission remarked: ". . . it is difficult to understand how, in the event of evacuation, an untrained person could take command of and operate a lifeboat, particularly in severe sea conditions" [11, p. 50].

Mobil and ODECO were also found lacking in their training of senior personnel in their emergency procedure roles, and the report emphasized the need for more drills [11, p. 153]. Furthermore, a comparison of the Mobil and ODECO contingency plans revealed several procedural inconsistencies, differences in criteria for the cessation of drilling, and disagreement over the person in charge. However, the significance of ODECO's Emergency Procedures Manual is debatable, in that one senior toolpusher who had left the Ocean Ranger a month before the sinking testified he had never seen it [11, p. 48]. Even so, it is interesting to note the commission's comments about the clear command structure of the two rigs that survived the storm that night compared with the ambiguous lines of authority and responsibility on the Ocean Ranger, reflecting a tension between industrial and marine matters on board [11, p. 151].

Mobil was criticized in the report for inadequacies in its standby responsibilities [11, p. 156]. The Commission concluded there was insufficient training of crew members in these tasks and poor communication of procedures. For example, the captain of the Seaforth Highlander had received no instructions from Mobil or his employers, Seaforth Fednav, as to the emergency standby role of his vessel, nor were there any posted aboard. He had only discovered this rescue role when reporting to the Hibernia site a week earlier than the night of the disaster. Consequently, Captain Duncan had received no specific instructions on standby distances and when the situation on the Ocean Ranger was communicated to him his vessel was eight miles away, largely due to maneuvers to protect his ship from storm damage. In fact, he testified that "the waves that night were so tremendous that he was reluctant to turn his ship, fearing the integrity of her structure and the safety of his crew" [11, pp. 125-126]. As the report made clear in a reference to the Seaforth Highlander's attempted rescue of the survivors in the lifeboat, the crew: ". . . strove valiantly to save the men in the lifeboat and displayed courage in the best traditions of the sea." But, the commission continued:

> Had the vessel been differently designed and better equipped with the crew trained in the use of that equipment, and had the men in the lifeboat been wearing survival suits, some might have been rescued [11, p. 153].

Finally, the commission criticized the federal government's search and rescue (SAR) attempts after the Ocean Ranger sank. The main point of criticism was the lack of a coordinated search and rescue center, accountable to a single federal minister; consequently, there had been no proactive extension of services to accommodate offshore oil activities. In addition, there were no purpose-built SAR vessels and aircraft, which were designed for primary use by the Canadian Coast Guard and Department of National Defence, respectively. They particularly criticized the use of the, then twenty-year-old,

Labrador model of helicopter, deemed unsuitable for sea rescue operations offshore [10, p. 162].

REGULATORY FAILURE: FRAGMENTATION AND JURISDICTIONAL AMBIGUITY

Overlaying all these problems identified by the commission was the failure of the health and safety regulatory regime in existence for the offshore industry at that time. Upon analysis, there were three categories of regulatory failure emerging from the Commission of Inquiry's report. The first was a lack of monitoring and enforcement such that there had been a number of serious contraventions of the existing regulations. For example, contrary to the U.S. Coast Guard Regulations, ODECO did not provide the rig with the required number of qualified marine personnel and had not met their requirements for lifesaving equipment, neither did the company have a valid Certificate of Inspection for the Ocean Ranger at the time of its loss. Mobil, contrary to COGLA Drilling Regulations, had failed to ensure that "every person employed on a drilling program receives instructions and training in respect of all operational and safety procedures that the person may be required to carry out during the course of his duties during such employment . . ." [11, p. 156].

The second category was comprised of deficiencies identified in the regulations as of February 1982, reflecting the contributing factors discussed earlier, referring mainly to specific design and construction; operational procedures; specific qualification and training needs, in relation to rig stability and general marine matters; and emergency preparedness. Many of these regulatory omissions were matched in the report by very specific recommendations, lending themselves to an extension of a prescriptive approach to regulating the industry. For example, recommendation number 9 required: "That all drilling units be equipped with remote draft sensing and reading devices" [11, p. 149]; and number 35 itemized exactly what a ballast control room operator's training should consist of, in contrast to the then regulation, which expressed training requirements in general terms only.

The third type of regulatory failure identified by the commission, leading to significant changes in the structure of the province's offshore health and safety regime, was the jurisdictional complexity and ambiguity at the time of the loss. There were two Canadian regulatory agencies that covered the offshore industry at that time: COGLA at the federal level, and the provincial Newfoundland and Labrador Petroleum Directorate. These bodies used an application and permit system, but the provincial Petroleum Directorate looked to COGLA to enforce its federal regulations on marine operations. However, the Ocean Ranger was registered in the United States, and COGLA relied on the American certification authorities to regulate this area. As pointed out in the Commission's Report, unfortunately:

COGLA and the Petroleum Directorate acted on the incorrect assumption that ODECO would comply with the requirements of the 1979 Certificate of Inspection, issued by the U.S. Coast Guard, and with the Booklet of Operating Conditions approved by the American Bureau of Shipping and the U.S. Coast Guard. [But] the U.S. Coast Guard did not monitor or follow up the conditions or requirements of the Certificate of Inspection . . . or maintain any check on its expiry date [11, p. 143].

To overcome this jurisdictional ambiguity, the commission recommended that Canada should enforce its own standards and that there should be one agency responsible for safety in the offshore oil industry that would have the authority to carry out its functions through memoranda of understanding agreed with all relevant government departments [10, Recommendations 86 and 87]. The commissioners recommended that:

. . . a Safety Branch of co-equal status and under a senior manager be established within the single regulatory agency with responsibility, *inter alia*, for the development, application and monitoring of safety standards and for the analysis of safety data [10, Recommendation 88].

This regulatory agency was to develop performance standards for operational safety, evacuation methods, and training. The latter was considered an interim measure only because the commission also recommended the establishment of an Offshore Petroleum Training Standards Board. Bearing in mind the unreported incidents leading up to the Ocean Ranger's loss (for example, the list incident only days before and the broken portlight), the commission stressed the importance of reporting and analyzing dangerous occurrences and significant events, including ". . . the failure of a safety system from which there is a lesson to be learned" [10, p. 153]. Hence, they recommended that:

. . . the information regarding significant events and all other information pertaining to human safety be standardised, the information be collected, collated and analysed by the proposed Safety Branch, and the results be disseminated to industry [10, p. 153].

Overall, the major thrust of the report published by the commission was the failure of industry and government to ensure safety for those working on the Ocean Ranger. Thus, it is difficult to reconcile the strong criticism aimed at the operator and contractor companies concerning their marginalization of marine safety in design, operations, and management with a decidedly conciliatory or dependent attitude toward the industry in other parts of the report, especially the second volume, published nearly a year after the first. For example, after very critically reviewing the lack of crucial training in systems vital to safety in the first report, the commission stated in Report Two:

It is generally recognised that there are certain areas such as industrial training where industry will know best what standard is necessary for competent

performance or where standards determined by external agencies are the
best to be adopted [10, p. 152].

This seems rather surprising, considering the poor record of the industry
leading up to the loss of the Ocean Ranger with regard to what amounted to
voluntary compliance in the absence of effective regulatory monitoring and
enforcement. Interestingly, whereas the first report was predominantly specific
and prescriptive in its recommendations, strengthening both the regulations themselves and their enforcement, the second report recommended extensive consultation and cooperation with the industry, moving further toward a goal-setting
model with its focus on principles, performance standards, and criteria. This could
partly explain why the province appears to have a "hybrid" regulatory regime,
containing elements of both the prescriptive and goal-setting models.

After the release of Report One, the federal government published a document
summarizing its action in response to every one of the commission's first set
of recommendations [12]. Subsequently, the government released an additional
document in 1986 in reaction to the second set of recommendations in Report
Two [13]. According to the federal government, they had rectified design weaknesses, improved emergency training on the rigs, improved the availability of
environmental information, established a more effective regulatory system,
worked with industry to develop better primary evacuation systems, and enhanced
emergency response procedures in consultation with industry.

However, an analysis of these 1985 and 1986 federal government reports
revealed a somewhat defensive or complacent tone at times, and a tendency to
weaken or fudge the mandatory nature of the original recommendations through
the establishment of interim standards, appeal to current practice, only acting on
part of the recommendation, or consultation with industry or advisory councils
before implementation.

By 1985, in response to fourteen of the first twenty recommendations dealing
with design, construction, and stability, the government had established Interim
Standards developed by an offshore sub-committee of the Marine Safety Advisory
Council, a consultative body representative of federal and provincial government agencies, industry, labor, and other groups. The provincial Petroleum
Directorate had already promulgated regulations governing these aspects in
1982, which required a Certificate of Fitness as a condition of development.
In its second batch of recommendations the commission criticized the Interim
Standards as not having the force of law as well as being restricted in
coverage, recommending a Certificate of Fitness at the federal level. As it
turned out, it was not until 1992 that the federal government legislated for this
latter requirement.

A significant number of the operational standards recommendations were,
according to the federal government, already current practice under either
Canadian Coast Guard (CCG) or COGLA regulations. In some cases the

procedure referred to by the government did not fully address the commission's requirement, as in their response to recommendation number 20 on critical systems, where interrelationships were ignored. In the series of recommendations on marine training, especially ballast control (numbers 34, 36, 39, and 46), current practice was to delegate responsibility to the master. In the light of what actually happened on the Ocean Ranger, this was a complacent and ineffective response. A very important factor in the commission's analysis was the command structure and the crucial need for the person in charge to be qualified in both industrial and marine matters (Recommendations 34 and 39), but the government's action based on current practice was confused and inadequate, and it only addressed part of the problem. This issue of the necessity that the senior person's qualifications be both industrial and marine was not truly addressed until the legislative amendments in 1992. The federal government's response to these specific recommendations begs the question of why policy and procedures had not been put in place to ensure that these Canadian current practices were followed when offshore drilling took place in Newfoundland waters. And even in the case of SAR, clearly a federal responsibility at the time of the loss, the government's current practice response to Recommendations 50 and 51 did not address all the shipping information problems identified by the commission on the night of the loss.

Although consultation with industry serves a useful function, when a Royal Commission investigates a disaster for two years, processing a large volume of testimony and technical data [11, Acknowledgments], we could argue that recommendations should be accepted at that stage without further consultation with industry, except on implementation. However, the recommended extension of the independent battery sources for the public address and the emergency alarm systems was reduced from six hours to only one hour after review by "COGLA/CCG/Industry" [12, Recommendation 62]. In addition, action on two recommendations in Report Two regarding damage stability was postponed on the grounds that the impact on rig design cost necessitated discussion of these recommendations with industry [13, Recommendations 99 and 100]. Given the scale of the disaster, and the number of lives lost only four years previously, it is instrumental to ask whose interests the government regulators were serving here. It also raises the question of conflicting production and safety agendas, pointed out by the commission in its report, and echoed by Lord Cullen in the later investigation of the Piper Alpha disaster [14].

Nevertheless, the majority of the changes recommended by the commission did eventually find their way into the regulatory framework, but not always in the form of mandatory requirements as worded in the original recommendations, and sometimes missing elements deemed important by the commission. However, the "Ocean Ranger amendments," completing the government's implementation of the recommendations, took until 1992 to work their way through the bureaucratic system. They consisted of changes to both federal and provincial legislation that introduced an override provision for the energy minister over all other federal legislation in emergency situations "where the safety of workers and operations are at risk"; the requirement of a Certificate of Fitness to obtain approval of oil and gas activities; an installation manager qualified in both marine and operational operations, in charge at all times; and the establishment of an Oil and Gas Administration Advisory Council together with an Offshore Oil and Gas Training Board [15].

In addition to regulatory change brought about by the Ocean Ranger, the British Piper Alpha disaster in 1988 influenced the Newfoundland safety regime, as it had in Norway [16]. Provincial regulatory requirements were introduced or strengthened, especially those regarding permit to work systems, the layout and accommodation facilities of the rig, fire walls, and temporary safe refuges [17].

THE CANADA-NEWFOUNDLAND OFFSHORE PETROLEUM BOARD: A NEW REGULATORY REGIME

By far the most notable change in the regulatory system, following the loss of the Ocean Ranger, was the establishment of the Canada-Newfoundland Offshore Petroleum Board (CNOPB) in 1986. In part this was the effect of a political compromise eventually reached between the federal and provincial governments over ownership of offshore resources. But the disaster and its aftermath constituted the crucial pressure to reach this agreement over jurisdiction. It was no coincidence that the new body's mandate and structure reflected specific recommendations in the Ocean Ranger report. For example, the commissioners had identified a need for a single regulatory agency responsible for safety offshore, with a separate Offshore Safety Division. The federal and Newfoundland governments passed parallel legislation, known as the Atlantic Accord Acts [18], which laid down the joint management of the petroleum board by both levels of government. Overall regulatory responsibility for the offshore in practice was achieved through memoranda of agreements between the new CNOPB and all relevant government departments and agencies, as recommended by the commission. This rationalization of overlapping and conflicting government agencies was certainly an improvement over the Newfoundland regulatory regime prior to the Ocean Ranger, but it did not go far enough.

When asked for their views of the province's offshore safety regime, the presidents of the Newfoundland and Labrador Federation of Labour (NLFL) and the Newfoundland and Labrador Employers Council, and the Executive Director of the Newfoundland and Labrador Building and Construction Trades Council (NLBCTC), all pointed first to a major problem with jurisdictional complexity and ambiguity. Some of their comments are on the following page:

. . . it's very complex . . . I'm still not absolutely clear . . . in terms of actual enforcement, it's very confusing . . . it definitely needs to be simplified [19].

. . . the system here is wrong in that the responsibility for occupational health and safety is too fragmented [20].

. . . the bigger risk may be in the future when other players come on board and if the regime is not in place then and tightened up . . . [by] the federal and provincial governments putting in place a complete regime that deals with the offshore that gives clear jurisdiction to one camp or another [21].

Indeed, despite the CNOPB being jointly managed, there are still some areas of the offshore that are federally regulated under the Canada Shipping Act and the Canada Labour Code—the supply and standby vessels, shuttle tanker ships, air transportation, and stevedoring. Although this dual jurisdiction is not unknown in Canadian industry elsewhere, for example, the pulp and paper sector, it does have the potential for confusion and inconsistencies in safety and labor standards offshore. In particular, while it is clear that ships are under the Canada Shipping Act, there is still some jurisdictional ambiguity in the Atlantic Accord legislation with regard to floating, production and storage offshore (FPSO) platforms. The criterion for whether such a vessel is covered by the CNOPB or federal jurisdiction rests upon whether it is:

. . . permanently attached to, permanently anchored to or permanently resting on the seabed or subsoil of the submarine areas of the offshore area [22].

It appears from this that, when the FPSO is in transit, it is federally regulated, whereas in the production mode, connected to the seabed, regulatory responsibility shifts to the CNOPB. This in itself causes complications. Moreover, there is a grey area concerning the point at which changeover in jurisdiction occurs during connection and disconnection. It is evident from interviews held at the Marine Safety Division of Transport Canada in 1998, that lawyers and other federal government officials were grappling with this jurisdictional problem before the Terra Nova FPSO sailed out to the field [23]. Now, over two years since the vessel arrived on the Grand Banks, the situation is still unresolved, although the CNOPB is working with Transport Canada to clarify it [24]. It may seem a merely technical matter, but, because a quick disconnect is usually in the face of an emergency, a jurisdictional conflict like this does not bode well. We should also note that the new White Rose project includes an FPSO.

This confusion regarding jurisdiction has undermined the effective regulation of occupational health and safety offshore as well. Matters not specified in the Atlantic Accord Acts, but covered in the provincial Occupational Health and Safety (OHS) and Workers Compensation Acts, have previously been interpreted by all parties as applying to the offshore. Hence, the CNOPB and other players involved worked according to a memorandum of understanding requiring the application of the provincial OHS Act covering safety committees (Sections 37-52) and the right to refuse unsafe work (Sections 21-22). However, in 1998, federal lawyers in the Department of Justice proposed a new interpretation of the Atlantic Accord Acts that would prevent the application of this provincial social legislation to the offshore [25]. The relevance of the "health" aspect of the draft set of offshore occupational health and safety regulations was also questioned. This development compounded what was already a complicated and ambiguous regulatory regime, and delayed still further the promulgation of health and safety regulations that had then been in draft form for more than ten years.

Upon trying to find an answer in 1998 for the unacceptably long delay in legalizing the draft regulations, it proved impossible to penetrate the bureaucratic maze, but it was apparent that a traditional federal-provincial rivalry was at work, worsened by earlier legal arguments over ownership and management of the oil off Newfoundland's shores. The evident tension in federal-provincial relationships illustrates the difficulty in fielding regulatory reform through an extremely complex bureaucratic structure involving a number of government departments at both federal and provincial levels, a potential problem raised by Morgan Cooper in his 1997 report to the provincial government on future offshore labor relations [26]. This was combined with a lack of commitment to designate sufficient personnel, especially in the Department of Justice, for a long enough period to finish the job. Both obstacles reflected a very weak political will to be proactive on offshore workplace safety in the provincial and federal governments.

The failure to promulgate these important regulations showed clearly that the jurisdictional problems identified by the Ocean Ranger Commission: "[as] . . . competing jurisdictions, administrative overlaps and lack of co-ordinated, consistent policy" [10, p. 152] had not been resolved by the establishment of the CNOPB. Not surprisingly, interviews with the presidents of the Employers' Council, the Federation of Labour, and the Building Trades Council as well as safety personnel in the Hibernia Management Development Company and the Terra Nova Alliance revealed that many of the parties with significant interests in provincial offshore development were critical of the current draft status of the health and safety regulations. Despite assurances by the CNOPB and the industry that the draft regulations are being applied as if they had been promulgated [27], the fact is that they do not have the force of law. Moreover, even if these regulations were promulgated in their existing form, there would still be uncertainty over the workers' legal rights to be represented on health and safety committees and to refuse unsafe work.

There is a sense of *déjà vu* here when we consider the British experience of regulatory development. Woolfson, Foster, and Beck could have been referring to this province when they described what happened in the United Kingdom as ". . . peculiar administrative fudge and delay: the two signal characteristics of offshore safety" [28, p. 252]. On a more encouraging note, it is important to report that on November 1, 2002, the federal and provincial governments of

Newfoundland and Nova Scotia released a discussion document outlining proposed amendments to the Atlantic Accord Acts. These amendments incorporate an offshore occupational health and safety regime that will include the draft regulations, rights and powers of occupational health and safety committees, right to refuse unsafe work without reprisal, right to appeal CNOPB decisions, and other relevant changes. This move is a huge step forward on the part of the governments involved, showing that at least there have been some constructive negotiations between the various levels in order to reach consensus on how to clarify the overall regime by consolidating all matters of health and safety into the Atlantic Accord Acts. Even so, we should not forget that the oil industry in Newfoundland has been in production mode since 1997 and that there are now two platforms offshore, with a third anticipated for the year 2005. Moreover, in 2002, the province marked the twentieth anniversary of the Ocean Ranger disaster, and it has to be questioned why it has taken so long to address the gaps and jurisdictional ambiguity regarding offshore safety. In the background section of the consultative document, the text assures the reader that "all levels of government and the CNOPB . . . are committed to proceeding in a timely manner" [29]. Given all governments' past records, it is to be hoped that they fulfill their promise.

Along with a history of jurisdictional ambiguity and weak political commitment since the Ocean Ranger, the regulatory framework has also been undermined by a potential conflict of interests between responsibility for safety and for energy policy. Indeed, the Ocean Ranger Commission warned of:

> . . . [the] inherent risk that, in the drive for energy self-sufficiency, particularly under conditions of economic stress, the price to be paid for accelerated production may be a lowered level of safety [10, p. 153].

The Cullen inquiry in the United Kingdom also identified these potentially competing interests [28] as has the International Labour Organization [30]. Despite this concern over the power and effectiveness of a government regulator, the CNOPB reports to the federal Department of Natural Resources and the provincial Department of Mines and Energy in both safety and resource development areas, creating conflicting lines of authority and responsibility [26]. Paralleling this tension is the potential gap in expertise, a concern expressed by a provincial labor leader:

> . . . the federal and provincial line departments are not people who have an OHS background. They're not people who would understand the need for an adequate OHS legislative regime. They are people who approach development from an entirely different perspective [19].

As pointed out by Cooper in his report to the provincial government, we can contrast this arrangement with both the Norwegian and British reporting relationships. Although responsible for both safety and petroleum development, the

Norwegian Petroleum Directorate (NPD) features a clear separation between accountability to the Ministry of Industry and Energy for resource development and to the Ministry of Local Government and Labour for safety [31]. It was evident from an interview conducted by the author with the head of the government department responsible for the NPD that pressures to modify industrial and, by extension, safety standards, were frequently coming from their own energy department as well as industry, and that this supervising department was able to act as a buffer between the regulatory agency in its safety role and a narrow drive toward production in a cost cutting era [32]. Indeed, a Norwegian expert on the offshore oil industry has confirmed the close relationship between the department responsible for resource development and the industry [16], as have Woolfson et al. in respect to the British sector [28]. Turning to the Health and Safety Executive (HSE) in Britain, responsibility for offshore safety was transferred to this single-purpose agency from the Department of Energy upon the recommendation of Lord Cullen.

Given the importance of this issue, the inclusion in the governments' November 2002 discussion document of a "clear separation of occupational health and safety issues and production issues" in its list of underlying principles represents a clear advancement in policy [33]. One of the proposed amendments related to this principle is the prohibition of the same CNOPB individual being appointed as chief safety officer, chief conservation officer and chief executive officer. But by far the most significant reform is the intention of establishing an independent appeal body for any order, decision, or directive of a CNOPB safety officer. This appeal body is to be "created under the auspices of the provincial Labour Relations Board created under the Labour Relations Act" [34] and is to include a federal government official. The route of appeal severs the line of final responsibility and accountability previously leading to the Mines and Energy departments of government, and this is a positive step. However, no change in general reporting relationships is to be gleaned from a reading of the discussion document. Therefore, it is to be assumed that the ongoing responsibility for the CNOPB's role in safety offshore remains with the departments, even if the decision of last resort lies with the appeal body. In any event, the proposed tripartite advisory council to provide advice to the CNOPB and appropriate ministers on occupational health and safety matters would, if established, provide some degree of counterbalance to the power of the energy departments and the industry.

Continuing with a focus on the role of the CNOPB, the Newfoundland Accord Act contains a provision for the agency to recommend changes to the regulations when it sees fit but given the restricted ability for research and development and relatively low staffing levels for safety, this potential power has been difficult to utilize effectively. In contrast, the HSE in Britain plays a proactive role in developing policy, legislation, and regulations, integrating its research activities with operational divisions and consulting with interested groups [35]. As an indication of the NPD's proactive thrust, when the Directorate decided in the 1980s to shift the regulatory framework toward an "internal control" system, it undertook an intensive campaign in order to win oil companies over to the new regime. This included education programs and workplace visits as well as the formulation of comprehensive regulations [16]. With an eye to encouraging a more proactive role in the CNOPB's responsibility for offshore safety, a proposed amendment grants it the authority to undertake its own or collaborative research initiatives. This formalizes the board's current participation in a major offshore-related and partnership-based health and safety research program [36] and paves the way for future such initiatives.

However, the reality of being proactive, in the same sense as other countries' regulatory agencies, is hampered by the CNOPB's historical lack of funding. The presidents of the province's Federation of Labour and the Employers' Council have both expressed concern at insufficient funding of the board in the area of workplace safety [37]. Even allowing for the relatively early stage of the province's industry, overall budget, including staff allocated to the safety respon-sibilities of the board, are low in comparison with the resources available to its Norwegian and British counterparts [26]. Not surprisingly, then, an interview in 1998 with a local labor leader revealed in the CNOPB a disturbing lack of awareness of a new air pocket re-breather system introduced earlier in the North Sea. Furthermore, a letter to the provincial Minister of Environment and Labour apparently produced no reaction either [19]. This piece of new technology is a potential lifesaver as it reduces the risk of drowning after a helicopter crash. On the positive side, the board has succeeded in developing some initiatives between 1999 and 2002, including stakeholder workshops on regulatory frame-works and pipe-handling activities, and the development with industry of training and qualification guidelines for production.

But the fact remains that resources allocated to the board just do not match up to the pattern of offshore oil activity in the province. In 1986, when most exploration had stopped, the budget jumped from $1.1 million to $4.5 million in 1988, and rose to its highest level of $5.7 million in 1993. In that year cuts were announced that would take the budget down to $3.9 million by 1995 [38]. After these cuts in 1993, the board announced a reduction in personnel from 58 to 43 over three years. It was the layoff of two safety personnel at this time that stalled the CNOPB's development of training standards [17]. By 1997, the year the newly constructed Hibernia platform was towed out, the CNOPB budget had dropped to $3.1 million. Since then, it has dropped even lower, reaching its lowest at $1.7 million in 1999, and slowly creeping up again to $2 million in 2000, $2.5 million in 2001, and still only $2.6 million in 2002, when Terra Nova production started. Only three people have been hired recently as safety officers in the face of a layoff of fifteen employees by the end of 1996. The stark contrast of a current budget of $2.6 million with a budget of $5.7 million during 1993, when there was virtually no activity offshore, reveals an illogical budget allocation and one that throws some doubt on the federal and provincial government commitment to offshore safety, despite current policy statements.

In terms of public debate, it is interesting to note the predominant emphasis on the employment benefits side of the CNOPB's regulatory function rather than on safety. Given the importance of jobs in a region plagued by high unemployment levels, this is perhaps understandable. An example of this trend is the legal challenge issued to the board and Petro-Canada by the city of St. John's mayor, who alleged the regulator was not enforcing its own conditions for relocation of engineering design jobs from England [39, 40]. The CNOPB's apparent lack of action regarding Terra Nova's application of U.K. welding standards and the hiring of non-Newfoundlanders for HMDC's seismic vessels have also been the subject of public debate, including criticism by labor leaders [41]. More recently, provincial economic benefits constituted a strong theme in the 2001 public hearings on the new White Rose development. The relative lack of attention paid to safety issues is in contrast with public debate in Norway where the media and public opinion demanded safer working conditions, adding significantly to the pressures for a strong regulatory regime in that country [16].

OFFSHORE SAFETY FROM THE
OCEAN RANGER TO 1996

Given the Ocean Ranger disaster in 1982 and its aftermath, it is instructive to ask how far safety practices offshore were improved. Even though accident statistics do not comprehensively answer this question, CNOPB figures are used in this section as the only publicly available indicators we have to work with. To put the following statistics in context, the Commission of Inquiry into the Ocean Ranger disaster released Report One in 1984 and Report Two in 1985, and the federal government's response to the commission's recommendations followed in 1985 and 1986. Based on CNOPB statistics for the numbers of wells drilled offshore, the years 1983, 1984, and 1985 constituted the peak of oil exploration [42].

According to the CNOPB's 1988-89 Annual Report [43], the lost time accidents (LTAs) offshore were at about 28 per million hours worked for the drilling rigs in 1984-85 (see Figure 1). Information was unavailable for the previous year 1983-84. Accident rates dropped quite significantly during the years 1985-86 to 1987-88, with the lowest rate at about 17 per million hours worked during 1986-87. However, it is disappointing to note the comparatively high level of accidents for 1984-85, at a time of peak offshore activity, only two years after the disaster and with the benefit of the commission's first report for a significant part of the year 1984-85. With no shortage of resources in such a large and powerful industry, it would not be unreasonable to expect a much more aggressive attempt to revamp critical and management systems offshore than is apparent in the safety figures for 1984-85. Moreover, given research pointing to underreporting

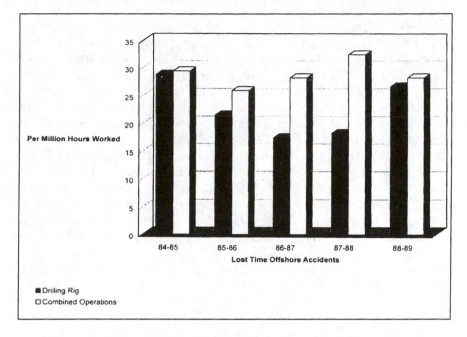

Figure 1. Offshore lost time accidents for drilling rigs and combined rates (1984-1989). **Source:** CNOPB Annual Report, 1988-1989, p. 21.

in accident statistics [44], it is quite possible that the accident rate in the 1984-85 year was underestimated. During interviews with labor representatives, local union activists in health and safety for nearly twenty years pointed to the potentially distorting effects of the safety incentive schemes prevalent in the offshore oil industry, and one specifically mentioned these systems in place on the drilling rigs at about the time of the Ocean Ranger [45].

It would be reasonable to assume that the drop in 1985-86 to 1987-88 was largely due to the impact of the reports, the establishment of the CNOPB, the introduction of Interim Standards, and the general tightening up of the regulatory framework. But if we consider the peak years of activity—1983 to 1985—this drop in LTAs was rather late in the day. It is also interesting to note that after this period of lower accident rates, during 1988-89 the LTAs rose to near 1984-85 levels again. By the following year, the trend had decreased, but not as low as the earlier 1985-86 to 1987-88 period. In 1989-90 the LTA rate was still at 22.4 per million hours.

If we turn to combined LTA rates, a relatively high rate of over 30 per million hours for 1987-88 (higher than 1984-85) was apparently due to an increase in accidents on supply and standby vessels. The CNOPB pointed to safety initiatives by the operators that had reduced the LTA rate by 50% by 1988-89. But the combined LTA rate in the latter year was still high. Considering the strong criticism of the design, operations, and management of supply/standby vessels in the report of the Ocean Ranger investigation, we could reasonably have expected that five years after the tragedy, safety procedures would have improved sufficiently to prevent such a level of accidents.

Bearing in mind research conducted in other countries into the effect of disasters on accident rates [28], the overall trend from 1984 to 1989 reveals an "Ocean Ranger" effect on the drilling rig LTAs, which seemed to fade away by 1988-89. But the combined LTA rate seems hardly affected at all, dropping most in 1985-86 but only as a little blip in an overall very slight reduction compared with 1984-85 levels. Based on the safety figures available during the five-year period reviewed, it would appear that safety practices and culture in the industry needed to change rather more effectively to make a real difference. By 1987 offshore employment had dropped to 7,147 person months from 10,526 person months in 1986, and by 1989 was only 1,619 person months. By 1991-92, the CNOPB had stopped reporting exploration activities and beginning in 1993 no more LTA charts were included.

SAFETY DURING CONSTRUCTION OF THE HIBERNIA PLATFORM FROM 1992-96

During the building of the platform at the Bull Arm site, there were two fatalities, in May 1992 and in September 1993, both resulting from severe injuries caused by falling from one level of the site to another. With the exception of the last year, 1996, the incidence rate per 100 employees was consistently higher than the provincial construction industry average (see Figure 2). The first year, 1992, was particularly high at 13.75, over double that of the industry average of 6.62. Only in the last year of the project, in 1996, was there a noticeable drop to 5.92, slightly less than the industry average of 6.59 [46]. Even allowing for back injuries, which comprise over 50% workplace accidents in the province [47], the high incidence of lumbar spine injuries, sometimes triple that of any other type, and overlifting as a major cause of injury, fits with the experience of women ironworkers on the site. A graphic description of one female rebar worker's exposure to high risk of back injury through the continued and excessive lifting of heavy vertical bars makes disturbing reading in a 1996 study. Moreover, unaccounted for in these Bull Arm figures is the degree of documented sexual harassment [48], now recognized as an occupational health and safety hazard [49].

The president of the Newfoundland and Labrador Building Trades Council criticized both government for lax enforcement of regulations and HMDC project management for implementing incentive systems for accident-free records. However, he viewed the main problem with safety as the high number and frequent change of contractors involved in the project. Significantly, the diffusion of accountability and responsibility resulting from increasingly more

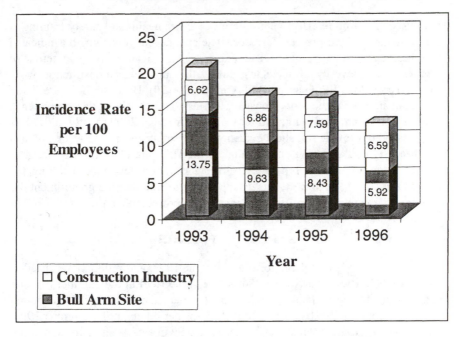

Figure 2. The incidence rate for the construction of the Hibernia
Platform (Bull Arm Site) and the provincial construction industry (1993-1996).
Source: Department of Environment and Labour, Government of
Newfoundland and Labrador, January 29, 1999.

complex operator-contractor relationships was identified as a significant problem
by the Ocean Ranger Commission of Inquiry. At Bull Arm this had apparently
resulted in low levels of commitment to safety. The president of the NLBTC
saw this as a much greater problem in the offshore oil industry than in the
construction industry in general: "So they have no stake . . . they just come in,
get the work done at the lowest possible cost and move off" [20]. A fragmentary
and shifting workforce meant a poorly functioning, sporadic safety committee
system with little or no continuity between different representatives for various
contractors and shifts. This view of the safety ramifications of a high level
of contractual employers onshore is consistent with Norwegian offshore safety
patterns. Analysis of accident rates has revealed a higher risk of injury to contractual employees compared to operators' employees, and one study found
that improvements in safety occurred only after the operating companies made
explicit demands on contractor companies [16].

Although starting with very high accident rates in the first year, the Bull Arm
figures show a steady improvement over the four years it took to build the
platform. In hindsight, the president of the NLBTC regretted that the unions had

not pushed for a more effective program of worker health and safety training at the beginning of the project. In a recent telephone conversation, he indicated that health and safety practice had improved significantly, both in terms of frequency and severity of accidents, during the subsequent construction work for the Terra Nova FPSO at the Bull Arm facility [50]. Because the vessel itself was built in Korea, the work consisted of installation of topside components, hook-up, and commissioning, and took place from May 2000 to July 2001. It is not possible to provide statistical evidence of the safety record at the Terra Nova site because, unlike during construction of the Hibernia platform, the accident figures were not tracked separately. Given the poor safety record during the Hibernia construction project, it is disappointing to find that the government did not monitor the next major offshore construction project in the province.

SAFETY OFFSHORE

Tow-out of the Hibernia platform was in June 1997, and production started in October 1997. The Terra Nova FPSO sailed to the field in the summer of 2001 and first oil flowed in January 2002. Lost time accident rates for the Hibernia platform were available from the CNOPB for the period up until December 1998. Subsequently, offshore statistics were released only in an aggregate form, making it more difficult to track safety indicators per type of installation (fixed or floating) or sectors (marine, production, or exploration), as is possible in Norway [16]. This unavailability of accident data is illustrative of recent criticisms in the province of the CNOPB's lack of transparency, acknowledged by the board, and apparently the subject of discussions to address them [51]. In any event, due to this gap in data, the next section focuses on early statistics from Hibernia, followed by a discussion of the aggregate offshore figures up to the year 2002.

THE HIBERNIA PLATFORM FROM JUNE 1997 TO DECEMBER 1998

The overall LTA rate for this eighteen-month period was shown as 14.91 per million hours in the table compiled by the CNOPB [52]. However, when we examine the pattern of LTAs in Figure 3 it is evident that there was considerable variation between months. For example, June and July 1997 showed an LTA rate of zero but this increased to 15.48 and 16.28 for August and September, respectively, dropping in October to 8.17, and jumping ten points to 18.75 in November before dropping again to 10.08 during the Christmas month. The variations between months were more extreme in the second year of production with the lowest LTA being zero in October 1998 and the highest rates occurring in April and July at 30.53 and 30.14, respectively. Upon further calculation, there is also a significant difference between the LTA rate of 10.12 per million hours for the half-year from June to December 1997, which included a start-up period,

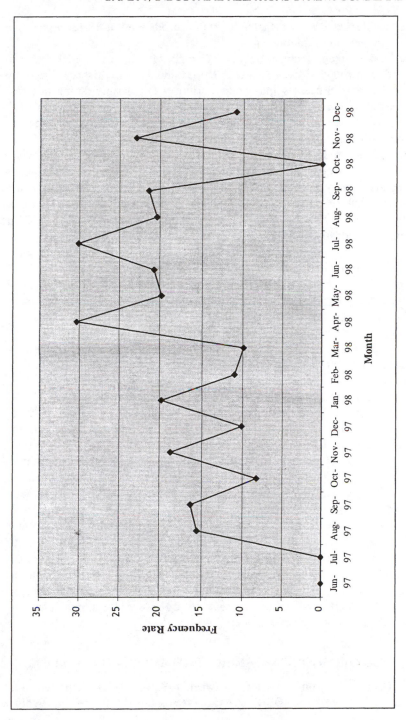

Figure 3. Lost time accidents for the offshore Hibernia Platform (June 1997-December 1998).
Source: CNOPB, Operations and Safety Division, March 1, 1999.

and the accident rate for the first full year of production at 18.18, arguably a more typical year of operations.

Care must be taken in comparing these current safety figures with LTA rates in the period following the Ocean Ranger up to the wind down of offshore oil activity in 1989, not only because some underreporting was probable during this past period but also because of HMDC's attempts to cultivate an open "no-blame" culture on the platform. In theory, if this culture has genuinely led to more open communication on safety issues, together with an increased tendency to report accidents, then the current Hibernia rates may well reflect this. In any event, because we cannot quantify the effect of an increased or decreased likelihood of reporting on either sets of figures, then there is a limit to how far we can compare the earlier, post-Ocean Ranger accident rates with those of the Hibernia platform. Nevertheless, even with this qualification, it should be noted that the CNOPB questioned the industry based on what they saw as an unacceptably high combined accident rate of 30 per million hours in 1987-88, leading to some concern at the Hibernia rates of more than 30 for April and July 1998.

The Hibernia platform is operating with a quality-audit model of safety, and safety and the environment are integrated with overall loss prevention, both characteristics reflecting an international trend. Occupational Health and Safety committees are elected on the basis of functional area and shift. The HDMC documents and interviews with safety personnel and the president of the corporation [53] indicated a genuine attempt to provide a safe workplace offshore. As the only production platform on the Grand Banks from 1997 until 2001, all eyes were on it during this earlier phase of oil development. Moreover, HMDC community-friendly public relations make it reasonable to assume that the company wants to be seen as a model employer offshore, and excellence in safety would be an inextricable part of this positive image.

Even allowing for limited access to offshore oil workers for interview purposes, informal meetings with employees and other information led to the initial conclusion in 1999 that many workers on the Hibernia platform would have expressed their confidence in the company when asked about safety. This is a positive note. Even so, the Ocean Ranger report suggested that, ". . . offshore workers appear to be reluctant to voice their concerns" [10, p. 167]. More recently, Woolfson et al. commented on the tendency of U.K. North Sea offshore oil workers to be overconfident regarding safety [28]. Furthermore, we should be aware that high levels of unemployment tend to increase feelings of job insecurity, potentially hampering willingness to speak out on safety issues, particularly in what was then a nonunion environment.

ALL OFFSHORE WORKERS FROM 1995 TO 2002

After a gap in reporting LTA rates between 1993 and 1996 when there was little activity offshore, the CNOPB's statistics (see Figure 4) show how in 1996/97

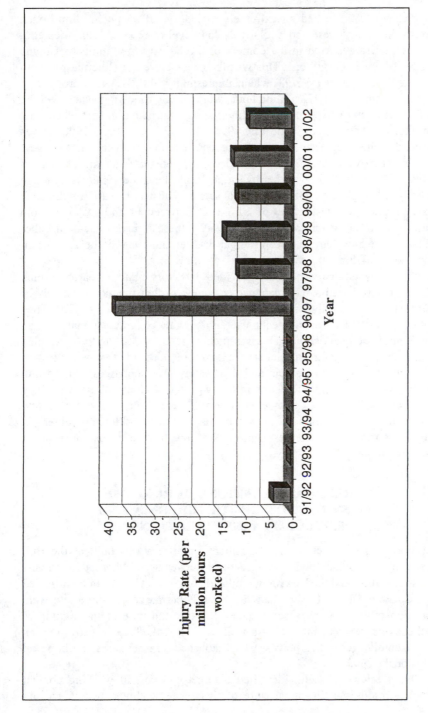

Figure 4. Reportable injuries offshore Newfoundland and Labrador (1991-2002).
Source: CNOPB Annual Report, 2001-2002, p. 23.

the aggregate LTA reached an extremely high level of 38 per million hours. Although this rate represented a relatively low level of reportable injuries at 5, they nevertheless occurred in the context of a relatively low number of hours worked offshore (132 million). This was the year before the Hibernia platform tow-out and first oil in 1997/98, when, interestingly, the LTA rate dropped to 11.15 in the context of 1,972 million hours worked. The following year, 1998/99, the LTA increased to 13.92; this was Hibernia's first production year when their rate peaked at 30 during April and July 1998. This LTA of 13.92 in 1998/99 was the second highest reported in Figure 4, even compared with the start-up year for the Terra Nova FPSO (2001/02). Indeed, it is encouraging to note that at 9.02 the LTA for 2001/02 was the lowest accident rate since 1996/97, although the latter year's high rate of 38 sets up what seems to be a downward trend, which in reality reveals a plateau effect of LTA rates between 11 and 13, apart from the last year. In any event, apart from 1996/97, these figures indicate a better trend than those between the Ocean Ranger disaster and 1988/89, before current developments offshore.

However, a cautionary note is provided by Norwegian research, which suggested quality-based safety management models often functioned merely as "paper systems" with only "marginal impact on drill floor practices" [16]. They tend to be couched in overly technical jargon with convoluted analyses; an example would be quantitative risk assessment (QRA). According to Norwegian studies, management safety specialists are therefore more able to take control, in effect excluding offshore workers and their safety representatives, calling into question any real worker participation in safety [54]. In a safety culture where any influence over safety needs a high level of technical expertise, well-trained safety committee members are crucial. One way of ensuring that workforce involvement is truly effective is union representation. We now turn to an examination of industrial relations in the industry.

INDUSTRIAL RELATIONS DURING THE CONSTRUCTION OF THE HIBERNIA AND TERRA NOVA INSTALLATIONS

The gravity base structure for the Hibernia platform was built at the Bull Arm site in the province under an agreement between the Hibernia Employers Association (HEA) and the Newfoundland and Labrador Oil Development Allied Trades Council (ODC). Labor relations at the Hibernia construction site were not as cooperative as they were predicted to be at the time of the signing of the collective agreement in 1990. As well as a no strike/lockout provision, an expedited conflict-resolution process was established for grievances, markup, and jurisdictional disputes.

In 1993 Kealey and Long identified a largely successful working context for dispute resolution: "As a measure of this success, almost two years into the project, there has been no recourse to third party arbitration" [55]. In the first three years of the project only four grievances reached the arbitration stage; one over the bargaining unit, two over shift changes, and the last over who could carry forth a grievance. However, by 1995 initial cooperation was breaking down as grievances reaching the arbitration stage skyrocketed, with roughly fifty grievances going to arbitration, over half of those in 1996 alone, and another fifty-six dropped or settled in a month of meetings between the ODC and the HEA in June 1995. In addition, the nature of many of the grievances was disturbing, with several grievances involving theft, drug, and alcohol problems [56].

There were four main labor relations issues running through the construction project. The first arose out of hiring procedures, with calls for local hiring affecting both the initial stages of the project and continuing throughout. Initial local complaints centered on the project being a union site and local hiring following seniority. In addition, unionized workers complained several times that work had been done by workers outside the province, or that outside "experts" had been brought in to do work while trained Newfoundlanders remained unemployed.

The second issue was employment equity, as many women complained of gender discrimination in both hiring and training practices. While the ODC encouraged women to apply for employment at the site, hired an equity promotion coordinator, and claimed to be actively seeking female welders, painters, and sandblowers, there were no equity promotion platform and no affirmative action quotas in the contract. Hiring was up to local unions. Many women who were hired filed human rights complaints (ninety complaints in total) claiming that they were the last to be called for work, resulting in low seniority and making them ineligible for training courses that would have ensured them of more work. A study by Women in Trades and Technology (WITT) has indicated that women made up less than 4% of the overall workforce at Hibernia, with the majority of those jobs in traditional women's work areas such as catering or clerical. Those women who did enter the construction trades noted pervasive harassment [48].

Third, there was a marked lack of trust between labor and management over the issues of grievances and arbitrations from 1994 onward. The record number of grievances going forward to arbitration in 1995 and 1996 showed a decided lack of step-three cooperation to solve issues independently without resorting to arbitration. Grievances were largely over discipline, shift scheduling, wrongful discharges, and management rights. With labor relations at an all-time low in 1995-96, several efforts were made by the ODC and the HEA to break the impasse, first with informal cooperation, and later with more formal meetings. With a large backlog of grievances and arbitrations awaiting settlement, both sides agreed to set up a committee of six members (three from each side) with a mandate to resolve all outstanding grievances. All unanimous decisions of the committee were binding, with those arbitrations that were not unanimous being sent back to the normal arbitration procedure. A preliminary analysis by Kealey and McBride indicates that the ODC opted to settle many of the grievances in exchange for a reduced fine for a wildcat strike that occurred in January 1995. This solution proved to be only temporary as the employers were complaining again in February 1996 of poor labor relations and another increase in arbitrations. In the latter stages of the project, the arbitration system again worsened, with the HEA demanding to have arbitrators removed for bias, and with both labor and management remaining intransigent on time limits, with the end result that even minor grievances ended up in front of arbitration, making it very difficult to deal with the larger issues [57].

Finally, there was a significant degree of jurisdictional conflict, despite the dispute resolution procedure in the Bull Arm Agreement. To avoid potential jurisdictional conflict between the fourteen unions on site, on-site prejob and markup conferences were required. Any disputes not resolved within fourteen days were to be referred to a specially appointed jurisdictional umpire, selected by mutual agreement. Procedures for settlement and penalties for noncompliance with any orders made were set down in the agreement. Final appeal beyond this umpire was to the building trades unions' Impartial Jurisdictional Disputes Board of the Building and Construction Trades Department of the American Federation of Labor-Congress of Industrial Organizations (AFL-CIO) [55].

In the first three years of the project the umpire was called in to address nine claims appeals (out of a total of 722 work assignments), with all but one being upheld as assigned [55]. No analysis has yet been done on the jurisdictional statistics post-1993; however, interviews have indicated that the umpire was much more frequently used in later years. On several occasions unions attempted to take jurisdictional disputes to conventional arbitration but in all instances they were referred back to the umpire. Indeed, by all indications, overall, this attempt to prevent jurisdictional conflict did not work very well. This would perhaps explain why the subsequent agreement between the newly formed Newfoundland and Labrador International Building Trades Petroleum Development Association (PDA) and Provincial Contractors Inc. Ltd. (PCL) covering Terra Nova construction work at the old Bull Arm site emphasized labor management cooperation, flexible work practices, and a single union concept [58].

Despite these attempts by the parties, there was divisiveness among the unions on the Terra Nova site from the beginning over the formation of the PDA, which involved international level leaders to the exclusion of some significant local players, resulting in a Labour Relations Board challenge over certification. Even though there was a no-strike/no lockout clause in the collective agreement, there were several illegal work stoppages, totaling 63,557 person-hours, representing 2.1% of the 2,987,033 person-hours worked up to October 1, 2000. Jurisdictional issues were central to all these walkouts but one, which was triggered by disciplinary dismissals [59, 60]. The labor relations and productivity problems were such that the provincial government commissioned a consultant, Morgan Cooper, to investigate and make recommendations for future offshore fabrication and construction projects.

In his report, Cooper attributes the poor labor relations climate during the Terra Nova project to a number of factors, including worker dissatisfaction with low-level wages compared with Hibernia, the lack of travel allowances, the absence of a jurisdictional dispute mechanism, and low morale. On the employer side, management of work processes featured delays, rework, and expansion of work, and labor relations were managed from outside the province. With regard to the unions, the PDA appeared unable to make the single-union concept work, revealing a lack of internal control over its member unions and the rank and file. As a result of this review and Cooper's recommendations, in 2001, the provincial government amended the rules governing the declaration of "special projects" such as oil and gas fabrication and construction projects, under the Labour Relations Act. These changes included the authorization of the Labour Relations Board to issue declarations of unlawful strikes or lockouts, as well as "directives to cease and desist from such unlawful acts"; the strengthening of penalties for those participating in unlawful strikes or lockouts; the prohibition of "union labelling" clauses in any council union's collective agreements; and the identification of mandatory criteria for both employers' organizations and councils of unions involved in collective bargaining [61].

Whether such confrontational labor relations at both construction sites affected offshore industrial relations is a moot point, but it is reasonable to assume that the high level of jurisdictional conflict reinforced the traditional union-avoidance strategies of the oil companies, and possibly made early attempts at organizing platform workers more difficult.

INDUSTRIAL RELATIONS OFFSHORE

For four years after the tow-out of the Hibernia platform in 1997, the offshore workers were largely unorganized, apart from shuttle tanker crews, unionized by the Fish, Food and Allied Workers/Canadian Auto Workers under an agreement notable for its twenty-five year length and a no-strike/lockout clause [62], and supply ship crews, represented by the Seafarers International Union. All labor informants interviewed for this research in 1998 were adamant that safety in the offshore oil industry would be problematic so long as the platform employees remained nonunion [63]. During union organizing drives in 2000 and 2001, safety was an important issue for workers, and when the Communications, Energy and Paperworkers (CEP) won their second certification attempt in October 2001, their representative included improved safety procedures in his list of items for negotiation, along with higher wages, a seniority list, and better benefits [64]. Hibernia is the first unionized offshore oil platform in North America, and offers the opportunity for more effective worker involvement in safety. In its 1997 government submission on the labor relations regime for offshore oil platforms, the Newfoundland and Labrador Federation of Labour listed as its first recommendation: "All platforms in the offshore oil industry, whether for exploration or production, should be unionized" [65]. Indeed, studies in a number of countries including Canada and Britain confirm the positive impact unions have on safety [66].

In an investigation into the disproportionately high incidence of fatalities in the British offshore sector up to the late 1970s by the Burgoyne Committee in 1980, two trade unionists had strongly argued this point:

> The token non-union committees that have been set up by employers . . . are no real answer to the need for genuine employee involvement. Until well-trained, union-appointed health and safety representatives are operating on all offshore installations and effective trade union based health and safety committees monitor events within each company and across the North Sea as a whole, there will be a quite inadequate offshore safety machinery. Unionisation and recognition is an important element in proper monitoring of accidents and full reporting of incidents. At the moment lack of union protection leaves employees totally exposed [67].

Later, in his report of the inquiry into the Piper Alpha disaster, Lord Cullen pointed to the advantage of union representation:

> . . . I am prepared to accept that the appointment of offshore safety representatives by trade unions could be of some benefit in making the work of safety representative and safety committees effective, mainly through the credibility and resistance to pressures which trade union backing would provide [14].

We know from recent studies by Woolfson et al. and Whyte that criticisms of nonunionized participation in health and safety still hold true in the British sector of the North Sea nearly two decades later [68]. Whyte's research showed that nonunion workers and committee representatives felt job insecurity undermined their ability to raise and pursue safety concerns. Moreover, a new more subtle form of employer retaliation than the old "not required back" (NRB) can be a barrier to open communication of health and safety concerns offshore in the U.K. sector [69]. In the context of cost cutting in the industry, this job insecurity is more acute and will reduce even further the likelihood of any real worker input into safety offshore in a nonunionized workplace.

Accordingly, both labor movement experience and research findings lead us to conclude that job security through union protection, together with union-based expertise in the field, provides the power base for workers to have a real influence in the design and implementation of occupational health and safety programs. The provincial Federation of Labour's three major recommendations for the health and safety regulatory regime offshore [70] dovetailed the establishment of crucial union-management safety committees at the workplace level with labor representation on a tripartite regulatory body responsible for offshore health and safety. Based on the worker participation provisions in the Norwegian model, the second and third recommendations read:

This regulatory framework should require the establishment of labor-management health and safety committees, with duties and powers similar to Norway's Working Environment Act.

In particular, we recommend that safety delegates on these committees be given the power in the last resort to stop work if they deem it as placing workers under serious risk, and that they be given legal protection against any loss resulting from this action.

After reviewing the Norwegian and British legislation regarding workforce participation in his report to the government, Cooper expressed concern that Newfoundland's health and safety legislation:

. . . [did] not provide for the election of safety delegates across defined safety areas, confer powers upon safety delegates to halt work, or require offshore installation managers to provide written response to government inspectors in circumstances where they refuse requests by safety delegates to halt work [26].

Later in his report recommending a labor relations regime suitable for the production phase offshore, he endorsed the tripartite approach to the development of offshore health and safety regulations in Norway and Britain:

. . . there are few obstacles and significant benefits to be attained through tripartite consultation in relation to the formation, administration and enforcement of offshore safety regulations and guidelines. A move toward tripartite consultation in the area of offshore safety will also alleviate the perception of many labor stakeholders that the CNOPB lacks the independence from the industry to regulate in the public interest [26].

Although the province's Employers' Council did not include a recommendation on tripartite consultation in their labor relations submission, the president of the council indicated during an interview with the author in 1998 that a tripartite advisory council on health and safety would be acceptable to her, although it was understood that the possibility would have to be discussed within the membership. It is encouraging to note the recently proposed regulatory reform to establish such a council, an idea more readily implemented by unionization of the platform workers in 2001.

In order to understand the events leading up to this dramatic change in offshore industrial relations, it is useful to start with a review of the relevant legislation. The province's Labour Relations Act, 1977, is in line with most Canadian labor law covering the private sector. It encapsulates a basic right for all employees to join a union of their choice and for the union to represent them in collective bargaining with the employer. It includes prohibition of unfair labor practices and requires formal certification of a union for it to have exclusive bargaining rights for a given bargaining unit. The legislation also sets the ground rules for the process and structure of collective bargaining and for decertification. It grants power to a tripartite Labour Relations Board to implement and enforce the legislation.

Acting on the labor relations consultant's recommendation, the Labour Relations Act was amended to require a platform-wide bargaining unit. Even allowing for criticisms of the rules on the certification process itself, for example, those on the requirement of a secret ballot vote, the current Newfoundland legislation is as conducive to organizing an industry as any in the country. Labor attempts to strengthen the access provision for the offshore in the legislation were resisted on the grounds that the Labour Relations Board already had the power to grant access to remote work sites. Nevertheless, the legislation provided a more positive framework than was available to U.K. unionists in the early stages of oil development there.

This was not for want of trying by the oil industry, who, along with the Newfoundland and Labrador Employers' Council, wanted a legal freeze on certification until offshore oil activities had reached "steady state" operations. Labor groups, including the Newfoundland and Labrador Federation of Labour and the Newfoundland and Labrador Oil Development Council, saw any freeze periods as inconsistent with the fundamental rights of all workers to choose union representation. Of course, to prevent applications for certification at the beginning of operations would reduce the likelihood of organization of the platforms in the longer term. In the end, Cooper concluded that the Labour Relations Board's existing powers to determine exactly what constituted an appropriate bargaining unit would enable it to deal satisfactorily with the start-up issue.

The legal requirement for a platform-wide bargaining unit was a double-edged sword. It went a long way toward addressing the industry's high level of concern for jurisdictional disputes and the potential they saw for undermining both continued production and safety. The strength of this view was apparent in their adamant opposition to a council of unions. In practice, a single bargaining unit widened the door to an industrial union organizing the platform. And in terms of current practice in Canadian industrial relations, there has generally been a clear recognition of the difference between the construction phase, the building trades unions' province, and the production phase, normally associated with an industrial union. Whereas building trade unions with conservative craft origins have traditionally believed in business unionism, the industrial unions have historically stood for social unionism. In the face of powerful oil companies, a united and strong stand on issues not only of health and safety but also on policies such as employment equity and sexual harassment are important.

The advantages of a more centralized bargaining structure, offering less opportunity for divide-and-rule tactics, were somewhat tempered by the realization that to organize a whole platform was a formidable task for any union. All occupational groups had to be organized at the same time and some were less open to unions than others. For example, drilling crews in particular are often very resistant to organizing attempts. This frame of mind is partly due to the organizational culture of many of the drilling companies whose origins are in the southern United States, where antilabor attitudes are common, frequently bolstered by right-to-work laws [71].

Moreover, even allowing for the small number of offshore workers interviewed in 1998, all of them, whether in production or exploration, revealed a negative attitude toward unions and unionization. A common thread in the workers' comments was that the tensions generated would undermine the cooperation and camaraderie that developed among workers on the platform. There was a perception of unions causing problems in work practices whereby one worker helps another out on any tasks that may have to be done. This was a reflection perhaps of the jurisdictional disputes commonly associated with unionism, and, historically, more particularly with the craft unions. Unions were seen as a potential problem for safety as well as productivity. This view of unions is not unexpected in American-based nonunion companies. And it is understandable in the context of the union-avoidance strategies followed by the oil companies, including, for example, an emphasis on employee participation, employer-employee communications, team concept, company as family, which leave little or no space for a union [72].

Added to these difficulties in organizing the offshore was a history of interunion tension, threatening to derail unionization as it had in Britain. The structure of the provincial labor movement still reflects the historical separation of craft-based construction unions from the mainstream labor movement in Canada, and jurisdictional conflict among building trades unions during the offshore construction phase has been noted. Potential rivalry among industrial unions interested in organizing the offshore became manifest in November 1999, when both the Fish, Food and Allied Workers Union (FFAW) and the Communications, Energy and Paperworkers Union applied to the Labour Relations Board for certification to represent the Hibernia platform workers. In order to apply, a union must have at least 40% support of the bargaining unit they propose, demonstrated by signed membership cards. Subsequently, there has to be a secret ballot vote whereby the union has to gain a simple majority support of those voting, provided 70 % of the bargaining unit vote. Because two unions applied, in the end neither could meet the initial 40% support threshold, the secret ballot vote conducted in February 2000 was not counted, and the board rejected both applications in March 2001 [73]. Shortly afterward, the CEP applied for certification on its own; this time it won the subsequent vote held in June 2001 and was certified by the board in October 2001. The HMDC challenged the board's jurisdiction to certify the CEP and filed for judicial review at the Supreme Court of Newfoundland. Court hearings have been held but a decision on certification from the Court is still pending, at the time of writing.

Meanwhile, the CEP has recently filed an unfair labor practice complaint with the Labour Relations Board, alleging that the HMDC has failed to negotiate with a certified bargaining agent, with the company arguing that they are not legally required to do so until certification is confirmed by the Supreme Court [74].

The outcome of this complaint is unknown at the time of writing. Earlier, both the CEP and FFAW had filed complaints of unfair labor practices with the Labour Relations Board, alleging that laying off twenty-five platform workers in February 2000 was illegal under the Labour Relations Act during the "freeze" period that prevents layoffs or changes in conditions of work before a certification vote is conducted. The board upheld the union arguments and ordered the HMDC to reinstate the laid-off workers with back pay. The HMDC filed for judicial review and in July 2002 the Newfoundland Supreme Court overturned the board's decision. [75]. These developments illustrate the obstacles that a union faces when organizing an industry with such a concerted union-avoidance strategy, but at least the legislative framework has provided the route to the CEP's certification, with the associated rights and due process that will benefit offshore workers. However, the CEP's subsequent appeal of the court's judgment was successful. In any event, the Terra Nova Alliance has accepted the organization of its FPSO by the CEP, which received legal certification from the Labor Relations Board in April 2003.

SOME CURRENT CONCERNS IN SAFETY OFFSHORE

Clearly, there have been significant improvements in both the regulatory regime and the industry's approach to offshore safety since the Ocean Ranger disaster, and the recent government discussion paper represents a significant step forward, although it remains to be seen how many of the proposals will result in regulatory reform. In the meantime, there are still some areas of concern, and it is to be hoped that, despite present difficulties, mature collective bargaining relationships will develop and the parties can work collaboratively toward their resolution.

Offshore Working Schedules

Labor informants with considerable experience in health and safety have identified the working schedule as a cause of increased health and safety risks [76]. Currently, the majority of work rotations on the production platforms are three weeks on and three weeks off. Each working period is made up of twenty-one days of twelve-hour days with no break; many workers also change from night to day shifts or vice versa at some stage in their hitch. Work-home tensions associated with regular periods of separation have been well documented in a number of studies [77], and these pressures increase the stress levels on the platform and have ramifications for health and safety at work.

Most important, the health and safety risks arising from fatigue and decreased levels of concentration in shift work are generally accepted [78]. As the medical director of Phillips Petroleum in Norway commented: "Sleep researchers are unanimous in concluding that shift working increases the threat of errors. . . . The offshore industry should refuse to accept the safety risk posed by sleep disruptions" [79]. He also reported a link between continuous shiftwork involving twelve-hour shifts for fourteen days without a break, and offshore workers losing their health certificates before retirement age, mainly due to musculo-skeletal and cardiovascular problems. The general significance of his observations are confirmed by an occupational physiologist at the regulatory body, the Norwegian Petroleum Directorate, who said, "A simple modelling of the data shows that six out of ten operator employees on the continental shelf will lose their medical certificate or all desire to work before they reach retirement" [80]. Compounding this impact of shiftwork in Newfoundland's case is the predominance of the long twenty-one day work rotation. Indeed, a study conducted by Shell Expro UK found that accident rates in its offshore workforce increased after ten days away from home [81]. The probability of chronic fatigue from long shifts and hitches is aggravated by disturbed rest time on the platform due to ever-present noise and vibration, and because of required activities taking place in rest time, for example, health and safety committee meetings, safety training, musters, and drills. Even if we acknowledge that these musters and drills are crucial in emergency preparedness training, sleep can sometimes be interrupted twice a night. As the president of the province's Federation of Labour commented:

> I think that the extended hours of work and the demands being made on employees outside their regular hours while they are offshore is cause for concern. I think there's a safety factor there. . . . I'm not quite sure that CNOPB is attempting to address these problems [19].

Shorter shifts and/or shorter work rotations would go a long way in alleviating these increased health and safety risks, although it is recognized that an increase in helicopter travel brings with it increased risks, too. However, a comparison with the Norwegian labor policy on offshore working hours is instructive. The Newfoundland government granted the HMDC an exemption from the province's Labour Standards Act to allow long rotations and shifts. In contrast, there was no exemption from the Norwegian Working Environment Act given to the industry, and the offshore unions and the companies negotiated a general pattern of work consisting of two weeks on, three weeks off; two weeks on, four weeks off. As argued by the OILC in the United Kingdom and other worker advocates, this results in a much lower annual working hour total for Norwegian contractual workers, at 1,612 hours, than for workers in the British North Sea, at 2,184 hours [82]. By comparison, the three week on and three week off pattern in Newfoundland is equivalent to 2,100 annual working hours, net of two weeks holidays.

According to a CNOPB representative, they are watching for any possible safety ramifications of the production platform working schedules, and are developing a database to enable analysis in this area. So far, they have not discerned any worrying patterns in LTAs, and, in their view, the research evidence is inconclusive [83]. The CNOPB's participation in a research project focusing on employment offshore, including the health and well-being of workers and their families, should assist the development of the most appropriate working schedules.

Training

Failure in operational and safety training was a crucial element in the loss of the Ocean Ranger. The commission recommended the development of training performance standards and the statutory establishment of an Offshore Petroleum Training Standards Board. The members of this board were to be "persons with first-hand knowledge of offshore operations, with special competence in training, and with the experience and insight of workers." Its purpose was to establish training and qualifications standards, certification and recertification requirements, verification and audit measures, and the requirement for, and approval of, training institutions and facilities. The board was to have a particular responsibility for a "program of certification of training in those skills which are judged to be critical to safety" including the delineation of certificate skills required for specific positions [10, p. 165]. The commission stressed that the content of safety training was fundamental and should be addressed without delay by the regulatory authority. Until the board was put in place, as an interim measure the then regulatory authority was to "immediately" establish uniform standards for basic safety and emergency training for regular and occasional offshore workers.

The urgency of this recommendation was apparently lost on the governments of the day. It was ten years after the tragedy before there was any legislative response to the commission's call for a more effective and monitored training system for the offshore. Among the "Ocean Ranger" amendments in 1992 was the establishment of an Offshore Oil and Gas Training Standards Advisory Board. To date, this board has not been established nor are there any indications that it will be in the future. An attempt by the CNOPB to develop training standards in 1993, eleven years after the Ocean Ranger sank, was stalled due to staff layoffs as a result of funding cuts. It is only in 2002 that the Canadian Association of Petroleum Producers (CAPP) updated their previous 1991 guidelines on training and qualification for drilling to include production [84], although oil has been flowing from 1997 onward.

Notwithstanding this long delay, there are clear advantages to the involvement of industry in developing training standards. One is the international experience in both operational and safety training brought to collaborative work with the CNOPB and with training agencies; the province's one-week basic survival training at the Marine Institute of Memorial University is as high a standard as any in the world. Nevertheless, it could be argued that provincial offshore training is industry driven in a way that does not reflect the Ocean Ranger Commissioners' recommendation of a training board, or, indeed, the regulatory amendment to establish one promised by the government in 1992.

A tripartite training advisory board along the lines of the British Offshore Petroleum Industry Training Organisation would enhance government's role and introduce valuable labor experience and expertise into the process, especially relevant now that the Hibernia platform is unionized and the government has recognized the advantages of a tripartite approach to policy development. It would reflect the original concerns of the commission, which specified the advantages of worker participation in the training board they recommended. Contractor as well as operator representation would ensure continuity and consistency.

Evacuation Systems

Following the failure of the evacuation system on the Ocean Ranger, in 1985 the commission recommended that:

> . . . government and industry without delay establish performance standards and initiate a joint major engineering development project to produce a safe primary evacuation system for offshore drilling rigs [10, Recommendation 107].

At the time of writing, there are still no performance standards in place, although in October 1998, sixteen years after the Ocean Ranger disaster, the federal government finally announced an initiative to develop some. This is a step in the right direction but progress is slow. In addition, the federal government is working through its departments of Transport Canada and Natural Resources Canada, along with its research agency, the National Research Council (NRC) and the industry (CAPP) to "create a research program in offshore escape, evacuation, and rescue (EER). The program's overall objective is to establish a baseline of evacuation systems' performance capability, based on environmental conditions off the East Coast of Canada." Currently, the emphasis is upon development of a database in EER at the NRC [85] and ongoing research at the NRC's Institute of Marine Dynamics to develop proper guidelines and techniques for performance evaluation and system approval, given this area's challenges in terms of waves, cold temperatures and ice [86]. All this is very positive but, once again, we have to ask why it has taken twenty years since the Ocean Ranger disaster before this kind of safety-related research really started to move forward, when other technological advances in drilling and reservoir management, designed to enhance oil production, have long been tackled and resolved and are already in place. In 1986 the government promised to develop a safe primary evacuation system jointly with industry. The following review of the evacuation system currently in place on the production platforms indicates that, so far, government has not completely fulfilled this promise.

On the Hibernia platform, helicopters cannot be relied upon as a primary means of evacuation due to distance from shore and likelihood of fog. Therefore, lifeboats are the primary evacuation method. Skyscape, a kevlar netting tube launched to rest on the sea with accessibility to four life rafts, is the second component of the evacuation system. The HMDC is also developing an innovatory dry form of evacuation, called GEMEVAC, a cable car concept to move personnel from the fixed platform to a supply/standby vessel. This latter system is currently being field tested and it exceeds regulatory requirements.

The overall evacuation system has been approved by the CNOPB. Nevertheless, it is useful to review the components of it and their combined effectiveness. Currently, Hibernia is equipped with TEMPSC (totally enclosed motor-propelled survival craft) launched by a PrOD (preferred orientation device), a boom and cable that pull the lifeboat away from the abandoned installation once launched. This would be a particular advantage in a platform fire, for example. In an explosion, which is an ever-present possibility with storage of oil and latterly gas on Hibernia, the surrounding ocean would also likely be on fire, and whether the PrOD could pull a lifeboat beyond this danger zone is uncertain. Although TEMPSC are designed for protection from ocean fires, how long this protection would last remains to be seen and depends critically on high levels of maintenance on the water spray apparatus. It also has to be borne in mind that the testing of lifeboats is generally conducted in reasonably fair sea states, and it is doubtful whether the PrOD device would work effectively in heavy, stormy seas such as on the night of the Ocean Ranger disaster.

Although an improvement on the traditional method of lifeboat launch, the PrOD system relies on essentially the same winch and release system that has impeded successful lifeboat launch in the past; indeed, it could be argued it aggravates the problem because it adds a third cable attached to the boom. A 1997 comparative study of four different evacuation systems conducted in the Institute for Marine Dynamics wave tank at St. John's pointed out that the PrOD:

> . . . incorporates the same release mechanisms that historically have had a high failure record with Davit systems [87].

The failure of lifeboat release mechanisms has been identified in a number of studies [88]. Consistent with these studies were the findings of a 1994 study by the Oil Companies International Marine Forum (OCIMF) to investigate what they described as the "disturbing frequency" of lifeboat accidents. They concluded that the major cause was the failure of winching and release launching mechanisms, compounded by human error [89]. These mechanical difficulties are magnified in heavy seas, as illustrated in the Ocean Ranger disaster [90]. It is of interest to note that the Canadian and British navies have stopped using lifeboats since not one was successfully launched in the Falkland War and they now use instead automatically inflated life rafts [91]. Of course, in highly trained marine personnel this system could work reasonably well, even bearing in mind the disadvantages of life rafts, but the same cannot be said for offshore oil workers who tend to be more industrial than marine in mindset. Norwegian union and management representatives, as well as the regulator's marine specialist, conveyed to the author their rejection of davit-launched lifeboats because of their poor record of accidents while maintaining and launching them. It is significant that only a small minority of old installations in Norway have this type of system, and, most important, only those with helicopters available on the platform as a primary means of evacuation are allowed to keep them [92].

Given the potential danger of launching a lifeboat, especially in heavy seas, when we build in the human element, the likelihood of problems occurring during evacuation expands significantly. In their study the OCIMF made a similar point: ". . . it is of concern that the potential for mistakes might reasonably be expected to increase during the stress of an emergency situation" [93]. Other research has highlighted the importance of building in the psychological, political, and cultural factors when designing evacuation systems [94]. Entering a totally enclosed lifeboat can be stressful in itself, especially if there is a lack of confidence in its successful launch and/or recovery. If launched, heat and fumes inside the boat, accentuated by a hot and bulky survival suit, adds to the potential stress of survivors inside. Because of a lifeboat's design, seasickness is common and if recovery is delayed for a significant period because of stormy seas, this becomes a real problem [95]. Taken together, all these known factors can affect the willingness of people to board a TEMPSC and their subsequent behavior, complicating and lengthening the evacuation process, ultimately jeopardizing its success. This has to be taken into account when designing evacuation systems and emergency response plans.

The dire effect of stress and panic on evacuation in a real emergency has been documented in the report of the inquiry into the death of a young offshore oil worker on the Ocean Odyssey in the United Kingdom [96]. Apparently adequate emergency response procedures were completely disrupted in the scramble to evacuate. The breakdown of communication and management systems ultimately resulted in one young man's death in a fire because he was ordered back to his station as radio operator while the rest of the crew evacuated the installation.

Some of the human factors are less likely to be a problem in a launching system that does not rely on complicated mechanisms and extensive maintenance, thus reducing the actual and perceived dangers of launch, especially in stormy seas. There are at least two launch systems available as alternatives to the currently used PrOD system, and they meet these criteria in addition to other advantages; therefore, we have to wonder why government and industry did not pursue these possibilities before the Hibernia tow-out, or conduct research and development of their own beforehand if these options were considered unsuitable. One alternative lifeboat system was developed through a private initiative in the province to address launching problems identified in the Ocean Ranger disaster and subsequent studies of lifeboat accidents. It uses a hinged deployment arm in a controlled gravity fall for launch, avoids the use of a conventional release mechanism, and can be launched at a heel and trim of 20 degrees. The other alternative is the free-fall system used predominantly in Norway. This launch system avoids the use of cables and winching mechanisms and with a skid launch will project the lifeboat away from an installation. Argument against its use off Newfoundland has been the potential problem with sea ice. But if there were ice, lifeboats would not be used in any case; on the Hibernia platform, Skyscape would be more appropriate. Like the deployment arm method, the free-fall launch system would involve extra weight, unpopular with the oil companies because of their continuing efforts to lower cost and increase deckload capacity. But it is possible to strengthen a rig or platform in order to install one of these options.

In the 1997 comparative study conducted at the National Research Council's Institute of Marine Dynamics in St. John's, both the hinged arm and 'free fall system of lifeboat launch were:

> a clear improvement over the Davit launch system in that they both delivered the TEMPSC a sufficient distance from the semisubmersible to enable it to avoid collision with the structure [97].

This wave tank study pronounced the PrOD system as a "modest improvement" over the conventional davit launch system but, as noted above, it was seen to have the disadvantage of essentially conventional winching and release mechanisms.

Given the strong emphasis placed upon evacuation in the Ocean Ranger report, available evidence on both fair and heavy weather launch problems caused by winch and release mechanisms currently used in the industry, available evidence on the impact of human factors on evacuation, and the existence of alternative systems, the question of why government and industry were not more proactive in this area becomes even more pertinent. Indeed, the selection of the current system appears to have reflected a more political or cost-driven process rather than one based on technical or safety criteria. When we consider the extreme unlikelihood that any future production platform will be fixed to the seabed because of the high costs involved, then it becomes even more important to factor in these potential problems with davit-launched lifeboats when designing evacuation systems. Even so, the Terra Nova FPSO will be fitted with PrOD lifeboats, although the drilling rig they have contracted does have free-fall lifeboats.

Skyscape is the second component of the Hibernia evacuation system accepted in the safety plan, but it is categorized by the British HSE as an escape system rather than a means of evacuation. This is because there is no protection from fire or the elements [98]. Indeed, it is questionable if it could be used at all during a fire because the structure would melt in the path of intense heat. In response to this possibility, the safety manager at HMDC pointed out that two Skyscapes are located at the accommodation, or "safe," end of the platform, and therefore unlikely to be near enough to a fire for this to happen [99]. Another concern would be the extreme difficulty in launching Skyscape in strong winds or heavy seas [100]. During a video presentation of the Hibernia evacuation systems, it was only demonstrated in flat-calm seas, in sharp contrast to the prevailing weather conditions on the Grand Banks. Moreover, that it cannot be used by injured personnel is an important limitation. Furthermore, the reliance on life rafts for escape raises the problems of instability in stormy seas; rapid drifting either into the dangerous area next to the abandoned installation or right away from it, hindering rescue; no protection from sea fires; and no independent source of power [98]. In the U.K. offshore sector, Skyscape is not commonly used, and, according to the HSE, has been installed only on unmanned installations for the evacuation of small visiting maintenance crews; furthermore, these unmanned structures are located in largely fair weather locations and the crew only travels out to them when weather conditions are favorable.

The dry evacuation system being field tested by HDMC, GEMEVAC, is a welcome shift in thinking, but there are some difficulties with the concept's operationalization. It is based on the Navy's Replenish at Sea (RAS) method of moving supplies between ships. However, in the navy, people are never transferred using this system because it is considered to be too dangerous. When it is absolutely necessary to transfer personnel at sea, the nonmechanical, traditional "jackstay" method is used with several well-trained people on both ships constantly adjusting the tension on the ropes to ensure the safety of the individual crossing over [101]. The HMDC's aim is to modify the RAS design to make it suitable for transporting personnel from the fixed platform to a waiting standby vessel; one set of moving variables is thus removed compared to RAS with two ships running alongside. Nevertheless, extremely high-level tension is required on the cables for such a system to work and each terminal has to be functioning effectively for this to be guaranteed. If the structural integrity of the installation is threatened or destroyed in, say, a fire or explosion, then in all likelihood the platform terminal will be dysfunctional and GEMEVAC will not work. Once the high tension fails the gondola will fall immediately, with potentially fatal consequences for occupants. In addition, the system needs highly trained and focused personnel to operate at both ends; in the event of an emergency this is often not the case [102], as noted earlier in the discussion. Moreover, it is doubtful whether this system could be used in stormy seas.

Up until February 1999, GEMEVAC had been run between the platform and supply boats 715 times in 67 field trials [103], but it failed twice with serious implications for safety. In October 1997, a welding joint gave way and the gondola crashed to the deck of the support ship; in July 1998, instead of slowing down as it approached the platform, the gondola slid out of control down the cable into the sea it was designed to avoid [104]. It is interesting to note that this cable car system had also been tested by Mobil Oil offshore Norway in the early 1980s, but trials were stopped by platform safety delegates and management in the Statfjord field when they feared that lives would be lost after a frightening near-miss incident [105].

In any event, the Hibernia platform has been on the Grand Banks for more than six years now and GEMEVAC is still not operational. The CNOPB has had to review the Hibernia safety plan in view of this failure [17]. It is instructive to ask why there has been such a delay in achieving full operations of this component of Hibernia's evacuation system. One local labor leader remarked:

> This is a new industry; all this should be tested and tried. . . . This is CNOPB. That would not happen in Norway. That rig would never have been allowed to let go its chain until all those systems were perfected . . . [until] the trial runs had been done [106].

Given the concerns raised during the course of the above discussion, it is reasonable to ask whether it would be possible to safely evacuate all workers off the Hibernia platform, or the FPSO, on such a night as when the Ocean Ranger sank. The commission's description of what happened in the attempted rescue of the survivors inside the one lifeboat that reached the support vessel serves as a reminder to all of us of the conditions out on the Grand Banks in the storm on February 15, 1982:

> . . . the swells exceeded 60 feet and there were 15 foot breaking waves . . . the seas were breaking over the stern of the ship and the spray froze instantly, hampering visibility and movement. . . . The lifeboat had completely capsized. The time was 2:38 a.m. . . . Jorgensen [first mate] told two seamen to launch a life raft in the hope that some of the men in the water would be able to climb aboard. Launching the life raft took some time because its securing lines were frozen and had to be cut. The men in the water, however, were immobilized and unable to make any effort to board the life raft or grasp lines thrown to them and within their reach. Stormy seas, inadequate retrieval equipment, and the immobility of the men in the water made the rescue attempts futile.
>
> During this time the Seaforth Highlander kept her stern to the wind and continued to take heavy seas on her afterdeck. The crews were forced to brace themselves against the bulwark and other solid objects to avoid being washed overboard. In spite of the hazardous and difficult conditions on the afterdeck, Jorgensen narrowly missed grasping a man who was washed against the port side of the supply vessel. One or two men in the water were able to hold onto the capsized lifeboat longer than the others. The lifeboat was very close to the ship's propeller and Captain Duncan decided to shut down one propeller for fear it would injure the men in the water. This reduction in power combined with strong winds and high waves forced his vessel off location. He was able to manoeuvre her back within 50-70 feet of the capsized lifeboat. By this time the men in the water had drifted downwind and attempts to retrieve them were unsuccessful [11, p. 110].

In a study of abandoning ships at sea by the Royal Institution of Naval Architects, some disturbing statistics emerged. The fatality rate of those attempting to evacuate from merchant ships in heavy weather was 35% and in calm conditions 5%; and 78% of what were called heavy weather incidents involved loss of life as a result of trying to evacuate as compared to 16 % of calm weather incidents that involved loss of life [107]. All these evacuation attempts used lifeboats and life rafts, essentially of the same launch design as those used now. Even allowing for the differences between a fixed installation, in the case of Hibernia, and a ship in distress, these figures show the extreme dangers of evacuation at sea, particularly in heavy weather. This point is all the more important when we remember the trend in the industry away from fixed to floating production platforms.

There have, of course, been some improvements in the design and operations of lifeboats and standby vessels since the Ocean Ranger disaster. However, it does seem as if there is a tendency in the industry to underestimate what a former HMDC president has identified as the harshest climate of any platform in the world [108], which is compounded by distance from shore. This is particularly disappointing when we recollect the design flaws identified by the Ocean Ranger Commission, which revealed a fatal lack of recognition of the effect of stormy seas on critical systems.

The underestimation of these considerations in designing an evacuation system may well be linked to the quantitative risk analysis (QRA) prevalent in what is known as loss prevention in the industry. Aside from a tendency to underestimate the complex interconnections in how an emergency or disaster unfolds [109], and the human element involved [110], most computer risk models will generally rate the risk of evacuation offshore as very low, especially on a fixed platform. As a result, the figures do not recommend a high level of attention and expenditure on systems that in all likelihood (according to the QRA) will not be used very much, if at all [111]. But if the consequences in terms of probability of escape, fatalities, and injuries in the event of an emergency evacuation were factored in effectively, then the calculation would be different from one where just the probability of having to evacuate is the crucial determinant. A Norwegian paper by Drager and Wiklund proposed some computer simulation models building in some of these additional factors [110].

The Ocean Ranger Commission criticized an industry mindset focused on research and development for production rather than on developing safe methods of evacuation for workers offshore. Unfortunately, it seems as if this mindset has resurfaced in the predominant assumptions underlying the most commonly used risk assessment models. The combination of an engineering model with what is fundamentally an insurance model in the development of safety management systems, while on the surface presenting a more rigorous and "scientific" methodology than worker-focused approaches to workplace health and safety, leads in effect to the marginalization of complexity and human factors.

Search and Rescue Helicopters

In 1983 the Ocean Ranger Commission criticized the federal government, not only for the fragmentation and inadequacy of search and rescue in general, but also for the age and inadequacy of the then twenty-year-old Labrador helicopters that were still in use at the time [10, p. 162]. In 1984, the federal government increased Newfoundland's SAR capability to three fixed-wing aircraft and three helicopters, to a level higher than the recommendations made by the commission [112]. Existing helicopters were upgraded, and included the addition of long-range fuel tanks.

However, the twin-rotor Labradors still in SAR service are now nearly forty years old. On October 2, 1998, one exploded in mid-air and crashed in Quebec, killing all six crew members. The fleet was grounded and given clearance on October 27. However, because the existing Labrador crews were so reluctant to fly the machines, their search and rescue duties were lifted temporarily. Bearing in mind the authority structure in the military, the crew members' response to the crash and the death of their crewmates was significant as well as understandable, given the history of the aging Labradors with their repeated engine-related safety problems. A 1992 crash that killed one man was thought to be caused by an engine problem, although investigators did not make a final determination. Two more recent grounding incidents erode confidence in the machines even further: a fire in the aircraft's deicing system on November 26, and a broken flight-control part on November 27, 1998. In spite of this troubling history of problems, on January 14, 1999, training and proficiency restrictions on the Labrador fleet were lifted and the machines were available once again for a full range of search and rescue missions [113].

Running alongside the potential danger of the aging Labrador fleet, the federal government's other SAR helicopter, the single-blade Sea King, has also been characterized by safety problems; hence, this newspaper report:

> Canada's geriatric Sea King helicopter fleet was grounded Thursday, further limiting search and rescue operations already strained by severe restrictions on the Labrador helicopters [114].

One of the Sea Kings had developed a fuel leak, and, upon inspection, four other aircraft were found with possible fuel-leak-related problems. In 1994, a similar problem had caused a Sea King helicopter to crash in a fireball, killing the pilot and copilot. A $4.8 billion replacement order for the Sea Kings was canceled by the federal government in its 1993 cutbacks, and the aircraft are expected to fly until at least 2004. The Labradors were originally due to be retired in 2001 [114], but it was not until the end of 2003 that all of the new Cormorant helicopters were operational [115]. By then, the Labradors were more than forty years old. Given that the Ocean Ranger Commissioners criticized the then twenty-year-old Labrador as substandard, and the federal government promised to upgrade SAR in its 1984 and 1985 reports, it has to be asked, once again, why it has taken the government so long to act.

THE POLITICS OF HEALTH
AND SAFETY

A corollary of the free market economics predominant at both levels of government in Canada is the elevation of the market over the political, cultural, and social [116]. Workplace health and safety has previously been marginalized through deregulation, administrative restructuring, and budget cuts. Occupational Health and Safety and Workers Compensation legislation has been reviewed across the country as part of a push toward deregulation. In the past few years, there has been a trend of transferring administrative responsibility for occupational health and safety to employer-funded workers' compensation commissions or boards, which is seen by many worker advocates as a retrograde step. This happened in Newfoundland in June 1998. Deficit budgeting in provincial governments has led to downsizing, weakening regulatory policy, and lack of enforcement in OHS. The restructuring of government departments has combined previously separate policy areas, diluting the importance and impact of OHS [117]. For example, in Newfoundland until the establishment of the new Department of Environment and Labour in March 1996, there was one assistant deputy minister (ADM) responsible for labor relations plus another for occupational health and safety. Afterward, one ADM oversaw both areas, with occupational health and safety shrunk into only a minor division of the department. The past few years have seen an improvement in this regard, with the reinstatement of a separate Department of Labour in February 2001, and an announcement in March 2002 of a $1.3 million increase in the budget allocation for the reorganization and expansion of its Occupational Health and Safety Division [118].

Turning again to the offshore, quality and audit safety management systems can work very well up to a point. Their predominance is related to a general movement toward regulation through goal setting rather than prescription, but they become truly effective only when complemented by a strong and well-resourced regulatory framework together with union-backed worker involvement. There are, of course, limits to how far we can transfer the Norwegian model to Canadian offshore development. What it does demonstrate, however, is that a strong, proactive government leads to a more effective regulatory framework for safety offshore and that oil companies can operate successfully in a unionized environment if they have to.

Even with the best safety personnel and systems, in the final analysis, an oil company exists to generate income for its shareholders and thus there is an inherent conflict between production and safety. This tension becomes more acute in cost-cutting mode. In June 1997, an HMDC safety manager acknowledged that Hibernia safety standards in some areas may not be the highest in use in the offshore oil industry. He added: "You have to have a safety culture that's appropriate for the area you're working with" [119]. Considering the ramifications of this comment, there is an urgent need for both levels of government to ensure that the offshore safety regulatory regime for the province is second to none. This is a challenge that demands vision, commitment and political will at the cabinet level, where ultimate responsibility and accountability for offshore oil workers' safety resides. The recent discussion paper incorporating health and safety into the Atlantic Accord Acts is an important first step toward regulatory reform, and unionization of the Hibernia platform offers all parties a good opportunity for a collaborative approach to resolution of the issues raised in this chapter.

ACKNOWLEDGMENTS

I would like to acknowledge the excellent research assistance of Michelle McBride and Amy Warren during the preparation of this chapter. Also, my thanks go to all the people I interviewed before writing it.

ENDNOTES

1. Det Norske Veritas (DNV), 1997.
2. Cable News Network, *Major Oil industry Accidents*, 2001, www.cnn.com/2001/WORLD/ americas/03/20/oil.accidents.
3. ILO (International Labour Organization), Occupational Safety and Health Branch, "Workers in Remote Areas," Working Paper (1995).
4. CNOPB (Canada-Newfoundland Offshore Petroleum Board), Hibernia (1998).
5. Terra Nova Alliance, Terra Nova Overview, 2000; www.terranovaproject.com/whatis/whatis.htm. CNOPB, *Annual Report*, 1998; Morgan Cooper, *Labour Relations Processes On Offshore Oil Production Platforms*, April 25, 1997.
6. Husky Energy, www.huskywhiterose.com, 2002.
7. CNOPB, *Annual Report*, 2001-2.
8. The 1998 unemployment rate for the province was 18.3% compared with Canada's average of 8.0%. This represents a rise in provincial unemployment approaching the 1996 level of 19.5% compared with Canada's 9.7%, after a slight decrease in 1997 to 17.5% compared with Canada's 8.6% (Statistics Canada, Series 71-201 and 71-001).
9. Canada, *Royal Commission of the Ocean Ranger Marine Disaster* (RCORMD), vol. 1 (1984), preface, iii. It is unfortunate that copies of this report are now no longer available from the government.

10. *Royal Commission of the Ocean Ranger Marine Disaster* (RCORMD), vol. 2 (1985), 147.

11. *Royal Commission of the Ocean Ranger Marine Disaster (RCORMD),* vol. 1, introduction, vii. 1984.

12. Canada, Department of Energy, Mines and Resources, *Summary of Action Taken by the Government of Canada in Relation to the Recommendation of the Royal Commission on the Ocean Ranger Marine Disaster*, April 1985.

13. Canada, Department of Energy, Mines and Resources, *Government of Canada Response to the Recommendations of the Royal Commission on the Ocean Ranger Marine Disaster*, April 1986.

14. Hon. Lord Cullen, *The Public Inquiry into the Piper Alpha Disaster*, Vols. 1 and 2 (London: HMSO, 1990).

15. *Daily Oil Bulletin*, February 21, 1992; Government of Canada, News Release: "Epp and Siddon Announce Proclamation of Amendments to the Oil and Gas Production and Conservation Act and Accord Acts," September 3, 1992. Government of Newfoundland and Labrador, News Release: "Minister of Mines and Energy Announces Proclamation of Amendments to the Canada-Newfoundland Atlantic Accord Implementation (Newfoundland) Act," September 4, 1992.

16. Helge Ryggvik, "Why Norway Was Different," in *Piper Alpha Ten Years After: Safety and Industrial Relations in the British and Norwegian Offshore Oil Industry*, ed. M. Beck, J. Foster, H. Ryggvik, and C. Woolfson (Oslo: Centre for Technology and Culture, 1998), 57-105.

17. Interview with Howard Pike, July 20, 1998.

18. Canada, *Canada-Newfoundland Atlantic Accord Implementation Act* (Ottawa: Queen's Printer, 1986). Newfoundland, *Canada-Newfoundland Atlantic Accord Implementation Newfoundland Act* (St. John's, 1986).

19. Interview with Elaine Price, president of the Newfoundland and Labrador Federation of Labour, June 16, 1998.

20. Interview with Bill Parsons, Executive Director of the Newfoundland and Labrador Building and Construction Trades Council (NLBCTC), July 21, 1998.

21. Interview with Marilyn Pike, president of the Newfoundland and Labrador Employers' Council, December 17, 1998.

22. Canada, *Canada-Newfoundland Atlantic Accord Implementation Act*, Section 1524(b).

23. Interview with Richard Day, director; Jan Swaan, manager; and Bob Gowier, of Compliance, Marine Safety and Environmental Programs, Government of Canada, November 10, 1998.

24. Telephone interview with Howard Pike, November 7, 2002.

25. Interview with Mike Hnetka, adviser, Regulations, Frontier Lands Management Division, Energy Resources Branch, Natural Resources Canada, Ottawa, November 9, 1998.

26. Morgan Cooper, *Labour Relations Processes on Offshore Oil Production Platforms*, April 25, 1997.

27. Interview with Harvey Smith, president, HMDC, December 17, 1998; Cooper, *Labour Relations Processes*; Jennifer Smith, "Hibernia Safety Measures Not up to North Sea Standards," *Evening Telegram*, June 15, 1997, 4.

28. C. A. Woolfson, J. Foster, and M. Beck, *Paying for the Piper*: Capital and Labour in Britain's Offshore Oil Industry (London: Mansell, 1997).

29. Governments of Canada, Newfoundland and Labrador, and Nova Scotia, *Proposed Amendments to the Accord Acts, to Incorporate an Offshore Occupational Health and Safety Regime,* St. John's, November 2002.

30. ILO, case no. 1389, 45. Cited in Cooper, *Labour Relations Processes,* 58.

31. Cooper, *Labour Relations Processes*; Ryggvik, "Why Norway Was Different."

32. Interview with Marianne Oistensen, director of the Safety and Working Environment, Ministry of Local Government, Government of Norway, Oslo, May 19, 1999.

33. Governments of Canada, Newfoundland and Labrador, and Nova Scotia, *Proposed Amendments to the Accord Acts,* 4.

34. Governments of Canada, Newfoundland and Labrador, and Nova Scotia, *Proposed Amendments to the Accord Acts,* 10.

35. Interview with Alan Sefton, director of Offshore Safety Division, HSE, UK, June 29, 1998.

36. The CNOPB is a partner in the "Offshore Employment—Implications for the Health and Well-Being of Individuals, Families and Communities" research project funded by SafetyNet, a Commmunity Research Alliance on Health and Safety in Marine and Coastal Work, based at Memorial University, St. John's, NF.

37. Interview with Marilyn Pike, December 17, 1998; letter from president, NLFL, to CNOPB, May 16, 1997 and personal communication.

38. The information in this paragraph, unless referenced separately, is from CNOPB, *Annual Reports,* 1987-2002.

39. Chris Flanagan, "Terra Nova Engineering Jobs Still Not Relocated to Province," *Evening Telegram,* March 21, 1998, 25.

40. William Hilliard, "Lawyers Battle City's Right to Fight Petroleum Board," *Evening Telegram,* September 1, 1998.

41. Chris Flanagan, "Seismic Worker Spat Spills: Immigration Canada Has no Authority Beyond 12-mile Limit," *Evening Telegram,* June 6, 1998, 22; interview with Bill Parsons, July 21, 1998.

42. CNOPB, *Annual Report,* 1990-1991. Unless otherwise noted, the figures referred to in this section are from CNOPB *Annual Reports,* 1987-1990.

43. CNOPB, *Annual Report,* 1988-1989, 21. Unfortunately, exact statistics were unavailable and Figure 1 has been reproduced from the CNOPB's Figure 5, 21. The overall trend can be clearly seen, however.

44. C. A. Woolfson, J. Foster, and M. Beck, *Paying for the Piper*; D. Tombs, "A Rather Tragic Blip," *Blowout: the OILC Magazine,* no. 55 (July/August 1998).

45. Interview with Bill Parsons, July 21, 1998; interview with Judy Vanta, chair of OHS Committee, NLFL, Labor representative on OHS Advisory Committee to government of Newfoundland and Labrador, January 12, 1999.

46. Figures provided by the Newfoundland Department of Environment and Labour, Occupational Health and Safety Division.

47. Telephone interview with Doug Carter, OHS, Department of Environment and Labour, January 29, 1999.

48. Brenda Grzetic, Mark Shrimpton, and Sue Skipton, WITT, *Women, Employment Equity and the Hibernia Construction Project: A Study of Women's Experiences on the Hibernia Construction Project, Mosquito Cove, Newfoundland.* St. John's, Report, June 1996.

49. Paula Arab, "Sexual Harassment Ruled Workplace Safety Hazard," *Evening Telegram*, August 23, 1997, 9.
50. Telephone interview with Bill Parsons, November 7, 2002.
51. Stephanie Porter, "Risky Business: Offshore Safety Standards Have Improved Since the Ocean Ranger Went Down, But There's Still Room to Get Better," *Gulf News* 29, no. 6, February 11, 2001; "Ocean Ranger Tragedy Raised Safety Issues," *Telegram*, February 16, 2002, B1; telephone interview with Howard Pike, November 7, 2002.
52. Personal communication from Howard Pike, letter dated March 1, 1999.
53. Interview with David Fitzgerald, HMDC, July 16, and August 25, 1998; interview with Harvey Smith, December 17, 1998. *Hibernia Environment, Safety and Quality AR 1997*, HMDC; *Hibernia Environment, Safety and Quality Management System, Hibernia Environment, Safety and Quality Handbook*, HMDC, October 1997. *The Hibernia Gainsharing Program, Program Description and Administrative Guide*, HMDC, undated.
54. Ryggvik, "Why Norway Was Different"; Petter Chr. Bonde, "Risk Analysis in the Norwegian Sector—Views from a Senior Safety Delegate," OFS/OILC Conference, *Offshore Safety in a Cost-Conscious Environment from British and Norwegian Perspectives*, Proceedings of Conference, Stavanger, Norway, November 15-16, 1994, 39-40.
55. Greg Kealey and Gene Long, *Labour and Hibernia: Conflict Resolution at Bull Arm, 1990-1992* (St. John's: ISER, 1993), 11.
56. Greg Kealey and Michelle McBride, "Labour Relations at the Hibernia Project, 1990-1997," Draft Report, forthcoming.
57. For more on labor relations at the construction site, see Kealey and McBride, "Labour Relations at the Hibernia Project."
58. Newfoundland and Labrador Employers Council Conference, St. John's, April 23, 1998.
59. Craig Westcott, "Oil Unions Look for Peace: Council Endorses Findings of Morgan Cooper Report," *Express*, March 21-27, 2001, 29.
60. Morgan Cooper, *Labour Relations Processes on Offshore Oil and Gas Fabrication and Construction Projects*, St. John's, January 2001.
61. Government of Newfoundland, Department of Labour, www.gov.nf.ca/labour/ whats_new.asp, 2002.
62. Collective Agreement, CAW/FFAW (Canadian Auto Workers/Fish, Food and Allied Workers), 1997.
63. Interviews with Bill Parsons, July 21, 1998; Elaine Price, June 16, 1998; Ron Smith, CEP (Communications, Energy and Paperworkers), December 3, 1998; Judy Vanta, NAPE (Newfoundland Association of Public Employees), January 12, 1999; Brian Kohler, CEP, December 8, 1998.
64. Michael MacDonald, "Hibernia First Unionized Offshore Oil Workers in North America," *Western Star*, October 11, 2001, 1.
65. NLFL, "Submission on the Labour Relations Framework for Production at the Hibernia Offshore Oilfield," February 13, 1997, 1.
66. Ontario Advisory Council on Occupational Health and Safety, *An Evaluation of Joint Health and Safety Committees in Ontario* (1986); Canadian Association for the Administrators of Labour Law; C. Tuohy and M. Simard, *The Impact of Joint Health and Safety Committees in Ontario and Quebec* (Canadian Association for

Administrators of Labour Law, 1993); B. Reilly, P. Paci, and P. Holl, "Unions, Safety Committees and Workplace Injuries," *British Journal of Industrial Relations* 33, no. 2 (1993); D. Walters and S. Gourlay, *Statutory Employee Involvement in Health and Safety at the Workplace*. Health and Safety Executive, report 20/1990 (London: HMSO, 1990); TUC, *The Future of Workplace Safety Representatives: A TUC Health and Safety Report* (London: Congress House, 1995); World Bank, *Workers in an Integrating World*. World Development Report (Oxford: Oxford University Press, 1995).

67. Note of Dissent, paragraph 26, quoted in Woolfson, et al. *Paying for the Piper. Public Inquiry into the Piper Alpha Disaster*, Vol. 2, 376, cited in Cooper, *Labour Relations Processes*, 68, and Woolfson et al., *Paying for the Piper*, 278.

68. C. A. Woolfson, J. Foster, and M. Beck, *Paying for the Piper*; Whtye, D., "Workforce Participation: Myth or Reality," Piper Alpha Tenth Anniversary Conference. University of Glasgow, July 3, 1998.

69. Interview with Jake Malloy, general secretary, OILC, July 6, 1998.

70. NLFL, *Submission*, February 13, 1997, 7, Recommendations 3-5.

71. Alberta Economic Development Authority, *Final Report: Joint Review Committee Right-to-Work Study* (November 1995); AFL-CIO, *A Tale of Two Nations: A Statistical Case for Free Collective Bargaining* (Washington: AFL-CIO Department of Organization and Field Services, 1994).

72. Morley Gunderson and Allen Ponak, *Union-Management Relations in Canada*, 3d ed. (Don Mills, ON: Addison-Wesley, 1995), especially chapter 5 by Mark Thompson, "The Management of Industrial Relations," which deals with the issue of union avoidance on a more general level. For specifics on the oil companies, see Woolfson et al., *Paying for the Piper*, ch. 2-4.

73. Williard Hilliard, "Unionization Fails on Hibernia Platform," *Telegram*, March 31, 2001, 1.

74. Information on the current status of the unfair labor practice complaints is from telephone conversations with Ron Smith, CEP, November 5, 2002 and March 16, 2004.

75. Moira Baird, "Hibernia Worker Still Awaiting Call," *Telegram*, December 6, 2001, A1; Moira Baird, "HMDC Appealing Board Order," *Telegram*, December 21, 2001, A1; CEP, "Union to Appeal Court Decision," media release, July 17, 2002; telephone conversation with Ron Smith, CEP, March 16, 2004.

76. Interview with Elaine Price, June 16, 1998; Ron Smith, CEP, December 3, 1998; Judy Vanta, NAPE, January 12, 1999; Brian Kohler, CEP, December 8, 1998.

77. R. Moore and P. Wyebrow, *Women in the North Sea Oil Industry* (Manchester: Equal Opportunities Commission, 1984); D. Clark, K. McCann, K. Morrice, and R. Taylor, "Work and Marriage in the Offshore Oil Industry," *International Journal of Social Economics* 12, no. 2 (1985): 36-47; D. Clark and R. Taylor, "Partings and Reunions: Marriage and Offshore in the British North Sea," in *Women, Work and Family in the British, Canadian and Norwegian Offshore Oilfields*, ed. J. Lewis et al.(London: Macmillan, 1988), 112-39; D.L. Collinson, "Shift-ing Lives: Work-Home Pressures in the North Sea Oil Industry," *Canadian Review of Sociology and Anthropology* 35 (1998): 301-24; G. Slaven and R. Flin, "Selecting Managers for a Hazardous Environment: Offshore Petroleum Installations," *Personnel Review* 23, no. 5 (1994): 4-14; V.J. Sutherland and C. Cooper, *Man and Accidents Offshore* (London: Eastern Press, 1986).

78. Timothy Monk, *Making Shiftwork Tolerable* (London: Taylor and Francis, 1992); Ilene Stones, *Rotational Shiftwork: A Summary of the Adverse Effects and Improvement Strategies* (Hamilton, ON: Canadian Centre for Occupational Health and Safety, 1987); W.P. Colquhoun and J. Rutenfranz, eds., *Studies of Shiftwork* (London: Taylor and Francis, 1980); James Walker, *Human Aspects of Shiftwork* (London: Institute of Personnel Management, 1978).

79. Tor Nome, quoted in Inger Ada, "Let My People Go," *Norwegian Petroleum Diary*, no. 2 (2000): 27.

80. Eirik Bjerkebaek, Safety and Working Environment Division, Norwegian Petroleum Directorate, quoted in Kristin Henanger, "Time and Toil Are Taking Their Toll," *Norwegian Petroleum Directorate*, no. 2 (2000): 18.

81. A. Alvarez, *Offshore* (Houghton Mifflin, 1986), 28. Cited in Cooper, *Labour Relations Processes*, 79, footnote 56.

82. OILC, *Submission to the European Commission Review Group for the Working Hours Directive*, undated.

83. Telephone interview with Howard Pike, January 29, 1999.

84. CAPP (Canadian Association of Petroleum Producers), *Guide: Canadian East Coast Offshore Petroleum Industry, Training and Qualification*, Calgary, February 2002.

85. National Research Council, Canada, *The Offshore Escape, Evacuation and Rescue Database and Web Site: Standards Information Workshop*, Escape, Evacuation and Rescue; www.nrc.ca/imd/eer/home_e.html, October 5, 2002.

86. National Research Council, Institute of Marine Dynamics, October 5, 2002; www.nrc.ca/imd/research.shtml#escape.

87. Offshore Design Associates Ltd., *Comparative Physical Model Study of Offshore Evacuation Systems* (St. John's, 1997), 9.

88. Richard Speight, "Lifeboat Release Mechanisms—Parts 1-3," in *Seaways* (August, September, and October 1995); Petrel Ocean Safety, *Escape and Evacuation Systems—Risk and Reliability, Summary and Review of Industry Studies of Evacuation Systems* (London, March 1996); and OCIMF (Oil Companies International Marine Forum) report, *Results of a Survey into Lifeboat Safety* (London, July 1994).

89. OCIMF report, *Results of a Survey into Lifeboat Safety*.

90. See endnote 10, regarding the Technical Appendix (E) of *Ocean Ranger* report.

91. Interview with Commander George A. Prudat, November 9, 1998, past commanding officer of a destroyer, with more than twenty years at sea during which he participated in several rescues.

92. Interviews with Peter A. Hansen, deputy leader and full-time representative at Statoil, OFS; Stein Rosengren, union coordinator at Statoil; and Finn Strand, health, safety, and environment manager, Oil Operations, Statoil; at Statoil offices, Stavanger, Norway, May 26, 1999; interview with Captain Finn Lien, marine evacuation and escape specialist at the Norwegian Petroleum Directorate, Stavanger, May 28, 1999.

93. OCIMF report, *Results of a Survey into Lifeboat Safety*, 7.

94. K. Mearns and Rhona Flin, "Decision Making in Emergencies: A Psychological Analysis." Paper presented at the Human Factors in Emergency Response Offshore Conference, European Seminar, 1993; Alan Waring, "Power and Culture—Their Implications for Safety Cases and EER." Paper presented at the Human Factors in Emergency Response Offshore Conference, European Seminar, 1993; M. Carey and

B. Kennedy, "Analysis of Human Failures During Evacuation, Escape and Rescue," consultant paper, 1993; B.P. Fitzgerald, M.D. Green, J. Pennington, and A.J. Smith, "A Human Factors Approach to the Effective Design of Evacuation Systems," *Loss Prevention Bulletin*, no. 097 (1997): 13-22; P. Stephens and D. Lucas, "Modelling the Human Response in Emergency Escape," consultant paper, September 1993.

95. J.P. Landolt and C. Monaco, "Seasickness in Totally-Enclosed Motor-Propelled Survival Craft: Remedial Measures," *Aviation, Space and Environmental Medicine* (March 1992): 219-225.

96. HSE (Health and Safety Executive) report OTO 96 009 (Ref. 1); EERTAG (Evacuations, Escape and Rescue Advisory Group), "An Assessment of the Evacuation of an Offshore Installation by TEMPSC: Based on an Analysis of Survivor Experience," November 1997, which identified primary issues of concern arising from the Ocean Odyssey incident of September 1988. EERTAG is a technical liaison group that is a forum for expertise in the area of evacuation, escape, and rescue, and comprises representatives from HSE, employer groups from different sectors of the industry including operator, rig owner, and standby ship companies, as well as the central labor federation in the UK (TUC). Telephone interview with David Menarry, HSE, UK, January 1999.

97. Offshore Design Associates Ltd., *Comparative Physical Model Study*, 9.

98. Telephone interview with David Menarry, January 1999.

99. Interview with David Fitzpatrick, HMDC, August 25, 1998.

100. Telephone interview with David Menarry, HSE, January 1999; interview with Captain Phillip McCarter, Master Mariner, Marine Institute, 5 March 1999.

101. See letter from Flag Officer Surface Flotilla, HM Naval Base, Portsmouth, UK, to C.F. Lafferty, Woking Surrey, UK, April 2, 1996; interview with Commander George A. Prudat, November 9, 1998.

102. Interview with Lieutenant-Commander Gavin Baker, March 4, 1999.

103. Telephone interview with Howard Pike, February 26, 1999.

104. Interview with Howard Pike, July 20, 1998; Interview with David Fitzpatrick, August 25, 1998; Chris Flanagan, "Ottawa Studying Safety Rules: Failure of Hibernia's GEMEVAC Rekindles Interest in Evacuation Systems," *Evening Telegram*, October 7, 1998, 6.

105. Interview with Peter A. Hansen, deputy leader, OFS, Senior Safety Delegate at Statoil for twelve years, on Statfjord B oil and gas platform, Norwegian North Sea, June 22, 2000.

106. Interview with Bill Parsons, June 12, 1998.

107. M.A.F. Pyman and P.R. Lyon, "Casualty Rates in Abandoning Ships at Sea," paper read in London at a Joint Meeting of the Royal Institution of Naval Architects, and the Nautical Institute, January 17, 1985..

108. This view takes into account an acknowledgment by HMDC president Harvey Smith of the most extreme weather conditions at Hibernia compared to other platforms in the world, in his presentation of February 5, 1999 at the graduating students' Business Day, Faculty of Business, Memorial University of Newfoundland.

109. Colin MacFarlane, "Some (Critical) Comments on Risk Analysis" in OFS/OILC, *Offshore Safety in a Cost Conscious Environment from British and Norwegian Perspectives*, Proceedings of Conference, November 15-16, 1994, Stavanger, Norway, 28-33.

110. K.H. Drager and J. Wiklund, "Advanced Computer Modelling for Solving Practical Problems in EER," A/S Quasar Consultants, Oslo, Norway, September 1993.

111. It should be noted here that in the early days of production, the Hibernia platform was evacuated more than once. The first evacuation took place on November 30, 1998, when a potentially hazardous gas leak was detected, just two weeks after oil production started. A total of 107 personnel were evacuated by helicopter to the oil rig Bill Shoemaker before the leak was traced to a small oil spill. On March 12, 1999, Hibernia oil production and drilling was halted after a gas and fire alarm went off in the drilling area, shutting down all power on the platform. A Hibernia helicopter and a coast guard rescue vessel were dispatched to the scene to evacuate the 230 workers on board but as no signs of gas or fire were detected the evacuation was called off (Chris Flanagan, "Production Halted After Alarm Sounds," *Evening Telegram*, March 12, 1999, 3). A second power outage occurred less than two weeks later on March 20, 1999 (Tracy Barron, "Hibernia Loses Power: Second Shutdown in Two Weeks," *Evening Telegram*, March 21, 1999, 2).

112. Robert Nishman, "Through the Portlights of the *Ocean Ranger*: Federalism, Energy and the American Development of the Canadian Eastern Offshore, 1955-1985." Masters thesis, Queen's University, 1991, 180.

113. Dean Beeby, "More Chopper Woes," *Evening Telegram*, November 27, 1998, 5; Dean Beeby, "Another Labrador Grounded Because of Engine Trouble," *Evening Telegram*, November 28, 1998, 5; "Troubled Choppers Fly Again," *Evening Telegram*, January 15, 1999, 5.

114. Dean Beeby, "Sea King Fleet Grounded," *Evening Telegram*, October 16, 1998, 1.

115. CH-149 Cormorant: Facts and Figures, Canadian Forces Aircraft; www.airforce.forces.ca/ equip/equip1b_e.ht, December 19, 2002.

116. D. Drache, and M. Gertler, "The World Economy and the Nation-State: The New International Order," in *The Era of Global Competition: State Policy and Market Power*, ed. Drache and Gertler (Montreal: McGill-Queen's University Press, 1991), 3-25.

117. Interview with Bill Parsons, July 21, 1998; interview with Judy Vanta, NAPE, January 12, 1999.

118. Government of Newfoundland and Labrador, Department of Labour, "Funding to Enhance Enforcement of Occupational Health and Safety Act," News Release, March 21, 2002; www.gov.nf.ca/releases/ 2002/labour/032ln48.htm.

119. Jennifer Smith, "Hibernia Safety Measures Not up to North Sea Standards," *Evening Telegram,* June 15, 1994, 4.

CHAPTER 4

BP's Baku-Tbilisi-Ceyhan Pipeline: The New Corporate Colonialism

James Marriott and Greg Muttitt

INTRODUCTION

In *Something New Under the Sun: An Environmental History of the Twentieth Century,* John McNeill summarizes the impact of oil explorations on native populations as follows:

> The Niger Delta (in Nigeria) at the end of the century, like Tampico (in Mexico) at the beginning, became a zone of sacrifice. The Ogoni, like the Huastec and Totonac, lacked the power to resist the coalition of forces that created and maintained the twentieth century's energy regime [1].

This book chapter has grown out of an international campaign to question the benefits of the Baku-Tbilisi-Ceyhan (BTC) pipeline, a campaign that is driven by a desire to prevent a future "zone of sacrifice." In December 2002, the organizations behind the campaign could claim some success when the oil corporation BP announced that there would be a six-month delay in the completion of the financing arrangements for the proposed $3.3 billion pipeline.

In this chapter we report on the contemporary struggle over the Baku-Tbilisi-Ceyhan project. First, we present some of the background on the pipeline project, then we describe the situation at present in relation to the actual and potential impacts of the project. Finally, we assess BP's efforts to cope with potential resistance to the pipeline project.

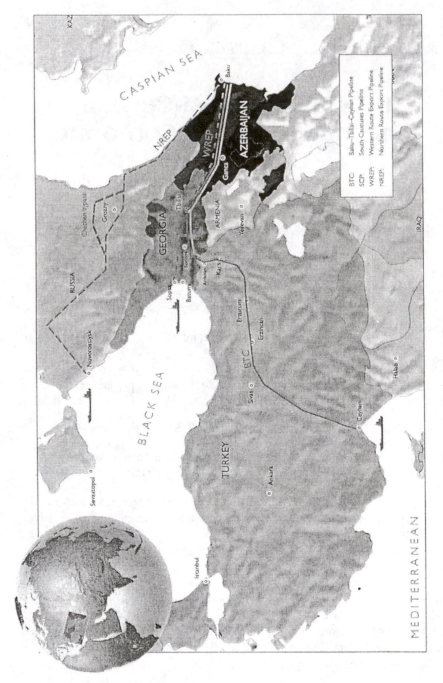

Figure 1. Map of the pipelines systems.

GLOBAL POLITICS AND THE HOST STATES

Azerbaijan is not a "new frontier" for oil. Pools of crude oil lying on the desert's surface have been utilized for hundreds of years. Drilling for oil began in Azerbaijani lands in the mid-19th century. Indeed, Baku is one of the birthplaces of the global oil industry.

The First Oil Boom, as it became known, followed the arrival of French and British entrepreneurs into this distant corner of the Russian Tsarist Empire. The Swedish/Russian industrialist Robert Nobel (whose family founded the Nobel Peace Prize) made his first oil investment in Baku in 1873, and by 1879 there were nine oil wells in the town. Once the railway from Baku to Tbilisi to Batumi on the Georgian Black Sea coast had been completed in 1883, development accelerated. The railway, partly financed by Rothschild's bank, provided a commercially viable export route for oil and answered the vital question: how to get Caspian oil onto the world market.

By 1900, there were 1,710 wells and Baku produced over half the world's oil. The heart of the industry was Nobel's Chiornyi Gorod, "the Black Town" on Baku's outskirts. Its name gives a clue to the industry's impact on the air, water, and soil. One visitor compared it to "confinement in a chimney pot" [2]. Nobel was followed by companies such as Shell, and later still by the Anglo-Persian Oil Company—which was later to become BP.

The rapidly expanding city of Baku was a hotbed of radicalism. The young Josef Stalin claimed to have organized strikes in Baku in 1905. Following the collapse of the Tsarist Empire in 1917, Baku had its own Bolshevik government, the Baku Soviet. Although this ended in September 1918, following the city's occupation by Turkish Forces, the Soviet had succeeded in nationalizing the oil industry and throwing out foreign companies.

Western companies returned a few months later, however, after the British Expeditionary Force had occupied Baku, and the Baku-Tbilisi-Batumi railway operated from November 1918 to August 1919, to ensure Western access to the oil. While the West reasserted its control, the Azerbaijanis fought a protracted conflict with the Armenians over the disputed mountainous area of Nagorno-Karabakh. This struggle halted only with the arrival of the Soviet Union's Red Army in 1920. The Red Army "facilitated" the establishment of the Azerbaijan Soviet Socialist Republic, and, in due course, the incorporation of the whole of the Caucasus and Caspian region into the Soviet Union. Once again, the Western oil companies had their assets nationalized and left.

During its Second Oil Boom, Baku became the heartland of the Soviet oil industry, with Azerbaijan producing 75% of Soviet oil up until the 1940s. In the seven decades within which the world economy was divided into the two sectors of planned and capitalist economies, Baku provided the skills base for the oil industry of the communist world. Following World War II, it was the technology of the Western Caspian that opened up the oil and gas fields of the Volga-Urals,

Kazakhstan, Uzbekistan, Turkmenistan, Western Siberia, Eastern Siberia, Ukraine, and, eventually, of satellite countries such as Vietnam.

THE COLLAPSE OF THE SOVIET UNION

Today Baku is surrounded by expanses of desert littered with hundreds of rusting Soviet oil derricks. Just 20 meters (60 feet) high, many of these drilling scaffolds are inactive, standing in pools of oil on the stony ground. The same derricks dot the shores of the Caspian. They are a relic of shallow-water offshore drilling which was developed intensively from 1949 onward. The Soviet oil industry, meanwhile, never successfully exploited the Caspian's deepwater offshore reserves. By the 1970s, oil production in Azerbaijani oil fields was declining with no new fields being opened up. The remaining deepwater reserves were beyond the reach of limited Soviet technology and capital. The stagnation of the Azerbaijan oil industry accelerated as the Soviet economy collapsed in the wake of perestroika. By the late 1980s, Azerbaijan produced only a fraction of Soviet oil. At the same time, the ghosts of the past came back to haunt Azerbaijan. Once again, Baku became a scene of conflict. In January 1990, hundreds of Azerbaijanis were killed in demonstrations against Soviet rule. The conflict in Nagorno-Karabakh flared up again between February 1988 and May 1994. In this brutal struggle, Azerbaijanis lost 20% of their country to Armenian occupation, thousands were killed, and some 800,000 refugees fled to Azerbaijan, now comprising about 13% of the country's population.

These conflicts have given rise to many of the forces that affect the current development of oil resources in the region. In the Azerbaijani-Armenian war, for instance, the United States, Russia, and Iran backed the Armenians. In 1992, the U.S. Congress passed Section 907 of the Freedom Support Act, which banned direct aid to Azerbaijan, while Russia gave the Armenians large stocks of armaments. Azerbaijan came out of the war, not only in further economic ruin, but also with a strong sense of isolation, a suspicion of Russian colonial interests, and a wariness toward the United States and Iran. This political setting was favorable to the entry of companies from Britain, Turkey, and other countries in Europe and the Middle East.

Since then, the political and cultural attention of Azerbaijan, as evidenced by everything from political speeches to product names and postage stamps, has continued to focus on the resolution of the Nagorno-Karabakh issue and the defense of the isolated Nakhchivan pocket, an area of Azerbaijan separated from the main territory. Within Azerbaijan, the oil industry is not viewed exclusively as a source of wealth for economic development, but also as a means to resolve the crucial Nagorno-Karabakh and Nakhchivan issues. Decisions about which foreign companies Azerbaijan should encourage, or where an export pipeline should run, are made with a view toward bolstering international support to resolve the conflict in Nagorno-Karabakh in Azerbaijan's favor. In Azerbaijan there is a view that the most significant "pressure" for building the Baku-Tbilisi-Ceyhan pipeline arises from the possibility that it will assist the state in the resolution of its historic struggle with Armenia.

THE BACKGROUND TO CONTEMPORARY DEVELOPMENT

Into this world of conflict stepped Steve Remp, chairman of Ramco, an independent oil company based in Aberdeen, Scotland. He arrived in 1989 to cultivate contacts in Baku, the city with the longest history of continuous oil production in the world and a city rich in indigenous oil development skills. It was not only the political climate that favored the British. The expertise developed in Britain's North Sea oil fields was well suited to the unexploited deepwater offshore fields of the Caspian. Indeed, some in the U.K. oil industry regarded Baku as a way of extending the life of Aberdeen as an oil city. Having made his contacts in Baku, Remp was charged with finding an oil company partner with the capital and technology to develop offshore Azerbaijan. He chose British Petroleum (BP).

On August 30, 1991, Azerbaijan declared its independence from the disintegrating Soviet Union, which formally dissolved four months later. The 1990s were a state-forming period for Azerbaijan which took place under the shadow of war, a struggling economy, and wealthy and powerful Western oil companies.

BP began negotiating with the Azerbaijani authorities in the middle of 1990, about a year prior to Azerbaijani independence. During the following three years, 1990-94, as Azerbaijan poured its resources into fighting Armenia, BP arranged with this fledgling and ever-weakening state what was to become known as the "Contract of the Century." Despite the chaotic political and social situation, BP Exploration, led by John Browne, now BP's chief executive, maintained a tenacious commitment to keeping a foothold in Azerbaijan.

On June 11, 1993, Azerbaijan's then president Abulfaz Elchibey signed a declaration with several Western oil companies: BP (United Kingdom), Statoil (Norway), Amoco (United States), TPAO (Turkey), Unocal (United States), McDermott (United States), and Pennzoil (United States) to develop the offshore Azeri, Chirag, and Guneshli oil fields as one unified project. But just twelve days later, incoming president Heydar Aliyev, canceled the contract as his first action after taking power in a coup on June 18.

According to Britain's *Sunday Times* newspaper, a Turkish secret service report alleged that BP backed the coup that ousted President Elchibey and installed President Aliyev. The report states that "As a result of our intelligence efforts, it has been understood that the two petrol giants, BP and Amoco, British and American respectively, which together form the AIOC (Azerbaijan International Operating Company), are behind the coup d'état carried out against Elchibey in 1993" [3].

Whatever the substance of these allegations, the position of the State Oil Company SOCAR (and hence Azerbaijan) was weakened significantly in the "Contract of the Century" signed in September 1994. The original declaration had granted SOCAR a 30% stake in the AIOC consortium formed to exploit the oil and gas fields, while the contract granted only a 20% stake. This share was reduced further to 10% when 5% was ceded to Exxon and 5% to Turkish Petroleum (TPAO) in spring 1995. The proximity of SOCAR to the Aliyev presidency was emphasized by the appointment, in May 1994, of the president's son Ilham Aliyev, to the post of vice president of SOCAR.

Over the thirteen years since the visit of Ramco's CEO Steve Remp, British government support for U.K. investment in Azerbaijan has been substantial. Perhaps it is no coincidence that one of the directors of Ramco is a former U.K. foreign minister, Malcolm Rifkind. In January 1998, Tim Eggar, who, as U.K. energy minister, made frequent trips to Baku between 1994 and 1996, including one for the signing of the "Contract of the Century," became chief executive of Monument Oil. Monument Oil took a stake in Azerbaijan's Inam oil and gas field in December 1998. These connections between the oil industry and the British government illustrate the stake held in development of the Azeri offshore fields—and ultimately the Baku-Tbilisi-Ceyhan (BTC) pipeline—by the U.K state, alongside the United States, as we shall see.

THE "CONTRACT OF THE CENTURY" AND "EARLY OIL"

With the signing of the "Contract of the Century" in September 1994 the first building block of the BTC pipeline was set in place. A massive inflow of foreign capital followed over the next three years as further agreements were signed to develop eight deepwater offshore oil and gas fields, involving seven more oil companies (Elf and Total of France, Agip of Italy, OIEC of Iran, Winterhall of Germany, and Mobil and Chevron of the United States). Effectively, the "Contract of the Century" sent a signal to the oil world that Azerbaijan was a safe bet for Western oil companies.

The AIOC's key function was to develop the Azeri, Chirag, and Guneshli offshore oil fields. In just three years the consortium refurbished the Chirag-1 oil platform at sea, a half-built platform that had been left unfinished by the Soviets, and built a new 230-kilometer (143-mile) undersea pipeline to a new oil and gas terminal at Sangachal on the Caspian coast just south of Baku.

On November 11, 1997, Terry Adams, then president of the AIOC, participated at the ceremony where Azerbaijan's president Heydar Aliyev and his son, Ilham Aliyev, vice president of SOCAR, smeared oil on their faces—the first "early oil" from deep below the seabed of the Caspian. The 230-kilometer undersea pipeline from Chirag-1 was merely the initial section of the oil export route that all parties knew was essential to opening up the Caspian reserves to the Western markets.

Five years earlier, in November 1992, BP, SOCAR, Botas (of Turkey), Pennzoil, and Amoco (of the United States) had signed an agreement to finance studies of three pipeline options: from Baku to Supsa (in Georgia), from Baku to Novorossiysk (in Russia), and from Baku to Ceyhan (in Turkey). The Ceyhan route could run from Azerbaijan to Turkey either through Georgia or Iran.

By the time oil was pumped from Chirag-1 in early 1998, it had been agreed that the Azerbaijani "early oil" would be exported via the Russian port of Novorossiysk, known as the Northern Route Export Pipeline (NREP). Although BP and its partner companies in the AIOC had previously signed an agreement with Russia and Georgia to export oil via their existing, dilapidated, Soviet-era pipelines, this proposal remained in doubt for two years. It is widely accepted that the go-ahead for the Northern Route in November 1997, was given by the United States under the proviso that it was for "early oil" only, was developed in parallel with the Western Route Export Pipeline (from Baku to Supsa in Georgia), while another route was found for the bulk of the Caspian oil.

Despite the November 1997 agreement for the Baku-Novorossiysk (Northern Route) pipeline, it took another four months before oil flowed. This was because the pipeline ran through Grozny, the capital of Chechnya. This pipeline development—by a BP-led consortium—was overshadowed by six years of brutal war and reprisal in Chechnya, which had started with the Chechen declaration of independence from Russia in September 1991. As British journalist Sebastian Smith wrote in his study of the first Chechen war (1991-96): "In the North Caucasus you have only to say 'nefteprovod,' or 'the oil pipeline,' and everyone knows what you mean. Not many people have ever seen it or really know exactly where it is, but there's no mistaking what pipeline you are talking about. The Baku-Novorossiysk pipeline has its own presence, like the mountains, and when people look at the war in Chechnya, they think of the pipeline" [4].

The Chechens wanted to control the pipeline that ran through their land, both because of its strategic importance and because of its potential to generate revenue from transit fees. The Russians, however, were determined to prevent this from happening, for the same reasons. When the Russian forces withdrew on the November 23, 1996, and presidential elections were held in Chechnya on January 27, 1997—resulting in the election of the rebel leader, Aslan Maskhadov—it looked like as if the Chechens had won. The Baku-Novorossiysk pipeline thus began its life passing through a semi-independent Chechnya. The Russian pipeline company Transneft thereafter delayed its opening as a result of complex negotiations with the new Chechen government, which demanded sovereign involvement in decision taking and a share of the transit fees along their section of the route.

Eventually, on March 24, 1998, a tanker of Azerbaijani crude oil left Novorossiysk. For the first time since 1920 Azerbaijani oil was back on the world market. The conflict in Chechnya soon reignited, however, and early in 1999, Transneft stopped pumping oil through the Baku-Novorossiysk pipeline. By

July 1999, AIOC oil was being shipped by rail through Dagestan to Novorossiysk so as to avoid the Chechen war zone. A new pipeline, the so-called Chechnya Bypass, was constructed by Transneft (opened in spring 2000) to carry oil from Baku to the Russian Black Sea terminal while avoiding Chechnya.

Meanwhile, on April 17, 1999, Georgia's president Eduard Shevardnadze, announced the opening of the Baku-Supsa (Western Route) pipeline. As he stood among the steel storage tanks of the Black Sea terminal, snipers kept watch over the crowd. Georgia had gone to great lengths to emphasize its ability to provide security, lining the pipeline with soldiers, and entering into a military cooperation agreement with Azerbaijan. The 830-kilometer (514-mile) pipeline from Baku to the purpose-built terminal at Supsa had been refurbished by AIOC's partner company, the Georgian International Oil Company. Shevardnadze was accompanied by President Aliyev of Azerbaijan and the then Caspian regional coordinator of the U.S. Department of Commerce, Richard Morningstar, as they watched the first loading of two oil tankers headed for Spain and Italy with Caspian oil.

THE GEOPOLITICS OF THE MAIN EXPORT PIPELINE

The two pipelines—Baku-Novorossiysk (Northern Route) and Baku-Supsa (Western Route)—have a combined capacity of 265,000 barrels of crude oil per day. But the combination of these two routes will never provide sufficient capacity to export the huge volumes of crude set to flow from the Caspian after 2005. Azerbaijani production is expected to increase to 600,000 barrels per day, and ultimately to 1 million barrels. Added to this is the likelihood of oil from countries further east, particularly Kazakhstan.

From Azerbaijan, there were five possible routes for the main pipeline:

1. to the Turkish Mediterranean town of Ceyhan and its port at Yumurtalik, either via Georgia or via Iran;
2. to the Iranian Persian Gulf port of Kharg Island via Iran, with the possibility of an "oil swap" (in which for each barrel of Azerbaijani oil refined in northern Iran, an extra barrel of Iranian oil would be piped across the country to the Gulf Coast for export) in the initial phase to decrease costs;
3. to the Pakistani Indian Ocean port of Gwadar, via an undersea pipeline across the Caspian, then via Turkmenistan, Afghanistan, and Pakistan (prior to the undersea pipeline being built, the oil would be transported across the Caspian by tanker);
4. to the China Sea port of Shanghai along the "Silk Road" eastward via the Caspian undersea pipeline (shipping by tanker in a first phase), through Turkmenistan, Uzbekistan, Tajikistan, and China; or

5. substantially upgrading the Baku-Supsa and/or the Baku-Novorossiysk pipelines and port terminals to enable them to carry larger volumes of oil. If this option were pursued, there would be a secondary pipeline on the other side of the Black Sea, involving some of the following countries: Ukraine, Slovakia, Romania, Bulgaria, Greece, Serbia, Montenegro, Albania, and Croatia. Competition over the choice of the route has been strong because the transit countries would gain not only revenue from pipeline "transit fees," but also a geopolitical position of great strategic importance to the West.

For some time, the most likely route has been to Ceyhan in Turkey via Georgia. The senior power in the region, the United States, has been determined, since the early 1990s, to prise the Caucasian and Central Asian states out of the Russian sphere of influence in which they have been enmeshed since the late eighteenth century. Key to this strategy is the involvement of U.S. companies in Caspian oil and gas developments, and the building up of a network of commodity arteries that avoid Russia. The involvement of U.S. oil majors was initially hindered in Azerbaijan by the U.S. government's support of Armenia during the war in the early 1990s between the two countries. But they have since rapidly made up ground after a late start.

The United States is just as keen to maintain the isolation of Iran. The Baku-Kharg Island route is a commercially attractive option, and, since early 1998, Iran has been opening doors to the West, in particular to European oil and energy companies. But the United States is determined not to place the Caspian reserves at the mercy of Iran, nor to increase the West's dependence on the stability of the Middle East and the compliance of the Gulf states.

The export route to Ceyhan in Turkey via Georgia would assist wider U.S. geopolitical aims, because it would bring to the Eastern Mediterranean a supply of oil that is non-OPEC, non-Arab, and from "secularised Muslim" sources. This could provide a secure source both for the West in general, and for Israel in particular, as Turkey is an ally of Israel and Ceyhan is a mere 483 kilometers from the Israeli port of Haifa.

Turkey itself is eager to regain the strategic position that it lost at the end of the Cold War, when it was NATO's bulwark on the Soviet Union's southern flank. Turkey's attempts to become part of the European Union have been constantly frustrated over the past decade, mostly on human rights grounds. The pipeline offers the possibility of renewing Turkey's strategic importance and furthering the Pan-Turkic Alliance in which the Turkish state binds itself into an eastern union with its Turkic "brother nations," Azerbaijan and Turkmenistan, and undermines the interests of its old enemy, Armenia.

For Turkish industrialists, these eastern connections open up a vast new export market and a new set of resources to feed an energy-hungry economy. Turkey has signed gas supply agreements with several countries in the region—Russia,

Azerbaijan, Iran, and Turkmenistan—despite its proven overestimated projections of future domestic gas demand [5]. These gas agreements may well enable Turkey to sell surplus gas supply, via a new pipeline between Turkey and Europe, transforming Turkey into a European energy gateway for gas.

Turkey has argued vociferously against any increases in oil shipments through the Bosphorus. Currently, the majority of tankers leaving Novorossiysk and Supsa pass through these narrow straits, which run between the Black Sea and the Mediterranean. Turkey, supported by some environmental groups, has argued that an increase in oil shipments in the straits would further raise the probability of a major environmental catastrophe—on the doorstep of Istanbul. Turkey's motives may not be so "green," however. The Bosphorus is classified as "international waters," not Turkish, so the Turkish state cannot collect transit fees and exercises limited control over this strategic oil route. In contrast, a pipeline crossing Central Anatolia on its way to Ceyhan would give it both revenues and political influence.

Both Azerbaijan and Georgia are eager to be considered a part of Europe and to revive the cultural and diplomatic ties of the late 19th century "First Oil Boom" (1870-1914). In July 1996, both countries applied to become members of the Council of Europe, and their eventual aim appears to be to become affiliates of the European Union and NATO, and to leave the Russian-dominated Commonwealth of Independent States. These aspirations neatly dovetail with the strategic desire of the United States to decrease Russian influence in the region.

On November 18, 1999, the ten-year struggle to come to an agreement on the Main Export Pipeline for Caspian Oil appeared to reach a conclusion. At the Organisation for Security and Cooperation in Europe Summit, under the watchful eye of U.S. President Clinton, the leaders of Azerbaijan, Turkey, Georgia, Turkmenistan, and Kazakhstan signed with the United States, the Istanbul Declaration on the building of the BTC oil pipeline. This agreement stressed that all the parties would provide comprehensive assistance in financing and constructing the Main Export Route until 2004. It looked as though the BTC pipeline had finally been launched.

GLOBAL POLITICS AND THE CORPORATIONS

The lead organization developing the Baku-Tbilisi-Ceyhan pipeline system is the oil company BP. It is planned that BP will manage construction and operation, and will coordinate with governments and other bodies and, of course, with its project partners.

While the aims, strategies and interrelations of nation states have been thoroughly studied, less attention has been given to the maneuverings of corporations. Yet the largest contemporary corporations are—in economic size, at least—of a scale similar to medium-sized states [6]. BP, for example, in 2001 had annual turnover of about US$175 billion [7], comparable to the GDP of Poland

($175 billion), just below that of Austria ($188 billion), and thirty times that of Azerbaijan ($5.7 billion) [8].

Geopolitics is especially important to corporations in the extractive industries. As producers of primary commodities, oil companies do not distinguish themselves by the quality or features of their product. No company sells gasoline that is "better" or more desirable than any other. The key to success in such an industry lies rather in strategy, in political and geographic positioning. Oil companies thus aim to gain control and ownership of the greatest possible quantity of cheaply extractable resources, and the means to deliver these to markets. They do so through a careful choice of locations and investments, and by forming alliances with other actors (governments and companies). Oil companies strive to ensure their longevity and strategic role in the world as actively as any nation state. Indeed their corporate survival requires careful tactics, diplomacy and planning.

BP—or the Anglo-Persian Oil Company as it was then known—began its life in 1908. Six years later, in 1914, the First Lord of the Admiralty, Winston Churchill, on behalf of the British state, bought a controlling stake in the company, so as to secure the supply of oil for Britain's World War I effort. Anglo-Persian became the fueling arm of the British Royal Navy. For the following sixty-two years, Anglo-Persian, or British Petroleum as it was renamed in the 1950s, was 51% owned by the British government. In 1976, however, the British government sold off its controlling stake, and since then the company has worked hard at finding a role for itself outside the shadow of the British state and its declining imperial legacy.

In the early 1990s, the government of Azerbaijan was being courted by British Petroleum (as BP was then known), but felt it could get a better deal if another company was competing with BP for Azerbaijani oil resources. The company that came to act as a counterweight to BP was the U.S. oil giant, Amoco [9]. For the following five years, Azerbaijan became a place of contest between a British corporation—British Petroleum—and a U.S. one—Amoco. But in August 1998, British Petroleum and Amoco announced their merger, which was completed in January 1999.

Since then, the key stake in Azerbaijan's economy has been controlled by a single British-American corporation (BP Amoco, later renamed BP). Since 1998, BP has been the primary player in the Western Caspian region. Today it has a 34.1% holding in the Azeri-Chirag-Guneshli oil field (which is by far Azerbaijan's largest), and a 30.1% stake in the associated BTC pipeline, and is the operator of both. It also has a 25.5% holding in the Shah Deniz gas field (Azerbaijan's only major gas field) and in the related South Caucasus (gas) Pipeline.

BP's 1998-99 merger with Amoco, and its subsequent takeover of another U.S. oil company, ARCO (announced in April 1999 and completed in April 2000), have set BP on a new course. The corporation now has a place among the ranks of the "super majors" of oil companies (alongside ExxonMobil and Shell).

Guided by chief executive John Browne, BP has become one of the "Three Sisters," the three giant companies that hold sway over the oil and gas world.

The Amoco merger and the ARCO takeover also brought an important geopolitical realignment for BP. Compared to its rivals, the company had made a late entry in the world's largest energy market, the United States of America. Its first retail presence on the Eastern Seaboard of the United States was established in spring 1969 with the purchase of the downstream assets of the U.S. oil company Sinclair. Only with the discovery of oil in Prudhoe Bay in Alaska (announced in September 1969), and BP's subsequent purchase of the rights to the controlling stake in the oil company SOHIO (completed in January 1970), did BP become a major player on the U.S. stage [10]. Since the merger with Amoco and takeover of ARCO, 36% of BP's shares are now held in the United States. Over the last four years, the company has boldly evolved from being a thoroughly British company to being a truly British-American corporation.

BP's enlargement coincided with key political events in the Caspian oil region. By the summer of 1998, the lack of an exit route for Azerbaijani oil was beginning to hinder investment in offshore development. The strategic desire of the United States to see a non-Iranian/non-Russian exit route for Caspian oil had been clear for the better part of seven years. The question was who would take up this challenge? BP's merger with Amoco was a relatively smooth five-month process. The merger with ARCO, however, took twelve months because of repeated objections from the U.S. Federal Trade Commission, the body that regulates takeovers and mergers in the United States. The commission's objections, though centered on BP's potential monopoly control of West Coast fuel supply, were colored by concerns that a "foreign" oil corporation would significantly intrude upon the U.S. domestic oil market [12].

Six months after the merger with ARCO, presidential candidate George W. Bush started making noises about taking action to prevent such foreign ownership: "This [Clinton] administration has left a lot of our offshore drilling under foreign hands such as Royal Dutch/Shell and BP" [13]. For two years, there had already been well-publicized disquiet about the "merger" of BP and Amoco, which had in reality also been a takeover. A joke reportedly making the rounds in the Texan oil city of Houston cut to the heart of the merger:

> "How do you pronounce BP Amoco?"
> "BP. The Amoco is silent."

In 2000, BP Amoco made the "takeover" official when the company renamed itself simply BP.

In the late 1990s, BP still needed to prove its loyalty to the U.S. administration, and driving forward the BTC pipeline was a part of that strategy. Up until the latter half of 1999, BP chief executive John Browne was publicly pouring cold water on the BTC oil pipeline. The pipelines from Baku to Supsa and from Baku to Novorossiysk were for exporting "early oil." For the later and much larger exports, there was a possibility that BP was thinking about a pipeline to Iran's Kharg Island, or a route from Baku to Ceyhan via Iran. After all, BP had opened an office in Tehran in early 1998 after nineteen years' absence from the country. Such a route would take the company back to its British Imperial birthplace. As the Anglo-Persian Oil Company, BP had begun its life in Iran, and the company's investment there had remained its biggest asset until it was ejected in 1951, when Iran nationalized its oil industry.

Alternatively, BP might support an expansion of the northern route through Russia to Novorossiysk, despite the conflict in Chechnya. After all, BP did not show much concern about reopening the route in 1997, so perhaps it felt that this pipeline could handle a much greater capacity. Throughout the 1990s, BP made several strategic investments in Russia, such as its stake in the Kovykta gas fields, through its investment in the Russian oil company Sidanco. BP bought 10% of Sidanco in 1997 for US$480 million, and in April 2002 acquired a further 15% for $380 million. In February 2003, BP combined its Sidanco shareholding with AAR Group's holding in TNK, paying AAR $6.75 billion. As a result, BP became a 50% shareholder in Russia's third largest oil company, now named TNK-BP. Again, BP's closeness to Russia might imply a strategy different from that espoused by the United States.

Publicly, BP did not express any clear preferences, but rather kept its options open, and conspicuously declined to support the Baku-Ceyhan (BTC) route until autumn 1999. From that point onward, BP began to say that the Baku-Ceyhan route might be possible, and by spring 2000, after the November 1999 OCSE Summit and the signing of the Istanbul Declaration on the BTC pipeline, BP committed itself to the project.

The BTC oil pipeline would bring Caspian crude to Ceyhan and the BP refinery at Mersin (100 kilometers west of Ceyhan). It is likely that this refinery will become a supplier of aviation fuel to the U.S. Air Force base at Incirlik 30 kilometers (18 miles) west of Ceyhan, and the U.S. Air Force base at Konya, 250 kilometers (155 miles) northwest of Mersin. Since the 1980s, Incirlik has been vital for U.S. military hegemony over the Middle East. Bombing raids were flown from Incirlik during the 1991 Gulf War and the 2002 Afghan War, and through the 1990s and early twenty-first century, the Northern No-Fly Zone over Iraq was enforced from Incirlik. The United States would have also used Incirlik to launch bombing raids on Iraq in 2003, if it had obtained permission from Turkey. If BP began its life as the fueling arm of the British Royal Navy, it could soon be seen as part of the fueling arm of the U.S. Air Force and the U.S. Navy.

Central to BP's support for BTC is the repositioning of this former British company as a British-American company that is careful to keep in line with the desires of Washington. During the four- or five-decade life span of most of BP's Caspian projects, the United States is likely to remain the leading world power. BP needs to keep itself aligned with that world power, while at the same time pursuing its own commercial logic.

BTC AND BP'S FUTURE GLOBAL STRATEGY

Beyond its wider geopolitical significance, the BTC pipeline is essential to the long-range commercial logic of BP. Without BTC, or an alternative, BP's presence in Azerbaijan would be almost redundant. Azerbaijan is key to BP's long-term strength. BP bases its future oil production growth on activities in five major "profit centres": Azerbaijan, Trinidad and Tobago, Asia-Pacific (mainly West Papua), the U.S. Gulf of Mexico, and Angola, plus its new investment in Russia.

BP has worked hard on consolidating its position in the Western Caspian. Through its corporate maneuvering, it does not have to share its crown in Azerbaijan, in contrast to oil companies in Kazakhstan, for example. BP today is effectively the key player in the Azerbaijani oil industry. Prior to January 1999, BP and Amoco each owned 17% of the Azerbaijan International Operating Company consortium. This distribution of power might have given SOCAR, the state oil company of Azerbaijan, some chance of playing one company off against the other. Since the January 1999 merger of BP and Amoco, however, BP has a 34% stake in AIOC. No other company has more than 10.3%, marking a major shift in the power dynamic within the AIOC, and, consequently, within Azerbaijan itself.

BP, after initially sharing the view of other oil companies that the Baku-Tbilisi-Ceyhan pipeline was economically unviable, was the first oil company to express public support for the project in October 1999. Within six months, it was negotiating government agreements in Washington, effectively acting as a fifth "government" alongside those of Azerbaijan, Georgia, Turkey, and the United States. Within twelve months, it was pulling other oil companies together to try to persuade them to join the project.

BP and its partners plan to spend more than US$13 billion dollars in Azerbaijan over the next six years, mainly on the construction phase of the Azeri-Chirag-Guneshli oil field, the Shah Deniz gas field, and the two corresponding pipelines, BTC and SCP, and the Sangachal Terminal Expansion [14]. BP's share of this investment ranges from 25.5% to 35.7%, depending on the project. This means that BP plans to invest about US$3.7 billion over six years, equivalent to at least 7% of all BP's investment in all countries in all sectors of the oil industry from field to forecourt. This is comparable to its expenditure in the North Sea (US$1,095 million in 2001), which currently accounts for 25% of the company's production [15].

BP is completely committed to the BTC pipeline project in terms of invested financial resources, not to mention its political and "emotional" investment. The sense of corporate pride and ambition attached to its presence in Azerbaijan in general and to the pipelines system in particular is substantial, and it is this that drives the "pressure to build" the Baku-Tbilisi-Ceyhan pipeline that comes from BP.

THE ACTUAL AND POTENTIAL IMPACTS
OF THE PIPELINE

At the time of writing, the construction of the Baku-Tbilisi-Ceyhan pipeline has not yet begun. Or so it would seem, for the precise definition of when the "construction begins" is a difficult task. Certainly the pipeline cannot be visited in the fields of Azerbaijan or mountains of Turkey. The physical process of excavating and pipe laying is not set to take place until spring 2003.

Since summer 2002, BP has repeatedly announced the start of construction [16] and certain elements of the pipeline are indeed being put in place.

Effectively, a pipeline is built five times. First it is built in law, with the formulation of contracts and legal agreements. Second, it is built in engineering, in technical drawings and computer models. Third, it is built in public relations, in glossy brochures, colorful photos of communities and landscapes, and promises about positive impacts on people on the route. Fourth, it is built in finance, constructing a complex package of loans and sponsor equity, each with its terms and definitions. Only after these four stages is it built in physical reality. The first two of these stages of construction are, as we write this chapter, broadly complete. The third and fourth are under way, and the fifth is just about to start.

The actual and potential impacts of the BTC pipeline can be grouped into eight categories which we discuss in detail below, namely:

1. the threat to fledgling democracies;
2. the mirage of new wealth;
3. the potential to exacerbate poverty;
4. the increasing militarization of the region;
5. the fear of re-igniting conflicts and the threat to human rights;
6. foreign standards and worsening working conditions in the oil sector;
7. the threat to the regional environment; and
8. the threat to the global environment.

1. The Threat to Fledgling Democracies

In August 2002, the Georgian nongovernmental organization Green Alternative, commented on the prospects of the BTC pipeline in the following words: "The requirement to compensate the [BTC] consortium for any disruption caused to the "economic equilibrium" of the project by new social and environmental laws severely curtails the development possibilities for our country" [17]. To comprehend this feeling of threat we need to understand the legal background of the BTC project.

Just over a decade after the collapse of the Soviet Union, the major priority for many Georgians and Azeris remains the development of strong, independent democracies in their countries. Many Turks meanwhile aspire to "modernity" and Westernization and, in particular, have their sights set on

European Union membership. These aspirations are threatened by the legal basis of the BTC pipeline.

The project is governed by an Intergovernmental Agreement (IGA) between the governments of Azerbaijan, Georgia, and Turkey, and by an individual Host Government Agreement (HGA) between each of the three governments and the BP-led consortium. These agreements are in effect the first actual manifestations of the BTC project. The existing agreements have largely exempted BP and its partners from any legal provisions in the three countries, present or future, that might conflict with the company's project plans. Furthermore, the IGA and the HGAs allow BP to demand compensation from the governments should any law (including environmental, social, or human rights law) make the pipeline less profitable [18].

Although the HGAs differ from country to country, they share a number of common elements. These are exemplified by the Turkish HGA [19] which:

- Exempts the BTC consortium from any obligations under Turkish law, aside from the Constitution, that conflict with the terms of the HGA/IGA. The HGA thus severely limits the Turkish government's executive and legislative powers to protect Turkish citizens from potential environmental damage and associated health and safety hazards.
- Requires Turkey to compensate the BTC consortium if new taxes or health or safety or environmental laws adversely affect the financial viability or profitability of the project. In practice this may prevent Turkey from enacting such laws, or from implementing them in the pipeline corridor (Paragraphs 7.2, vi and xi). This has the real potential to place Turkey in direct contravention of international and European laws by which Turkey is currently bound, or would be bound in the future if its application to join the European Union were accepted.
- Grants BP and its partners the power to terminate the HGA, but denies that power to the Turkish government, except in extraordinary circumstances (Paragraphs 3.2, 3.4, 11.4). This effectively denies a future Turkish government the ability to amend the agreement so as to afford its citizens greater protection (Paragraph 16.1).
- Grants the consortium an effective right to restrict the geographical development of villages, without compensation (for example, by prohibiting construction of buildings or planting of trees in the pipeline corridor) (Paragraph 4.1, iii). It would also be for the consortium to decide whether *it* can build structures over the buried pipeline, regardless of how severely those structures interfere with the use of the adjacent land (for example, by blocking movements of livestock). Meanwhile, the consortium can bar the construction of any other buildings that it considers close enough to pose a security threat— even on land the consortium does not own.

Other provisions in the HGA include unfettered access to water, regardless of the needs of local communities (Paragraph 4.1, iv), and an exemption from liability in the event of an oil spill or any other harm caused by the pipeline consortium. The Turkish government can intervene only in the case of an "imminent" and "material" threat to the public, the environment, or national security (Paragraph 5.2, iii). The preservation of the stability of the project prevails over any other considerations. It is unclear what would be seen as constituting an "imminent and material threat" and who would decide if such a threat existed. The high threshold of damage required before action is taken is at odds with any recognized concept of precaution in matters of environmental protection. Local populations would have no redress where the government has not acted or has failed to act to protect its interests. Finally, the HGA specifies that any arbitration proceeding shall be carried out in the English language (Paragraph 18.6). This exclusion of any other language places the Turkish government and any other non-English-speaking parties at a disadvantage.

In essence, a strip of Turkey approximately 1,000 kilometers (620 miles) long is, through these agreements, transferred to the legal control of BP and other oil companies. The environment, human rights, and development organization, the Corner House, argues that "Turkey is now divided into three countries: the area where Turkish law applies; the Kurdish areas under official or de facto military rule; and a strip running the entire length of the country from North to South, where BP is the effective government" [20].

We noted earlier that BP began negotiating with Azerbaijan while the country was in the midst of the process of gaining independence from the Soviet Union. The new Azeri state was formed under the shadow of war and a major international oil corporation. This process has not come to a halt, for the IGA and the HGAs considerably constrain the ability of a fledgling democracy, such as Georgia, to frame its own environmental and social laws.

Even where there is room for environmental protection specified in the agreements, this has not prevented BP from attempting to constrain environmental action. For example, in Georgia, the Host Government Agreement provides for a project environmental and social impact assessment (ESIA) to be subject to approval by the government. But in late 2002, as the Georgian government considered the ESIA, and especially the issue of the impact of the pipeline on its valuable Borjomi mineral water springs, which the BTC pipeline would pass close to, BP placed heavy pressure on the Georgian president to rapidly approve the ESIA. The Georgian environment minister, Nino Chkhobadze, who had the ultimate responsibility for approval of the ESIA, had indicated that she would not do so with the current route, at least until further studies had been carried out.

On November 21, 2002, the presidents of BP Azerbaijan and the State Oil Company of Azerbaijan Republic, David Woodward and Natiq Aliyev, wrote to Georgia's President Shevardnadze, stressing the need to approve the ESIA by November 30. The letter hinted that if BTC were delayed, the Shah Deniz gas development in offshore Azerbaijan (from which Georgia was anxious to obtain gas supplies) would also be held up. In relation to alternative routes avoiding Borjomi, the letter stated "we believe it may be necessary to inform experts who visit with you in the coming weeks that routes through this district are and will remain unacceptable" [21].

The U.S. special adviser to the Caspian Region, Steven Mann, was called to Georgia on November 25, supposedly to mediate between BP and the Georgian government. He opened the discussions with the comment that "The agreed route of the oil pipeline goes through the Borjomi Gorge. If the approval of this project is delayed any further, I cannot see any opportunity for the implementation of other projects in Georgia. I repeat that delaying the Baku-Ceyhan project will block the Baku Tbilisi-Erzurum gas pipeline project" [22].

Following the warnings of Woodward, Aliyev, and Mann, both Shevardnadze and Gia Chanturia, president of the Georgian International Oil Corporation, promised that the approval would be given on time. Meanwhile, Environment Minister Chkhobadze wrote a letter to BP chief executive officer John Browne, in which she complained that "BP representatives are requesting the Georgian Government to violate our own environmental legislation" by requiring a route through the Borjomi protected area [23]. Finally, on the night of December 1-2, after extensive negotiations, Chkhobadze bowed to the pressure from Mann, Chanturia, and Shevardnadze and signed the ESIA approval in the early hours.

This incident made a mockery of the purpose of the ESIA, namely, to identify problems and agree on mitigatory measures prior to the ESIA being approved. Furthermore, it demonstrated that the pressure to build the pipeline, from the point of view of BP and the United States, is such that the legal process of the host governments can effectively be bullied out of the way.

A further dimension in which the BTC project threatens to undermine the development of an efficient democratic society is in its potential to stimulate corruption. Azerbaijan is ranked by Transparency International as the world's eighth most corrupt country [24]. High levels of corruption have also been reported in Georgia. In Turkey, the World Bank says that contractors have traditionally been asked to pay up to 15% of the value of state contracts to politicians as "state contributions" [25]. Nongovernmental organizations (NGOs) report that villagers have had to pay bribes of $500 to secure pipeline jobs, in some cases being forced to sell cattle and property to raise the money. A complaint has also been made to the World Bank regarding contract rigging in the award of a contract by the Georgian International Oil Company for work on the environmental and social impact assessment for BTC [26].

Instances such as these demonstrate that widespread corruption is likely to result in revenues from the project being creamed off or used for the benefit of the elite—and thus denying them to the poor and to those most affected by the pipeline. Furthermore, these practices entrench the status quo and undermine the evolution of a strong rule of law and an open democracy.

2. The Mirage of New Wealth

Azerbaijan, Georgia, and Turkey see future oil and gas revenues—from taxes, shares of resources and pipeline transit fees—as a means of bringing them prosperity. However, it appears that the pipeline project is unlikely to assist the process of state-building.

One of the major elements of the preconstruction phase of the BTC pipeline has been the establishment of the commercial framework for the project, including taxation and transit fee arrangements. As discussed above, despite pressure from the U.S. government, BP had declined to support the Baku-Tbilisi-Ceyhan pipeline route until November 1999. It would appear that part of this reluctance was based on cost considerations, insofar as BP's change of heart coincided with Turkey's guarantee of the construction cost of the Turkish section of the pipeline. Under this agreement, any cost above US$1.4 billion would be covered by the Turkish state. This undertaking was clearly of great benefit for the oil companies in the BTC consortium. Some analysts estimated that the guarantee at this cost figure shaved $600 million off the project cost to the companies [27].

For a project the scale of the BTC pipeline, which is subject to complex political, economic, social, and environmental tensions and possible delays, construction risk is a crucial factor. The Trans Alaska Pipeline System (TAPS), for example, was originally planned to cost US$900 million, but by the end of construction the project cost had soared to $7.7 billion. Even on the Forties Pipeline System, which did not have the unexpected delay experienced by TAPS, overspending pushed up the cost from an original estimate of £330 million (US$800 million) to £750 million ($1.2 billion).

Beyond the issue of indirect subsidies, it should be asked whether this deal will get worse over time, during the forty or more years of BTC's operational life. A common thread running through BP's existing projects is the company's effectiveness in minimizing the amount of revenue that goes to the host state: either by lobbying to change the tax system in its favor, or by using accounting techniques to minimize its tax liability [28]. The history of BP's operations in Alaska, Colombia, and Scotland illustrates how the company has been able to drive down the host state's tax revenue long after the construction of a pipeline system, indeed throughout its period of operation. For example, as late as July 2002, BP was still battling with the U.K. Exchequer over its tax and royalties payments; nearly twenty-seven years after the opening of the Forties Pipeline System [29].

There are already indications that Azerbaijan, Georgia, and Turkey will have similar experiences. As part of the Baku-Supsa pipeline project, Georgia was expecting to be paid a port fee for the use of the Supsa port, as well as a transit fee for the land passage of the pipeline. However, in the period following the opening of the port in April 1999, tankers refused to pay anything for being loaded at Supsa. This resulted in an estimated loss to the Georgian state of US$2.5 million per year.

In June 2002, a Greek tanker was detained by the port authorities at Supsa for its unsettled account. BP intervened and forced the authorities to release the tanker without payment, pointing to the terms of the Host Government Agreement for the pipeline. The agreement does not specify a precise arrangement for tankers. BP claimed that this means that tankers cannot be taxed, but the Georgian government believed that no such restriction could be inferred from the contract. BP threatened to go to international arbitration if Georgia attempted to charge the tankers [30].

Today host governments are specifically precluded from adjusting the terms of the HGAs without approval from BP and the other BTC consortium members. While BP cannot unilaterally change the contract either, the Supsa case illustrates how BP utilizes its political strength to insist on an interpretation of the HGA that is beneficial to itself. It appears that this interpretation is likely at each stage to decrease the revenue coming from the project to the host governments, with Azerbaijan, Georgia, and Turkey becoming less likely to achieve their hoped-for prosperity through the means of the BTC pipeline.

3. The Potential to Exacerbate Poverty

Azerbaijan, Georgia, and Turkey currently suffer high levels of economic hardship and poverty. Unfortunately, for many communities living along the pipeline route, the project stands to actually exacerbate poverty.

In Turkey alone, up to an estimated 20,000 families would have their land impacted by the BTC pipeline route. While, in theory, BP has said that it will compensate people for their land, in practice, the company is likely to pay only for a narrow corridor containing the pipe itself, even though a much wider area will be damaged or destroyed by construction activities. In the case of BP's OCENSA pipeline project in Colombia, built in the mid-1990s, landowners are still fighting in court to be compensated for the impact on their livelihoods [31]. A similar pattern already occurred around the Baku-Supsa "Early Oil" pipeline project, built by BP in 1997-99, along the same planned route as the BTC [32]. The East Anatolian Natural Gas Pipeline (NGP), built in 2000-2001 by Botas, along the planned route as BTC through much of Turkey, revealed the same pattern [33]. Even for the narrow strip of land directly occupied by the pipeline, there have been many complaints that compensation for the NGP project generally undervalued land. For example, no more compensation was paid for fertile, productive land than for unusable rocky slopes in the mountains. Botas is set to construct the Turkish section of the BTC pipeline, under contract to BP. Therefore, it is widely expected that compensation for land taken by the BTC pipeline would be the same as that offered by the NGP project.

As well as private property, community and public property stand to be lost. Roads to villages, for example, were badly damaged by heavy machinery driving over them during construction of both BP's Baku-Supsa "Early Oil" pipeline in Azerbaijan and Georgia, and Botas's NGP pipeline in Turkey. BP and Botas, respectively, promised at the time to rebuild these roads after construction; a promise that was not kept. In at least one village, Baku-Supsa construction activities damaged a water pipeline supplying the village. BP refused to repair the water line, and the villagers had to pay for the work themselves [34]. As the BTC pipeline in Azerbaijan and Georgia is planned to run on the same route as the Baku-Supsa pipeline, many communities that have suffered from broken promises are deeply skeptical of BP's current proposals to ensure minimum disruption during the process of construction.

Even if damage were repaired, the economic structure of major oil and gas deals is problematic. Oxfam America explains in its recent report, *Extractive Sectors and the Poor,* that:

> Not all forms of economic activity are equally good at promoting develop-ment. . . . Extractive sectors tend to be capital-intensive and use little unskilled and semi-skilled labor; they are geographically concentrated and create small pockets of wealth that typically fail to spread; they produce social and environmental problems that fall heavily on the poor; they follow a boom-and-bust cycle that creates insecurity for the poor; and they are generally run by the state, or by large corporations, in ways that lead to high rates of corruption, repression and conflict [35].

Echoing this analysis, there has been much debate about whether Azerbaijan might suffer from "Dutch Disease," the name for the phenomenon whereby an economy regresses rather than grows due to oil investment. One of the main drivers for this phenomenon is that the economy's capacity is taken up by the oil development, sucking resources out of other sectors. Meanwhile, there are major impacts on wages and currency exchange. Since the mid-1990s, the real exchange rate of Azerbaijan's currency—the manat—has appreciated markedly due to oil revenues, severely damaging the nonoil sector's competitiveness [36]. The overdependence on a single commodity makes the country vulnerable to the damaging impacts of the sharp price fluctuations that characterize the oil market.

Concerns about adverse effects on the economy are not restricted to Azerbaijan. BP estimates that 10,000 construction workers will be employed in total along the whole pipeline route. This would create a massive influx into the region that would force up food and housing prices, making life more expensive and more difficult for local people. The impact of the construction of a major pipeline such as BTC is eloquently portrayed by Alaskan journalist and author John Strohmeyer in his description of the building of the Trans Alaska Pipeline System:

> [It was a] massive invasion of men and machines slicing an 800-mile (1,287 km) corridor north to south across Alaska. There was an urgency to work on the pipeline that was like the fervor of a military expedition. Crews landed by land, sea and air all along the route. Then they raced to see who could move fastest. Nineteen camps, with random names like Happy Valley, Kennedy,

and Sheep Creek, were built along the route. Each had a narrow, prefabricated dormitory, complete with dining hall, rec room, and first-aid station. Support planes, barges, and trucks brought in a steady stream of supplies, from the latest tools to thick sirloin steaks [37].

The experience of the "Early Oil" project has already highlighted the social impact of major oil infrastructure construction. The port of Supsa, before the arrival of the Baku-Supsa pipeline, was a thriving market town. Then during the two years in which local men were employed building the terminal, consequent labor shortages caused the rest of the economy to collapse. Once the temporary construction phase was over, there was no work to return to. A report on the Web site, Eurasianet, describes the scene three years later:

> Outside the train station men sit and wait. And wait. And wait. There is no work in Supsa, so the most predominant image is groups of men of all ages sitting and waiting. Waiting for the day to end, for the next bottle of wine, vodka or chichi (Georgian vodka made from the skins of grapes, a by-product from the wine making process). Waiting and watching [38].

As we have detailed above, the Georgian environment minister has been deeply concerned about the potential impacts of the BTC pipeline on the mineral water springs in the Borjomi district of Georgia. Possible pollution from the oil project would undermine or even destroy the mineral water company, which accounts for 10 % of Georgia's exports and is the major source of employment in the area [39]. Even the prospect of the BTC has meant severe reputational damage to the Borjomi plant. Significantly, the mineral waters provide a sustainable form of economic activity, jobs in the bottling plant and export facilities are long term, compared to the temporary employment that the BTC construction might offer. BP has refused to reconsider the routing to avoid the important springs.

Many in Azerbaijan feel that the very concept of BTC is flawed. The BTC is an export pipeline, designed to carry Azerbaijan's oil to the world market. Local NGOs and opposition political parties argue that Azerbaijan would benefit far more from the value-added revenue in refining and the country should retain and develop its ability to process the oil [40]. Over the past decade, the focus on oil export has led to severe contraction of Azerbaijan's petrochemical industry. Drawing on its long oil history, Azerbaijan still has people trained to work in refining, and continues to turn out petroleum engineers from its university. But with the high level of unemployment, especially in skilled jobs, thousands of highly educated Azerbaijanis have already left the country for elsewhere in the Former Soviet Union, the Middle East, or for the West. Refined oil products are now imported, which is bad for the country's balance of payments. Meanwhile, there is no quality car oil in Azerbaijan. The main product available is "mazut," a heavy, low-quality oil product that is used for generating electricity.

It seems that the main potential benefits to communities from the BTC pipeline arise from employment opportunities during the construction phase. In Azerbaijan and Georgia, BP has set up registration centers in major towns along the route, where local people can put their names down to be considered for work. Communities that had the experience of the Baku-Supsa pipeline are generally quite skeptical about employment prospects because between 1997 and 1999, BP promised great employment opportunities that did not materialize. A few villages had some of their residents employed on low wages and with unfavorable contracts. Most villages had no one employed at all. However, for those without this experience, the registration process has served only to encourage unrealistic expectations about possible employment levels. For example, in the town of Tetri Ts'karo in Georgia an estimated 2,000 people have registered for work [41]. But if construction proceeds, only about 1,700 people will be employed in the whole of Georgia, at least half of whom would be foreign, and many more of whom would be nonlocal, from elsewhere in Georgia. Thus, at most, 50-100 people from Tetri Ts'karo might get jobs, out of the 2,000 people hoping for them. Even those jobs would be for only a few months.

Finally, when international NGOs traveled to the pipeline region on two fact-finding missions in summer 2002, they were told many times that the two biggest development priorities were better roads and a secure energy supply. Currently, the regions that the pipeline would pass through suffer from great energy poverty. Although communities along the route in Azerbaijan and Georgia used to have electricity and gas during the Soviet era, they now lack secure supplies of energy. Few villages now have either piped gas or electricity. For cooking and heating householders have to buy expensive gas canisters when they can. While a million barrels of oil and 20 million cubic meters of gas would pass through these villages every day, it is unlikely that the villages will have a secure supply of energy. These kinds of perceptions fuel the sense that the BTC pipeline will exacerbate poverty.

4. The Increasing Militarization of the Region

The BTC pipeline would pass just ten miles from Nagorno-Karabakh, the area of Azerbaijan occupied by Armenia, where a bloody six-year conflict killed thousands and created 800,000 refugees. It would also pass through Georgia, which remains unstable, with separatist movements in Abkhazia and South Ossetia—movements that the Georgian government tried to violently suppress during the 1990s. Just across the border into Russia, and still only seventy miles from the BTC pipeline route, the horrific conflict in Chechnya continues. The Caucasus region also saw related conflicts in neighboring Dagestan in 1999, as well as fighting between the Russian republics of North Ossetia and Ingushetia in 1992. In Turkey, the BTC route passes through the edge of the area of the conflict between the Turkish state and the Kurdistan Workers Party (PKK), which is currently under a fragile ceasefire.

Against this background of persistent conflict, Azerbaijan, Georgia, and Turkey are heavily militarized. Due to the unresolved conflict with Armenia, Azerbaijan retains strong armed forces, which consumes an important share of its budget. Georgia has a smaller military capacity, but is extremely security conscious. It relies instead on external military support, especially from the United States. Turkey has a substantial military capacity, military expenditure accounting for an enormous 4.5% of GDP [42].

Russia and the Western powers have been in competition in the south Caucasus region throughout the past decade. After the collapse of the Soviet Union, Azerbaijan and Georgia resisted Russian attempts to bring them more into security arrangements of the Commonwealth of Independent States. They both became members of the NATO-led "Partnership for Peace" initiative, and have also joined the Georgia, Ukraine, Uzbekistan, Azerbaijan, Moldova regional cooperation group, known as GUUAM.

Since September 11, 2001, Georgia and Azerbaijan have significantly increased their cooperation with the United States. Both countries provided the United States with rights to fly over their territories for military operations. In March 2002, the U.S. Defense Department pledged US$4.4 million in military aid to Azerbaijan with the reported aims of countering terrorism, promoting stability in the Caucasus, and developing trade and transport corridors. In February 2002, the U.S. government said it would provide Georgia with military support worth US$64 million, and promised to dispatch 180 crack troops and to train up to 2,000 Georgians in antiterrorism and counterinsurgency operations, chiefly in the Pankisi Gorge, where Al Qaida fighters (as well as Chechens) are believed to have taken refuge.

Meanwhile, Turkish officers have served as advisers to the Azerbaijani armed forces. Turkey will reportedly modernize Azerbaijan's armed forces within the framework of a new program named "Arms in Exchange for Gas" [43]. On April 30, 2002, Azerbaijan, Georgia, and Turkey, agreed on accords on security issues. The Georgian defense minister indicated that Georgia is interested in sending officers to study in military schools in Azerbaijan.

There are clear indications that the host states plan to militarize the corridor of the pipeline system. These plans carry grave risks for stability in the region and for human rights. Since 1999, Georgia has already lined the Baku-Supsa pipeline with military posts and has been conducting joint military exercises with Azerbaijan to promote pipeline security. On July 3, 2001, BP vice president John Sullivan and Georgian president Eduard Shevardnadze discussed security for the construction and operation of the BTC oil and South Caucasus (gas) pipelines. At the meeting they agreed to set up an interdepartmental commission with the participation of law enforcement structures, which would guarantee the security of the construction and operation of the oil and gas pipelines [44]. A few days before this meeting, President Shevardnadze publicly announced that the Georgian State Guard Service would be responsible for the security of the transportation of Caspian oil and gas resources through Georgia. He also revealed that a special unit of the service had been policing the Baku-Supsa oil pipeline for the past two years [45].

The region has become further militarized since September 11, 2001, with U.S.-led antiterrorism initiatives emphasizing the need to increase security along the east-west energy corridor. In April 2002, Azerbaijan and Georgia signed a new military agreement designed to increase oil and gas pipeline security, along-side antiterrorist and antiseparatism efforts. Following increasing U.S. deployment in Georgia in 2002, a BP spokeswoman commented that, "The pipelines will of course benefit from the military presence" [46].

Given the volatile past of the region, and the international nature of the BTC pipeline, there are well-grounded fears, both locally and internationally, that the oil transport infrastructure could spark conflict between states. Even if these fears are not realized, the very possibility of conflict means that Azerbaijan and Georgia, in particular, would be diverting much needed resources into military expenditure. A stark illustration of this process is the Georgian government's agreement in January 2003 to purchase aerial surveillance systems from the U.S. firm Northrop Grumman, at a cost of at least $4.5 million, explicitly to monitor the BTC pipeline system when constructed [47].

5. The Fear of Reigniting Conflicts and the Threat to Human Rights

The construction of the pipeline has the potential to trigger tensions and conflicts within the states. As a major symbol both of the state's power and of Western intervention in the country, there is a strong likelihood that the BTC will be targeted by rebel groups and terrorists. These threats affect people both directly and indirectly. Directly, acts of sabotage can affect local people. The comparison with BP's OCENSA pipeline in Colombia, where the civil conflict bears some parallels with that in Turkey, is instructive. In one of the worst tragedies of Colombia's conflict, at least seventy people were killed in the village of Machuca (in Antioquia state) in October 1998 when the ELN guerrilla group blew up BP's OCENSA pipeline. According to press reports, one survivor described a fifty-meter fireball roaring along a river before hitting the village, where it engulfed wooden homes where villagers were sleeping [48].

Ominously, there is already evidence that some groups may be disposed to sabotage the BTC pipeline system. Upon returning to Baku from internal exile in 1997, ex-president and Azerbaijan Popular Front (AzPF) chairman Abulfaz Elchibey warned that AzPF partisans in the Gazakh and Agstafa regions might take military action against the Baku-Supsa pipeline if the project did not "serve the interests of the Azerbaijani people" [49].

In Turkey, the PKK has a history of targeting oil installations. During the height of their armed conflict with Turkish security forces in the 1990s, the PKK identified Turkish pipelines and oil refineries in the Kurdish regions as legitimate military targets. In December 1991, the PKK destroyed TPAO's Selmo oil wells near the city of Batman with rocket fire. Then, within less than five weeks, between August 31 and October 5, 1992, the PKK attacked three different pipeline sites in the Kurdish regions. First, on August 31, Shell Oil's depots near the Kurdish stronghold of Diyarbakir were attacked and oil tanks were set on fire. Less than two weeks later, on September 12, the PKK raided the Selmo oil fields a second time, setting fires and killing three engineers. Then, at the beginning of October, the Turkish Petroleum (TPAO) pumping stations and factories near Sason were attacked and set on fire. Six months later, in January 1997, the PKK attacked the Kirkuk-Yumurtalik pipeline again, this time in the town of Mardin in southeastern Turkey [50].

In December 2002, U.S. experts also warned of a serious danger of "megaterrorist acts" against oil infrastructure projects in the Caspian, based on a statement by the head of Egyptian Islamic Jihad (part of Al Qaida, which has had a Baku cell for ten years) that "the USA's and Western countries' economic interests" will be targeted [51].

Indirectly, security measures to protect the pipeline can also impact any innocent civilians, whether deliberately or not. For example, the potential creation of a "militarised corridor" along the pipeline's route in Turkey's Kurdish regions poses serious risks of an escalation in state violence in these war-ravaged regions. Responsibility for the security of the pipeline in Turkey would rest with the Turkish State Gendarmerie. The Gendarmerie has a lamentable human rights record, and, during the fifteen-year civil conflict with the PKK, has been involved in clearance and displacement of numerous Kurdish villages. The Council of Europe passed a highly critical resolution in July 2002, condemning the severe and ongoing human rights abuses committed by Turkish security forces and naming the Gendarmerie as one of the forces in urgent need of reform [52]. Considering Turkey's continued failure to commit to serious human rights reform and the ongoing impunity of those responsible for torture and extrajudicial killing, the increased militarization that would accompany the development of the BTC pipeline could also bring with it a blow to peace in Turkey. The PKK's three-year ceasefire, would not be aided by an increased military presence in the Kurdish areas, where people continue to suffer gross human rights violations at the hands of the state. In its agreements with the Gendarmerie, BP has failed to incorporate clauses stipulating that human rights must be upheld [53].

The HGA also paves the way for the BTC consortium to demand protection from Turkish security forces, without safeguards against human rights abuses being stipulated. Under the vague wording of the agreement, paramilitary units could be placed along the pipeline route to preempt "civil disturbance" or "terrorist" activities (Paragraph 12.1). These provisions would do nothing to quell regional and international concerns that the construction of the BTC pipeline would reignite smouldering conflicts and stimulate further human rights abuses.

6. Foreign Standards and Worsening Working Conditions in the Oil Sector

In their study of the North Sea oil industry, Woolfson, Foster, and Beck argue that the development of the U.K. sector has been marked by the implementation of an external production regime, the exclusion of trade unions, the lack of an effective health and safety system, the disaggregated structure of management, and the weakness of the indigenous supply base. The causes behind this lie, in part, in the role played by the United States in development of the U.K. North Sea, and in the sense of urgency with which it was developed.

Similar forces may influence the Caspian developments. These include:

- The West's insecurity about energy supplies from the Middle East, which in the early 1970s was due to the Arab-Israeli war and OPEC, and today arises because of militant Islam and Iraq.
- BP's own insecurity about its oil supply, which in the 1970s arose from nationalizations in Iran, Iraq, and Libya; and in the 1990s arises from the decline of its fields in the North Sea and Alaska.
- Like the North Sea, Azerbaijan in plain economic terms is not particularly attractive, mainly because of the cost of getting Caspian oil to Western markets. As in the North Sea, development in the Caspian is driven by political motives, or, more specifically, the dominance of U.S. interests.

Many of the patterns of poor working conditions observable in the U.K. North Sea are already evident in the Western Caspian. But in Azerbaijan two factors exacerbate the problems. First, there is no capacity for external scrutiny. Second, corruption is endemic in Azerbaijan.

In the North Sea, improvements in safety and working conditions that have come about in the past thirteen years are largely due to pressure from the unions. In the U.K. North Sea, there is an independent trade union movement, an uncorrupted judiciary, and a strong culture of investigative journalism. In Azerbaijan, independent unions are not permitted, and those who attempt to organize the workforce face intimidation, sacking, and possible arrest. Opposition political parties and independent media are also severely marginalized.

In Azerbaijan, international oil companies do not recognize independent trades unions, and have no contacts with them. The only active independent union, the Committee for Oil Industry Workers' Rights Protection (COIWRP) has not been able to register as an NGO with the Ministry of Justice. Instead the companies only recognize the official, state-controlled Azerbaijan Trade Union (ATU), the so-called "yellow" union. This union was created in 1997 in a meeting in the main hall of the SOCAR (state oil company) building. According to COIWRP, the hall holds 250 people. The front ten rows of the ATU inauguration meeting were filled with SOCAR managers, including Natiq Aliyev (president of SOCAR). Head of the union Jahangir Aliyev (no relation) was appointed personally by

Natiq Aliyev, and everything Jahangir says must be approved by Natiq. Since 1999, SOCAR's annual report has claimed a progressive attitude to union rights, but this refers only to the official ATU union.

The ATU not only lacks independence, but, according to COIWRP, actively works with SOCAR to undermine the rights of workers. In 1999, a joint decree by SOCAR and the ATU called for changes to three articles of the labor code that had stated that permanent workplaces should not be allowed to employ people on short-term contracts. Following the SOCAR/ATU initiative, this protection was abolished. Now many workers have been put on short contracts, even those who have worked for a long time for a company, can now be switched to short-term contracts and laid off within a year [54].

In 1999, Azerbaijan's labor law was amended with a new article that states that workers may be fined or jailed for protesting. These two new provisions make it easy for companies to neutralize any organizing by workers. The cochair and one of the founders of the COIWRP union, Mirvarie Gahramanly, has been subject to repeated intimidation. She has been arrested three times, the first time in 1998 after she criticized SOCAR vice-president Ilham Aliyev (the son of Heydar Aliyev, the president of Azerbaijan). She was arrested again in January 1999, after she made a statement against SOCAR corruption. When she visited the United States, in March 2002, to meet congressional representatives and to talk to the media about oil industry worker conditions in Azerbaijan, she was first demoted from her job in SOCAR, and then fired. She was then arrested again on her return [55].

Corruption in the oil industry not only undermines the rule of law and democratic practice, but it also affects working conditions and safety. The COIWRP reports one case from 2001 where an oil company allocated and recorded expenditure of $50 each for the purchase of safety suits. The company ended up with inferior suits worth $10 each, which were not fit for their purpose. The remaining $40 was somehow "lost" in the transaction [56].

Corruption also bleeds into discrimination. In Azerbaijan, employees of foreign oil companies are subject to a two-tier system that favors foreign workers over Azerbaijanis, in which Azerbaijani people are only able to get unqualified and unskilled jobs. As a result of this discrimination, Azerbaijanis earn considerably less than foreign staff. Even President Aliyev complained about the wage gap, claiming, in May 2001, that foreigners were earning three times as much as locals [57].

The COIWRP union reports that, when BP hires Azerbaijani people, it selects English-speakers rather than those with technical skills. There is also a strong degree of nepotism, such that it is possible to get a job only if one is a friend or relative of a manager, or of a member of the recruitment staff. This bias affects not only direct company employees. As in the North Sea, many functions are outsourced, and oil companies favor foreign subcontractors over Azerbaijani companies. Tender terms of reference are often weighted in favor of foreign companies, and Azerbaijani companies sometimes struggle even to obtain copies of the terms of reference for tenders [58]. Even for those who do get a job, there is great insecurity. Since 1997, 1,400 oil industry workers have been laid off by foreign companies. Employment contracts offer little or no protection. Some contracts are written only in English, which Azerbaijani speakers have to sign even though they do not understand them.

Evidently, since the signing of the "Contract of the Century" in 1994, there has been no improvement in working conditions in the Azeri oil sector. The building of the Western-sponsored offshore oil fields has led, and now the BTC pipeline will lead, to further growth in the number of onshore jobs, both in the construction and in the operation phases. Unfortunately, there is little confidence that this growth will lead to any improvement in working conditions either onshore or offshore.

7. The Threat to the Regional Environment

According to BP's regional affairs director for the BTC Pipeline, Barry Halton, there is a "showstopper environmental benefit to this project. It will mean that the oil doesn't have to go through the Bosphorus," preventing another 1,000 tanker movements per year through this highly sensitive zone [59]. Halton's argument is that the amount of oil that is currently transported across the Black Sea, via the overcrowded Bosphorus Straits, and into the Mediterranean on its journey from the oil ports of Supsa and Novorossiysk, will not have to increase. However positive this sounds, it should be noted that BP is not offering a "benefit" to the Bosphorus, for example, by reducing the excessive tanker traffic; but rather it is offering to refrain from introducing a further risk by not actually increasing tanker traffic. In fact, BP is responsible for a large part of the increase in Bosphorus tanker traffic since 1997, by pumping oil to Supsa and Novorossiysk.

Unfortunately, the BTC pipeline would merely relocate the problem. A risk not imposed on the Bosphorus would become a risk brought to the Gulf of Iskenderun, on Turkey's southern coast. There, just south of Ceyhan, three supertankers would load at the Yumurtalik terminal every day. The scale of this relocated threat to the environment is abundantly clear to those living near Yumurtalik who are well acquainted with the terrible storms that take place in the Gulf of Iskenderun about twice a year. These storms are called Yarikkaya, which translates as "the rock cut in two pieces" and are infamous for sinking ships [60].

The fishermen of Yumurtalik stand to be some of those most affected by the whole BTC development. In the community of Yumurtalik alone, 180 families are completely dependent for their livelihoods on fishing. The fishermen would be affected in four ways:

- The tanker terminal is a security area in which they are not allowed to fish— thus with the expansion of the terminal they would lose some of their fishing

grounds. Meanwhile, the passage of supertankers from the terminal would both cause disruption and further restrict available fishing areas.
• Their catches of fish would be likely to be reduced due to persistent pollution from the terminal, from discharge of ballast water and of hold-cleaning water.
• In the event of major spills, they would risk sustaining substantial, or devastating damage, to their livelihoods.
• Much of their sales are to people on summer vacations (mainly from the Ceyhan area), an income source that could be reduced if the sea were considered polluted, leading to a decline in tourism.

The experience of the "Early Oil" project gives some cause for concern. Officials of the Supsa port authority worry that they are not being allowed to check tankers in accordance with international conventions, even though the port carries responsibility for spill prevention and contingency plans. BP has supported the argument of shipping companies at Supsa that they should be exempt from regulation [61]. Furthermore, according to the Georgian environmental organization Green Alternatives, the standards of the Supsa oil terminal do not meet guidelines for special zones under the 1973-78 MARPOL Convention for the Prevention of Pollution from Ships, which require oil terminals to be equipped with adequate reception and wastewater facilities [62].

It is also instructive to look at the example of the Trans Alaska Pipeline System, built in the mid-1970s by Alyeska, a consortium led by BP. It was after loading at the Alyeska-run terminal at the southern end of that system that, in March 1989, the Exxon Valdez oil tanker ran aground in Prince William Sound, spilling 258,000 barrels of crude oil and creating one of the world's worst environmental disasters. The TAPS pipeline was, on paper, one of the safest ever built. After sustained public challenges against the project, TAPS was constructed according to technically very sophisticated designs, leading to great confidence that it would be environmentally safe. Yet, as the final chapters of this volume suggest, throughout its operation, and continuing today, the pipeline system has suffered from a lax attitude to safety standards combined with hostility to regulation and harassment of workers and others who have attempted to raise concerns about the safety problems.

Against this background, it is not reassuring that similar promises have been made in BP's consultation leaflet on the BTC, distributed in Azerbaijan, that the pipeline "will be built to the highest international standards" [63]. About Alyeska, BP said in 1976: "this pipeline is being built to conform to the highest standards for quality and safety, thus ensuring both its environmental and operational integrity" [64].

Part of the reason why the Exxon Valdez spill became a major environmental disaster was that responsibility was not clearly defined. The Alyeska consortium, which operated the Valdez terminal, had statutory responsibility and had developed a contingency plan along with regulators, but hours after the grounding it handed over responsibility to the ship owner, Exxon. The companies later shifted responsibility again, publicly blaming the captain of the tanker [65]. In the case of the Turkish section of the BTC pipeline system, including the Yumurtalik terminal, there is the added complication in the assignment of responsibility, that the pipeline would be operated by the Turkish pipeline company Botas, through a turnkey agreement.

Meanwhile, environment group WWF has pointed out that the environmental assessment for the project considers only a worst-case spill in the Gulf of Iskenderun of 10,000 metric tons of oil. Yet the facility is anticipated to be for 80,000-300,000 metric ton tankers. For reference, WWF points out that a 10,000-metric-ton spills is approximately the size of the *Erika* tanker spill off France. *Exxon Valdez* (about 40,000 metric tons), *Braer* (70,000 plus), and *Sea Empress* (84,000) were all much larger and each of these vessels was much smaller (except the *Sea Empress*) than the vessels which would be used at the Ceyhan terminal [66].

Away from the coast there are other threats to the environment in the immediate vicinity of the proposed pipeline. Turkey lies in a major earthquake zone, and on the North Anatolian fault. One of the most serious fault lines in Turkey runs directly from Sivas through Erzincan to Erzurum, exactly the intended route of the Baku-Tbilisi-Ceyhan pipeline. By a conservative estimate, there have been at least seventeen major earthquakes since 1924, measuring from 5.5 to 7.9 on the Richter scale, directly along the pipeline route. Erzincan has been completely destroyed and rebuilt on two separate occasions: after the 1939 earthquake, which measured 7.9 and killed almost 33,000 people, and again, more recently, in 1992, after a 6.8 earthquake killed 653. In 1983, Erzurum was hit by a 6.9 earthquake, which killed nearly 1,200 people. The entire region is permanently under duress. In the first seven months of 2002, there were no fewer than forty-four minor earthquakes (all less than 4.5 on the Richter scale), in various locations along the pipeline route [67].

The BTC pipeline system would be in place for at least forty years—making it almost inevitable that a major earthquake would seriously affect it at some point in its lifetime. BP has addressed the earthquake risk by giving assurances that the pipeline crosses fault lines at an optimized angle. In the TAPS pipeline, BP allowed for earthquakes by building the line such that it could move and bend during earth tremors. In Turkey no such flexibility is set to be in the pipeline, because it would be buried underground.

Finally, the BTC pipeline poses a threat to the environment as an indirect result of military or civil conflict. We have noted above that there is risk of the pipeline coming under attack either as a result of war between states, terrorism, or guerrilla activity. Inevitably, any such attacks on the BTC oil transfer system could result in a major spill. For all the above reasons, there is widespread concern, especially among local and international conservation groups, that the proposed pipeline poses a major threat to the regional environment.

8. The Threat to the Global Environment

The global environmental threat of climate change is a problem that is conclusively accepted by scientists and governments alike. Under the UN Framework Convention on Climate Change, industrialized countries are committed to first stabilizing and then reducing their emissions of greenhouse gases, principally caused by the burning of fossil fuels.

The 2001 report of the world's highest scientific authority on climate change, the United Nations body known as the Intergovernmental Panel on Climate Change (IPCC), is unequivocal: "There is new and stronger evidence that most of the warming observed over the last 50 years is attributable to human activities." The panel predicts that global warming will continue. According to its projections, global temperature will increase by between 1.4 and 5.8 Celsius against 1990 levels by 2100. The IPCC warns that this rate and level of change is "very likely to be without precedent" during at least the past 10,000 years [68]. Scientists have already documented a wide range of impacts that are consistent with global warming. These include changes in sea level, snow cover, the extent of ice and rainfall, along with more persistent, frequent, and intense El Niño events, coral reef bleaching, and shifts in plant and animal habitats, some of which are likely to result in extinction. All these changes impact on human beings, for instance, by affecting water supply, agriculture, infrastructure, and disease patterns.

The distribution of greenhouse gas emissions around the world is highly imbalanced. For example, on average, each person in the United States emits 5.5 metric tons of carbon per year (in the form of carbon dioxide from fossil fuel consumption and cement production), while India's per capita rate is 0.3 metric tons per capita per year [69]. While it is accepted by most governments that the concentrations of greenhouse gases in the atmosphere must be stabilized, by reducing emissions thereof, there are strong arguments that the rights of nations and regions to emit greenhouse gases should be shared equitably on a per capita basis—essentially arguing that the atmosphere is a global commons, and that no one, therefore, has any greater rights to it than anyone else. Such arguments have been made most forcefully by the London-based Global Commons Institute, but are now gaining currency within some governmental and even business circles [70].

In fact, those least responsible for climate change suffer its worst impacts. According to the IPCC: "The impacts of climate change will fall disproportionately upon developing countries and the poor persons within all countries, and thereby exacerbate inequities in health status and access to adequate food, clean water and other resources." This is because climate change will be more severe in tropical and sub tropical regions, where most developing countries are located, and because poorer people are usually more vulnerable in that they have fewer resources to protect themselves.

If one accepts the arguments for equity in distribution of atmospheric rights, one might allow for growth in certain developing countries' per capita emissions, up to an equitable level. This has to be within a framework of global reductions, and, in particular, drastic cuts in the emissions of the more polluting industrialized countries. Within this context, it is contradictory to be bringing new sources of oil to Western markets, which would facilitate an increase rather than a reduction in their fossil fuel burning.

The one million barrels per day of oil passing along the BTC pipeline would contribute 160 million metric tons of the greenhouse gas carbon dioxide to the atmosphere. This is equivalent to nearly 30% of the total emissions of the United Kingdom (557 million metric tons), and two and a half times the amount of emissions the United Kingdom is committed to cutting under the Kyoto Protocol. Carbon dioxide released into the atmosphere has a life span of 50 to 200 years. So, fossil fuels burned today could contribute to global warming for the next two centuries. The operational lifespan of the proposed BTC pipeline is projected to be at least forty years; thus, the pipelines would be bringing oil and gas to the world market until at least 2040. With this in mind, we can calculate that the fossil fuel infrastructure that BP is currently working to put in place would have an impact on the earth's climate stretching to the year 2240.

Thus, in the realm of climate change, the Azerbaijan-Georgia-Turkey pipeline system would have its longest-lasting impact. But this, the greatest of all the pipeline's environmental impacts and one of the greatest of its social impacts, is barely considered in BP's Environmental and Social Impact Assessment study [71]. BP takes responsibility only for the greenhouse gas emissions of the machines building and operating the pipeline, not for those of the oil it would bring to the West. This final issue is clearly the most fundamental, for no matter how safe and sensitive its construction and operation are, it suggests that this pipeline to export Caspian oil to the West should never be built.

RESISTANCE AND PUBLIC RELATIONS MANAGEMENT

In May 2002, seventy-four international nongovernmental organizations sent a letter to the presidents of six of the international financial institutions considering backing the pipeline project. The letter raised concerns about the project including transparency, corruption, poverty, resettlement, ethnic minorities, militarization, and climate change. It also urged the institutions to impose conditions that would mitigate the project's impacts [72].

As we write this chapter, an international campaign on the Baku-Tbilisi-Ceyhan pipeline is gathering momentum. In the autumn of 2002, major demonstrations against the project took place in the Georgian capital of Tbilisi, outside the offices of BP and the Georgian International Operating Company, while several environmental groups have come out with strong criticisms of BP and the project.

This opposition has been fueled by widespread outrage at BP's refusal to consider rerouting the pipeline to avoid the Borjomi mineral springs. It also takes place against a background of complaints from villagers on the impact of the building of the Baku-Supsa "Early Oil" pipeline through Azerbaijan and Georgia by BP in 1998-99. That pipeline caused considerable damage to land and livelihoods, and there was a widely held belief that BP did not keep its promises about social development or employment. Georgian villagers also protested against the BTC pipeline plans during the consultation process through summer 2002 [73].

In Azerbaijan, several NGOs and opposition parties have been critical of the project, despite severe repression by the state authorities. The Caucasus NGO Confederation has published critical comments on the BTC, and in early 2003 a new watchdog, Oil and Bank Watch, was set up. Meanwhile, there have been major protests in the Nardaran district of Baku, against the unfair distribution of oil wealth. This level of opposition is notable for Azerbaijan, where any criticism of state policies is met with intimidation and punishment. Indeed, in February 2003, Ilham Aliyev, the son of president Heydar Aliyev, said on Azerbaijan television that opponents of BTC would be considered opponents of the national interests of Azerbaijan and would therefore be "repulsed" [74].

In Turkey, the strongest protests have been in the port of Yumurtalik, where local people are so frustrated that they are receiving no benefits from the pipeline that they have threatened to blockade construction in protest [75]. As in Azerbaijan, the penalties for criticizing the state in Turkey can be high. However, despite these risks, along the route a number of landowners have threatened protests.

In the United Kingdom, throughout the second half of 2002, and into early 2003, public meetings have taken place opposing the pipeline plans, along with several public demonstrations. On October 28, 2002, a public hearing was held in the House of Lords, questioning the appropriateness of British public money being used to help finance the BTC, with delegates from Azerbaijan, Georgia, Turkey, Alaska, Colombia, and Scotland.

Several important international NGOs have begun to devote substantial resources to the issue, in the United States, Europe, and Japan, as well as in the three host countries. These include Friends of the Earth International, the Kurdish Human Rights Project, World Wide Fund for Nature, Oxfam, Amnesty International, and CEE Bankwatch Network. The latter, an international network spanning twelve countries of Central and Eastern Europe and the Former Soviet Union, has made its campaign against the BTC one of its major priorities [76].

Meanwhile, the international press has regularly reported on the growing concerns over the BTC project—with features appearing in the *Financial Times*, the *Times*, the *Guardian*, the *Observer*, *Agency France Press*, and the *Village Voice*, the *Washington Post* as well as in the Turkish, Azeri, Georgian, and Iranian media.

Vociferous opposition to major infrastructure projects is certainly not uncommon. However, what is particular about this campaign is that it is taking place prior to the construction of the main export route pipeline. More commonly, international opposition begins after construction has started, and particularly during a pipeline's operation phase, when human rights have already been violated, or the environment despoiled.

Part of the reason for the preemptive nature of this campaign is that the late 1980s and 1990s have seen increased international awareness of human rights and environmental issues connected with oil and gas development. From the Exxon Valdez oil spill and the Piper Alpha explosion in the late 1980s, to environment and human rights issues in Nigeria and Colombia in the mid-1990s, there is a growing recognition that the social impact of the oil industry can be severe.

This chapter has highlighted how development of the BTC pipeline project is central to BP's strategy, and how the company is thoroughly committed to it. Meanwhile, there are a number of outstanding social and environmental problems with the project, which presents difficulties for BP in two ways. First, difficulties arise from the fact that since the late 1990s BP has deliberately portrayed itself as environmentally and socially responsible, or even as "Beyond Petroleum." This has become a key part of the company's brand, especially in relation to its internal culture and the morale of staff. If the Baku-Tbilisi-Ceyhan pipeline were to lead to major public criticism of the company for environmental and social damage, this positioning would be set back, or even undermined. Second, and perhaps more significantly, the Baku-Tbilisi-Ceyhan pipeline is far more a political project than an economic one. Therefore, BP is interested in the project only if what chief executive John Browne has referred to as "free money," is offered by governments to subsidize the construction [77].

The structure of the financing of the BTC is already taking shape. BP talks confidently of the pipeline being funded by a 30% equity/70% debt arrangement. This means that 30% of the finance would be provided by the members of the BTC Co. consortium of oil companies, while 70% would be provided by loans from banks, led, supported and guaranteed by taxpayers' money—the International Finance Corporation (IFC, an arm of the World Bank), the European Bank for Reconstruction and Development (EBRD) and national export credit agencies. This gives these banks and international financial institutions a strong degree of influence over the project.

Nongovernmental organizations have argued that, if such public money is offered, the pipeline must be in the public interest, at least to the extent of meeting the guidelines given by the public financial institutions who are approached for funding. This is the lynchpin upon which much of the international campaign has focused, with NGOs pressurizing international finance institutions (IFIs) to ensure that they adhere strictly to their environmental and social guidelines, while questioning the validity of Western governments providing the project with public money.

The BTC Co. consortium, led by BP, aimed for the financing of the pipeline system to be arranged by early 2003; in time for the start of construction in April 2003. However, in December it was announced that the decision on financing by the IFC and the EBRD would be delayed until at least September 2003, due to unresolved environmental and social issues in the project. This was apparently on account of the pressures on the IFIs coming from the international campaign. BTC Co. has surprisingly decided to press ahead with construction regardless. As we write this chapter, there are signs that another delay is possible, which would leave BP and its partners very exposed, as their own budget for the project is likely to expire in autumn 2003.

BP's Strategy to Manage the Issues

BP has adopted three strategies to address these issues. First, the company has ensured, through the Host Government Agreements, that the profitability of the project would not be compromised if any action were taken by the host governments to mitigate its environmental and social impacts. These agreements either exempt the pipeline from any such actions, or otherwise ensure compensation for BP and its partners from the governments. Furthermore, the HGAs specifically indemnify the oil company consortium against legal liability for any adverse impacts.

Second, BP has accepted the requirement to improve the environmental and social aspects of the project on a voluntary basis only. For at least three constituencies—the general public, the public financial institutions, and its own employees—the project is thus described as beneficial. Meanwhile, BP is not legally committed to keep any of its promises. The experience of the "Early Oil" pipeline from Baku to Supsa indicates that promises made by the company in the past were not kept. While these promises limited opposition to the Baku-Supsa pipeline, this approach is less likely to be effective now with those communities that feel they have already been betrayed once. BP's voluntarist approach is especially targeted at international financial institutions, which would not be able to publicly justify their support for the project unless there are public benefits. The most notable aspect of BP's voluntarism is its emphasis on social investment projects [78].

The third aspect of BP's strategy is its tactic of entering into private dialogues, or other constructive relationships, with NGOs. This has been pursued to the greatest extent in Azerbaijan, where in November 2002, a number of NGOs were sponsored by BP to launch the "International Public Support Coalition for the Baku-Tbilisi-Ceyhan Pipeline." Meanwhile, BP has been reluctant to debate these issues publicly, declining an invitation to discuss the project in the British House of Lords in October 2002, and failing to invite some of the key NGOs working on the project to a private NGO seminar in March 2003 [79].

Managing the Issue by Outsourcing Responsibility

The oil industry is familiar with the concept of "outsourcing." Very often up to 90% of the staff working on oil installations are employed not by the company that owns and operates the installation, but by its contractors, by engineering, drilling, geological, construction, catering, or other contracting companies.

Exactly this process, familiar at the operational level of oil platforms and refineries, can now be seen at the corporate, management level of oil companies, a trend that has taken place mainly over the past twenty years. At this level, the organizational transformation process in BP is well illustrated by a parallel architectural transformation.

Thirty years ago, BP's corporate center was a unified institution that carried out all its work "in-house." It was based in the many-storied office block that was its headquarters at the time, the Britannic Tower in the city of London. On the top floors were the offices of the chief executive and of the board, while further down below were the offices of the company accountants, the company personnel department, the company legal department, the company advertising department, and so on. The tower symbolized the nature and structure of the corporation at that time; a large hierarchical block.

Today, BP is less like a "block" and more like a "web" of interconnecting companies, contractors and other institutions. Its corporate headquarters are split between 1 St. James Square, in Piccadilly, London, and Britannic House in Finsbury Circus, both much smaller, terraced office buildings. In these, the core coordinating functions of the company are carried out, while a vast range of company activities is "outsourced" to other smaller companies and institutions. For example, BP's accounts are no longer kept by people directly on BP's payroll, but by employees of accounting giant PricewaterhouseCoopers in London and in Portugal. BP's global human resources function, as the personnel department is now known, is today partly carried out by Exult, a California-based company.

This same process of outsourcing is at work in the BTC pipeline system. A wide range of companies is carrying out work on the project on behalf of BP, as illustrated in the diagram. Engineering is outsourced to the U.S. company, Bechtel; financial advice to Lazard Brothers in London; environmental impact assessments to the consultancies ERM and URS; publications to the agency McQuillan Young, also in London, and so on.

The notion that these outsourced companies and organizations are working on behalf of BP merits closer inspection. Although BP is the operator of the BTC pipeline, this is not because it owns the project in its entirety, but rather because it is the lead company in the consortium of companies that together are the sponsors of the pipeline.

What does this extended web of interconnecting companies mean for establishing responsibility if something goes wrong? When BP's involvement in human rights abuses in Colombia was uncovered, it led to the sacking of

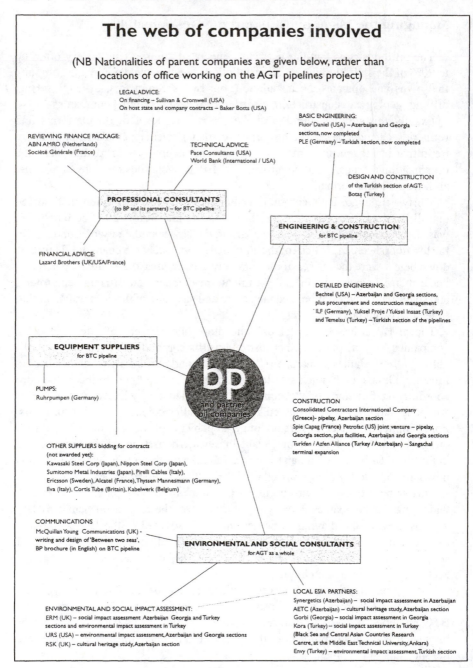

The web of companies involved

(NB Nationalities of parent companies are given below, rather than
locations of office working on the AGT pipelines project)

LEGAL ADVICE:
On financing – Sullivan & Cromwell (USA)
On host state and company contracts – Baker Botts (USA)

BASIC ENGINEERING:
Fluor Daniel (USA) – Azerbaijan and Georgia
sections, now completed
PLE (Germany) – Turkish section, now completed

REVIEWING FINANCE PACKAGE:
ABN AMRO (Netherlands)
Société Générale (France)

TECHNICAL ADVICE:
Pace Consultants (USA)
World Bank (International / USA)

DESIGN AND CONSTRUCTION
of the Turkish section of AGT:
Botaş (Turkey)

PROFESSIONAL CONSULTANTS
(to BP and its partners) – for BTC pipeline

ENGINEERING & CONSTRUCTION
for BTC pipeline

FINANCIAL ADVICE:
Lazard Brothers (UK/USA/France)

DETAILED ENGINEERING:
Bechtel (USA) – Azerbaijan and Georgia sections,
plus procurement and construction management
ILF (Germany), Yuksel Proje / Yuksel Insaat (Turkey)
and Temelsu (Turkey) – Turkish section of the pipelines

EQUIPMENT SUPPLIERS
for BTC pipeline

PUMPS:
Ruhrpumpen (Germany)

CONSTRUCTION
Consolidated Contractors International Company
(Greece)- pipelay, Azerbaijan section
Spie Capag (France) Petrofac (US) joint venture – pipelay,
Georgia section, plus facilities, Azerbaijan and Georgia sections
Turkfen / Azfen Alliance (Turkey / Azerbaijan) – Sangachal
terminal expansion

OTHER SUPPLIERS bidding for contracts
(not awarded yet):
Kawasaki Steel Corp (Japan), Nippon Steel Corp (Japan),
Sumitomo Metal Industries (Japan), Pirelli Cables (Italy),
Ericsson (Sweden), Alcatel (France), Thyssen Mannesmann (Germany),
Ilva (Italy), Cortis Tube (Britain), Kabelwerk (Belgium)

COMMUNICATIONS
McQuillan Young Communications (UK) -
writing and design of 'Between two seas',
BP brochure (in English) on BTC pipeline

ENVIRONMENTAL AND SOCIAL CONSULTANTS
for AGT as a whole

LOCAL ESIA PARTNERS:
Synergetics (Azerbaijan) – social impact assessment in Azerbaijan
AETC (Azerbaijan) – cultural heritage study, Azerbaijan section
Gorbi (Georgia) – social impact assessment in Georgia
Kora (Turkey) – social impact assessment in Turkey
(Black Sea and Central Asian Countries Research
Centre, at the Middle East Technical University, Ankara)
Envy (Turkey) – environmental impact assessment, Turkish section

ENVIRONMENTAL AND SOCIAL IMPACT ASSESSMENT:
ERM (UK) – social impact assessment Azerbaijan Georgia and Turkey
sections and environmental impact assessment in Turkey
URS (USA) – environmental impact assessment, Azerbaijan and Georgia sections
RSK (UK) – cultural heritage study, Azerbaijan section

Figure 2. The web of companies involved in the BTC.

Roger Brown, a manager of BP's security contractor, Defence Systems Colombia (DSC), and publicly blamed Brown and DSC for any malpractice. In the North Sea, outsourced engineering, geological, construction, and other contractors are forced to bid for contracts with BP. Generally those with the lower costs get the work. As a result, pay, conditions, and safety are far worse for employees of contractors (over 80 perent of the North Sea workforce) than for those directly employed by BP.

It is a complex web of companies and institutions that drives forward the pipelines project, that creates the sheer momentum of BTC, and it is also this complex web that helps to manage public opposition. Let us reflect upon this complex web in the context of a leaflet, which was a key tool in the process of conducting interviews in villages in Azerbaijan as part of the environmental and social impact study. Consider the chain of responsibility in the consultation process of the BTC pipeline. The person who conducted the interviews as part of the Environmental and Social Impact Assessment may have been employed by the Baku-based firm, Synergetics. This company is in turn contracted by ERM. ERM-Baku is itself a subsidiary of ERM in London, which has gained the contract for this work from BP Exploration Azerbaijan. BP is the operator of the pipeline projects on behalf of the BTC Co. consortium, to whom it is answerable. The members of BTC Co. are only the minority financiers of the BTC project, however, and thus have to negotiate with the major financiers, including the International Finance Corporation and the European Bank for Reconstruction and Development, together with several export credit agencies and commercial banks.

When the affected villager in Azerbaijan talks with the interviewer who hands him or her a copy of the leaflet, does he or she realize that they are not really talking to the company, not really talking to "the people who are building the pipeline?" And as for the employee of Synergetics who conducts the interviews, how much does this person know of the true nature of the web that they are representing? How much does this employee feel personally responsible for what he or she is representing? And how much anxiety does the employee feel about the possibility of things going wrong, of the pipeline having an adverse environmental and social impact?

THE STRUGGLE OVER POSSIBLE FUTURES

At the time of writing, the future of the Baku-Tbilisi-Ceyhan Pipeline looks less certain that it did a year ago in early 2002. Nonetheless, the intensity of the "pressure to build" from the host states, foreign powers, and from the multinational oil corporations led by BP, is such that it seems almost inconceivable that this project could fail to go ahead. However, as we have described, resistance to the pipeline is growing, both locally and internationally, and this may yet overcome the seemingly insurmountable odds to create a different future to that conceived of by BP and its partners.

ENDNOTES

1. J. McNeill, *Something New Under the Sun: An Environmental History of the Twentieth Century* (London: Penguin, 2000), 304.
2. D. Yergin, *The Prize* (New York: Simon and Schuster, 1991), 59.
3. D. Leppard, P. Nuki, and G. Walsh, "BP Accused of Backing 'Arms for Oil' Coup," *Sunday Times*, March 26, 2000,
4. S. Smith, *Allah's Mountains: Politics and War in the Russian Caucasus* (London and New York: IB Tauris 1998), 73.
5. M. Lelyveld, "Wage Gap Becomes Sore Point," Radio Free Europe—Radio Liberty, May 10, 2001, www.rferl.org/; Radio Free Europe/Radio Liberty, "Turkey: Slashed Gas Forecast May Spell Trouble for Neighbours," January 4, 2002, www.rferl.org/; Y. Solylemez, "Turkey as an Energy Terminal in the 21st Century," *Turkish Daily News Special*, February 15, 2002.
6. S. Anderson and J. Cavanagh, "Top 200—The Rise of Corporate Global Power," December 4, 2000 (Washington, DC: Institute for Policy Studies).
7. BP, *Annual Accounts*, 2001, 6.
8. World Bank, *World Development Indicators Database: Total GDP 2001* (Washington, DC: August 2002).
9. D. Morgan and D.B. Ottaway, series of three articles: "Azerbaijan's Riches Alter the Chessboard," "Grasping the Potential," and "A British Coup," *Washington Post*, October 4, 1998, A1-A3.
10. J. H. Bamberg, *British Petroleum and Global Oil, 1950-1975: The Challenge of Nationalism.* Vol. 3 of *The History of British Petroleum* (Cambridge: Cambridge University Press, 2001).
11. BP, *Annual Accounts*, 2000, 6.
12. "BP Fights back at US Regulator, *Daily Telegraph* March 3, 2000 (London); "Protecting a Precious Commodity in a Volatile State," *Financial Times*, March 16, 2000.
13. "Bush to Attack Gore on Oil Ownership," *Financial Times*, October 2, 2000.
14. R. Paniguian, BP Group, vice president for the Caspian and Middle East, presentation to 2002 Deutsche Bank Oil and Gas Conference, London, May 2002.
15. BP, Financial and Operating Information 1997-2001 (London, 2001).
16. Kazakh Commercial Television (Almaty), "Building of Baku-Ceyhan Oil Pipeline Starts in Turkey—Kazakh TV," in Russian, 1030 GMT, June 18, 2002, recorded and translated by BBC Monitoring Central Asia Unit; Interfax News Agency News Bulletin, "Georgia Starts Implementing Baku-Tbilisi-Ceyhan Project—Shevardnadze," January 13, 2002; BBC News, "Caspian Oil Project Forges Ahead," September 18, 2002; Agence France Presse, "Turkey Starts Work on East-West Oil Pipeline," September 26, 2002; AssA-Irada, "BTC Construction Starts in Turkey," December 10, 2002, recorded by Financial Times Information.
17. Press Release from Cornerhouse, FOEI (Amsterdam), CRBM, KHRP, PLATFORM, CEE Bankwatch Network (Prague), Ilisu Dam Campaign, "Oil Companies Colonise Turkey: MAI by the Back Door?" August 30, 2002.
18. Campagna per la Riforma della Banca Mondiale (Rome), Kurdish Human Rights Project (London), The Corner House (Sturminster Newton, Dorset, UK), Ilisu Dam Campaign (Oxford, UK), and Platform (London), "Preliminary Analysis of the Implications of the Host Government Agreement Between Turkey and the BTC Consortium," October 2002.

19. Host Government Agreement between and among the Government of the Republic of Turkey and the State Oil Company of the Azerbaijan Republic, BP Exploration (Caspian Sea) Ltd, Statoil BTC Caspian AS, Ramco Hazar Energy Limited, Turkiye Petrolleri AO, Unocal BTC Pipeline Ltd, Itochu Oil Exploration (Azerbaijan) Inc., and Delta Hess (BTC) Limited, October 19, 2000.

20. Corner House, "Oil Companies Colonise Turkey." See [17].

21. D. Woodward and N. Aliyev, letter to Eduard Shevardnadze, November 7, 2002; reproduced on Web site of CEE Bankwatch Network, at:
www.bankwatch.org/issues/oilclima/baku-ceyhan/downloads/letter-shevardnadze-1102.pdf.

22. Rustavi-2 TV (Tbilisi), in Georgian, 1700 GMT, November 25, 2002, recorded and translated by BBC Monitoring Former Soviet Union—Political

23. N. Chkhobadze, letter to John Browne, November 26, 2002; reproduced on Web site of CEE Bankwatch Network:
www.bankwatch.org/issues/oilclima/baku-ceyhan/downloads/letter_georgianminister_1102.doc.

24. Transparency International, Corruption Perceptions Index 2002, August 2002.

25. L. Boulton, "Turkey Set to Unveil Action Plan to Fight Corruption," *Financial Times*, February 6, 2002,

26. Eurasianet, "Rigged Bid Allegations Halt World Bank Loan," October 17, 2002; available at: www.eurasianet.org/departments/business/articles/eav101702a_pr.shtml.

27. Sunday Business, "Lazard Win Puts Caspian Oil Deal Firmly on Line," July 1, 2001.

28. G. Muttitt and J. Marriott, "Some Common Concerns—Imagining BP's Azerbaijan-Georgia-Turkey Pipelines System" (London: PLATFORM, the Corner House, Friends of the Earth International, Campagna per la Riforma della Banca Mondiale, CEE Bankwatch Network & Kurdish Human Rights Project, 2002), ch. 2.

29. Ibid., ch. 8.

30. Caucasus Environmental NGO Network, CENN-INFO mailing, "Uncertain Future of Supsa Port," July 10, 2002.

31. A. Higginbottom, "BP's Colombian Pipeline Subsidiaries Have Driven Peasants off Their Land," Colombia Solidarity Campaign, January 2003.

32. International Fact-Finding Mission, Green Alternative (Tbilisi), CEE Bankwatch, Campagna per la Riforma della Banca Mondiale, PLATFORM, Friends of the Earth US (Washington, DC), Bank Information Center (Washington, DC), Preliminary Report: Azerbaijan, Georgia, Turkey Pipelines project, Georgian Section, July 2002.

33. International Fact-Finding Mission, International Fact Finding Mission (Campagna per la Riforma della Banca Mondiale, Kurdish Human Rights Project, The Corner House, Ilisu Dam Campaign and PLATFORM), Preliminary Report: AGT Pipelines project, Turkish Section, August 2002.

34. International Fact-Finding Mission, see [32].

35. M. Ross, *Extractive Sectors and the Poor* (Boston: Oxfam America, 2001), 4.

36. M. Kaldor and Y. Said, "Oil and Human Rights in Azerbaijan," in *Human Rights and the Oil Industry*, ed. A. Edie, H. Bergesen, and P. Goyer (Oxford: Intersentia, 2000), 96.

37. J. Strohmeyer, *Extreme Conditions: Big Oil and the Transformation of Alaska* (Anchorage: Cascade Press, 1993.

38. M. Corso, "A Look at a Georgian Port Along the Proposed Caspian Oil Route," Eurasianet, January 2, 2002; available at: www.eurasianet.org/departments/culture/articles/eav020102.shtml.
39. E-mail from Badri Japaridze (managing director, Georgia Glass & Mineral Water Company) to Nino Gujaraidze (Green Alternative), January 13, 2003.
40. International Fact-Finding Mission, Second International Fact Finding Mission to Baku-Tbilisi-Ceyhan Pipeline, Turkish Section (Campagna per la Riforma della Banca Mondiale, Kurdish Human Rights Project, The Corner House and PLATFORM), Human Rights and Environment Report, May 2003.
41. International Fact-Finding Mission, see [32].
42. Central Intelligence Agency, *World Factbook 2002* (Washington, DC: CIA, 2002).
43. R. Mirqadirov, "Russia Disturbed at Plans To Reoutfit Azerbaijan's Armed Forces: Moscow Is Especially Peeved at Turkey's Possible Involvement," *Baku Zerkalo*, April 4, 2002.
44. Interfax News Agency, "BP Arranging Security for Gas Pipeline in Georgia," July 4, 2001 (Moscow).
45. Georgian Radio (Tbilisi), "Georgian President Confident About Success of Oil, Gas Pipeline Projects," in Georgian, 0605 GMT, June 25, 2001, recorded and translated by BBC Monitoring Former Soviet Union—Political.
46. N. Paton Walsh, "Oil Fuels US Army Role in Georgia," *Observer*, May 12, 2002.
47. Civil Georgia magazine, "Major Birds in the Air, Northrop Grumman to Fly over Georgia," January 8, 2003 (Tblisi: United Nations Association of Georgia).
48. J. Kotler, "Death Toll Mounts, Guerrilla Role Probed in Pipeline Explosion," *Associated Press*, October 19, 1998.
49. D.I. Hoffman, "Oil and Development in Post-Soviet Azerbaijan," *NBR Analysis* 10, no. 3 (August 1999): 5-28.
50. Muttitt and Marriott, "Some Common Concerns," 118-119. See [28].
51. *Ekho* (newspaper, Baku), "USA Warns of Al-Qaida Threat to Azeri Oil Pipelines: Baku paper," reproduced by BBC Monitoring, December 21, 2002.
52. KHRP (Kurdish Human Rights Project) press release, "Council of Europe Adopts New Resolution on Turkish Security Forces in Light of Continuing Human Rights Abuses," July 10, 2002 (London).
53. J. Eastham, "BP and the Baku Pipeline: Whose Standards Are High Enough?" on Web site of *Ethical Corporation* magazine, January 27, 2003 (London); available at: www.ethicalcorp.com/login.asp?mode=premium&Referrer=content%2Easp%3F ContentID%3D352.
54. International Fact-Finding Mission, see [55].
55. International Fact-Finding Mission, International Fact Finding Mission (Green Alternative, National Ecological Centre of Ukraine, CEE Bankwatch, Campagna per la Riforma della Banca Mondiale, PLATFORM, Friends of the Earth US, Bank Information Center, Ilisu Dam Campaign, The Corner House, Kurdish Human Rights Project), Preliminary Report: Azerbaijan, Georgia, Turkey Pipelines project, Azerbaijan Section, September 2002.
56. Ibid.
57. See [5].
58. See [55].

59. B. Halton, interview with Caspar Henderson Globolog column, "The Baku–Ceyhan Oil Pipeline: BP Replies," December 3, 2002; available at: www.opendemocracy.net.

60. International Fact-Finding Mission, see [33].

61. "Uncertain Future of Supsa Port," see [30].

62. M. Kochladze, "Kolkhety Lowland—Towards Sustainable Development?!" Tbilisi: Green Alternative and CEE Bankwatch Network, June 2001.

63. BP, Financial and Operating Information, see [15].

64. *Alyeska Reports* newsletter 2, no. 3 (July 1976): 16, quoted in Townsend Environmental, "The Promises Issue—Commitments and Representations by Alyeska and Its Owner Companies Regarding the Trans Alaska Pipeline System," report for Chuck Hamel and Dan Lawn (undated).

65. A. Rowell, "The Exxon Valdez: A Case of Corporate Virtual Reality," March 1994, Amsterdam: Greenpeace International.

66. WWF, 2002, table of WWF concerns vs BTC response.

67. Boğaziçi Üniversitesi, Kandilli Rasathanesi ve Deprem Araştırma Enstitüsü (Kandilli Observatory and Earthquake Research Centre), latest earthquakes, listed on Web site: www.koeri.boun.edu.tr/.

68. IPCC (Intergovernmental Panel on Climate Change), Third Assessment Report, Climate Change 2001: Synthesis Report, Summary for Policy Makers, 2001.

69. G. Marland, T.A. Boden, and R. J. Andres, "Global, Regional, and National Fossil Fuel CO_2 Emissions," in Trends: A Compendium of Data on Global Change, Carbon Dioxide Information Analysis Center, Oak Ridge National Laboratory, U.S. Department of Energy (Oak Ridge, TN: 2002).

70. Global Commons Institute; see Web site: www.gci.org.uk/.

71. BTC Co. Environmental and Social Overview: Baku-Tbilisi-Ceyhan Pipeline Project (summary of project ESIAs for Azerbaijan, Georgia and Turkey), September 2002.

72. Kochladze, "Kolkhety Lowland" see [62].

73. G. Kupatadze, "Georgian Villagers Haggle with Oil Giant," IWPR Caucasus Reporting Service, no. 140, August 1, 2002 (London).

74. Media-Press News Agency (Baku), "Azeri Leader's Son Says Armenia Behind Attempts to Thwart Strategic Pipeline," in Russian, 1415 GMT, February 24, 2003, recorded and translated by BBC Monitoring International Reports, February 25, 2003.

75. R. Khatchadourian, "Crude Measures: At the Gates of a Global Oil Rush, Turkish Fishermen Threaten a Blockade," *Village Voice*, February 12-18, 2003 (New York).

76. See: www.bankwatch.org.

77. R. Corzine, "Wisdom of Baku Pipeline Queried," *Financial Times*, November 4, 1998, 4.

78. BTC Co., "Breaking New Ground: Working with the Community to Enhance the Social Benefits of Oil Development and Export," March 2003.

79. Lustgarten, Anders, and N. Hildyard, "Experts' Seminar on BP's Pipeline Record and Baku-Ceyhan Pipeline," seminar report, October 28, 2002 (Oxford: Baku Ceyhan Campaign).

CHAPTER 5

Northern Exposure

Michael Gillard, Melissa Jones,
and Andrew Rowell

INTRODUCTION

On April 1, 1999, BP Amoco, Britain's number one company, announced its intention to take over Atlantic Richfield Co. (ARCO), the American oil giant that made its name and fortune from three decades of exploitation of Alaska's North Slope. The announcement, made to a stock market fueled by merger mania, was no April Fools. The $30 billion acquisition promised BP a near monopoly on oil in Alaska. "We shall also become the largest non-state owned oil producer in the world, as well as the largest oil and gas producer in both the United States and the United Kingdom," BP Amoco cochairman, Peter Sutherland boasted to reporters. The newly merged BP Amoco-ARCO giant would control 74% of North Slope oil fields and 72% of the Trans Alaska Pipeline System (TAPS), which snakes its way south through 800 miles of unforgiving terrain.

The TAPS stands stark against the changing landscape, suspended on huge stilts above the often frozen tundra. Crossing arctic mountain ranges, plains, seismic faults, and rivers and sometimes burrowing beneath the frozen earth, TAPS is the umbilical cord for Alaska's oil industry. From the North Slope oil fields to the sprawling Valdez Marine terminal, it takes nearly five days for the crude to reach tankers docking almost daily in Prince William Sound. The ecosystems and desolate wildlife refuges criss-crossed by TAPS are home to moose, wolves, polar bears, and grizzlies. Bald eagles, the national symbol, can also be seen soaring above the migrating caribou herds. But for the communities living in the pipeline corridor and near remote pumping stations, the shimmering outline and rumble of TAPS is a reminder that this metallic cash cow and those who control it deliver 80% of state revenue.

A SEMBLANCE OF COMPETITION

The champagne was still on ice at BP's London headquarters as the proposed merger awaited the final result of antitrust investigations in Alaska and Washington. Alaska governor, Tony Knowles, had demanded stiff terms in order to ensure competition. He wanted BP Amoco to divest just over 360,000 acres of land leased from the state for exploration and development, which in any case was a legal requirement under state law, and for the oil giant to sell off some producing oil fields to create a semblance of competition. Even with these concessions, the self-styled green oil giant would still have unrivaled power to further influence key public policy debates on future exploration areas in the state such as the coveted oil and gas inside the Arctic National Wildlife Reserve, also known as the American Serengeti.

At the beginning of September 1999, ARCO and BP Amoco shareholders met separately to decide on the merger. They voted overwhelmingly—97% and 99%, respectively—in favor of the acquisition. And, problematically for Governor Knowles, so too did the fund managers for the Alaskan state, which owns 2.7 million shares in BP Amoco and 95,000 shares in ARCO, collectively worth $71 million. Although most people expected the merger to go through, the debate in Alaska nevertheless adopted a particularly fiery tone. One local congressman even raised the spectre of a "neocolonial state"—language normally used by peasant farmer communities fighting the excesses of multinationals operating in the underdeveloped world.

To neutralize criticism, BP Amoco dipped into its enormous PR budget and bombarded Alaskans with wholesome television ads extolling the local benefits of "downsizing" operational costs and 'upsizing' shareholder dividends and boardroom bonuses. Safety and pipeline integrity, viewers were assured, would remain a number one priority for Alyeska, the company that operates TAPS and the Valdez Marine Terminal on behalf of the consortium led by BP Amoco, the majority shareholder with 50%.

Eventually, to make the deal more palatable and neutralize antitrust legal action, the two companies agreed with the state to sell some of their Alaska holdings, reducing their combined share of the state's oil production from 70% to 55%. The Alyeska pipeline carries more than 15% of America's domestic oil production servicing the economically vital West Coast "downstream" oil industry. The states of California, Washington, and Oregon and the Federal Trade Commission went to federal court in San Francisco in February 1999 over concerns that the merger would give BP monopoly-like control not only over Alaska North Slope crude oil production but also over sales to West Coast refineries in violation of antitrust laws. After a year of delay caused by legal action, the merger deal received approval in April 2000, conditional on the sale of ARCO's Alaska assets to Phillips Petroleum. Nevertheless, with its ARCO acquisition, BP Amoco now owned 27% of the crude oil and natural gas tapped from Alaska's North Slope at Prudhoe Bay, and at the same time became the world's second largest nongovernment-owned oil company.)

Alyeska, named after the native word for mainland, had other important shareholders like ARCO, Exxon, and Mobil. But it was a BP man who had held the last three presidencies. Earlier in 1999 there was cause for a more silent celebration inside the consortium. Alyeska president, Bob Malone, received warm corporate back slaps from the vulnerable owners for getting them through the tenth anniversary of the Exxon Valdez oil disaster, which fell that year only days before the merger was announced. Some insiders believed Malone was appointed specifically for the crucial task of persuading the world that this "dark chapter" in Alyeska's history could never happen again. The muted celebration over this corporate sleight of hand was short-lived however. For while Malone was spinning the media tales of state-of-the-art equipment, lessons learned, environmental rejuvenation, and transparency, a collection of his senior employees were preparing evidence of impending disaster, forged inspection reports, a culture of intimidation, and "lip service" to safety.

THE LETTER

On July 12, 1999, a fourteen-page letter with supporting evidence from six anonymous Alyeska whistleblowers arrived on the desks of BP Amoco chief executive, John Browne in London, two Democratic congressmen in Washington, and interior secretary, Bruce Babbitt. The whistleblowers' concerns and personal testimony were simultaneously revealed in the *Guardian* newspaper in London. The six men and women said they represented a larger group of employees who were too afraid to speak out because of an entrenched culture of harassment and retaliation in the Alaskan oil industry. Their motivation, they said, was the safety of the pipeline, its employees, and the fragile Alaskan environment. Their convincing evidence exposed a life-threatening "gamble" by Alyeska with all three. A battle between safety and the bottom line—one where senior oil executives and their contractors, motivated by budget schedules and bonuses, actively undermined technicians and inspectors tasked with upholding safety-related checks and balances. "I am just so surprised when (Alyeska) goes another day, week, month without an accident," said one whistleblower. Another went further, believing the disaster will be worse than Exxon Valdez spill because human life will be lost: "It's not a matter of *if* it is going to happen, it's *when* it is going to happen."

The Exxon Valdez spill occurred twenty-five miles offshore. But the whistleblowers feared the next disaster would occur somewhere along the pipeline or at the Valdez Marine Terminal. In particular, they were concerned about the Tanker Vapor Recovery System (TVRS), which captures volatile and potentially harmful gases as crude oil is loaded onto tankers at Valdez. The whistleblowers also described a twenty-two-year-old leaking oil pipeline carrying one million barrels per day, whose owners wish to extend its lifetime without spending the necessary money to make it safe. It was the classic bandage-over-retrofit approach. "I don't want to be associated with a situation where the pipeline ruptures and we spill oil all over the tundra or somebody gets seriously injured. If we keep allowing things to happen it's going to get somebody killed. It is not what we promised we would do," said one whistleblower. The group provided the government and Alaskans with a catalogue of offenses and mismanagement. They said they were forced to speak out because these issues had been raised with Alyeska executives, but the company had turned a blind eye or covered up the problems. "It's more dangerous now than it ever was because Alyeksa is being run by spin-doctors," said one. Collectively they believed that Alyeska's Quality Assurance Program (QAP), which is vital to the safe operation of TAPS, represented an "imminent threat." It cannot be regarded as safe, and noncompliance with the QAP could cause death, severe injury, uncontained oil spills, and narrow design safety margins.

REVELATIONS

Specifically, the whistleblowers provided the government with evidence about major compliance failures, illegalities and mismanagement. These included claims that:

- Alyeska executives turned a blind eye to "the culture of harassment, intimidation, retaliation, and discrimination (HIRD)."
- Alyeska's quality assurance program was "deliberately undermined" by middle management. "The pipeline operates as a system, and one of the key components is the quality program. If it is not working properly, then the pipeline cannot be said to be working properly," said one whistleblower.
- The true state of pipeline corrosion was unknown and Alyeska was "extremely lucky" there had been no major spill since 1996 when 30,000 gallons leaked near a river. According to documents in our possession, in 1998 Alyeska found 60% corrosion of one pipeline section extending to one of the welds that holds it together. A U.S. pipeline safety report admitted "current technology does not provide for accurate detection of corrosion under the weld." There are an estimated 71,000 welds on TAPS.
- Record keeping was "totally dysfunctional" and illegal under Alyeska's "Right of Way" lease agreement with the government. Records, like engineering designs, are "critical" to determining the condition of and maintaining the pipeline. "Without this knowledge, incongruent design features could be installed that could lead to disaster."
- Alyeska had spent more than $90 million since the mid-1970s trying to correct shoddy record keeping, but the whistleblowers said this effort had been unsuccessful, and they accused Alyeska of "hiding" the seriousness of these problems from government regulators.

- Maintenance and inspection records before 1996 were lost, and audit results were falsified to make it seem otherwise.
- Alyeska executive management instructed middle managers "to disregard and/or circumvent" a series of legally binding compliance manuals and codes of conduct, and to "tone down, alter or delete negative reports including internal audits and surveillance reports." To issue such negative reports, they were told, could "negatively influence" their employment prospects.
- The whistleblowers believed that the combination of volatile gases, mismanagement, procedural violations, and hardware failures, represented all the conditions necessary for a fatal explosion at the Tanker Vapor Recovery System. Design changes on the TVRS did not comply with the quality program and involved "numerous deviations and circumventions." Inspection documents were also falsified; therefore, the TVRS could not be qualified as safe. Internal Alyeska documents seen by the authors also showed that its Quality Plan was not "consistent" with the one approved by regulators.
- The TVRS safety valves were designed to shut the system down in an emergency. Internal U.S. government documents also seen by the authors showed that for the first nine months of the TVRS's operation, these safety valves were not qualified as safe.

U.S. government regulators had also raised their own concerns about the safety of the TAPS prior to these revelations. In March 1999, the Office of Pipeline Safety fined Alyeska for code violations. In April that year, leaked documents showed that Dan Lawn, an outspoken local government regulator, called for the TVRS to be "shut down" due to continuing operational and procedural violations. Lawn warned of "dire consequences" if Alyeska did not stop "improvising on the fly." He wrote: "I believe we have come close (to a disaster), at least twice, in the last two or three months."

In ending their "revelations" letter, the whistleblowers called for "immediate intervention." Specifically, they wanted Secretary of the Interior Bruce Babbitt and John Browne at BP Amoco to send independent auditors to verify the evidence they were willing to provide. "If a third party audit came in tomorrow they would have many of the repeat findings (from an earlier 1993 audit) which would put in question the renewal of the lease," said one whistleblower.

The letter also made clear the group of six's complete disregard for the government regulators. "The Joint Pipeline Office, the U.S. Coast Guard, and local U.S. Office of Pipeline Safety are all totally useless and most untrustworthy. They are, in fact, allied with Alyeska in squelching dissent from concerned employees." As for Alyeska, history, they suggested, has shown that the company was "not capable of policing their own behavior" despite the willingness of government regulators to let them.

DISASTER

In 1990, the state Oil Spill Commission was formed after the Exxon Valdez spill of 11 million gallons in Prince William Sound. It concluded that Exxon, BP, ARCO, Mobil, and the government had all been complacent. "Privatization, self-regulation and neglect" were also identified as root causes of the spill. According to the commission "the disaster could have been prevented by simple adherence to the original rules" but "concern for profits . . . obliterated concern for safe operations."

Democratic Congressman George Miller later testified that Alyeska and its owners "knew that they could not effectively respond to a spill in Prince William Sound" and "had secretly decided (they) would not." Miller is one of the two congressmen who received the whistleblowers' letter in July 1999.

The six senior employees felt the government regulator was unwilling to bite the hand that feeds it. Meanwhile, Alyeska was only too willing to take the financial penalties when it occasionally got caught ignoring safety controls. As Congressman Miller also pointed out back in 1990, acting out of compliance is cheaper than acting in compliance. In other words, it costs Alyeska less to bandage the problems as they arise than to carry out a proper retrofit of an aging pipeline at the end of its design life, or keeping its legally binding promises to the Alaskan people and Washington.

DEATH THREATS

It was in 1993 that the last group of senior inspectors blew the whistle on Alyeska's deliberate failure to honor its commitments to safety and the environment so soon after the promises resulting from the Valdez spill. There followed explosive congressional hearings in Washington where Alyeska's major owners were heavily criticized for their lack of transparency and accountability. Democratic committee chairman, Congressman John Dingell, reminded the oil companies of Alyeska's record of "harassment and intimidation of inspectors, including deaths threats" and threats of broken arms if Nonconformance Reports were written. "One wonders how richly stocked is Alyeska's closet with an assortment of skeletons involving mismanagement, misbehavior and perhaps worse?" remarked the congressman, who also received the whistleblowers' letter.

In 1993, a battered Alyeska was forced to comply with a massive audit repair program to solve the "major problems" its executives eventually admitted. Repair schedules were set and agreed to, but six years later the new whistleblowers claim that many of the same "imminent threats" identified in that 1993 audit remain unaddressed. This, they said, was one of their main reasons for speaking out in July. Rather than spend money ensuring full compliance with safety and quality procedures, the whistleblowers accuse Alyeska of adopting the language of change while continuing with the practice of cost-and-corner cutting, intimidation, and blacklists.

SPEAKING OUT

Speaking out in Alaska remains a dangerous decision, as the recent case of senior engineering designer, Jeannie Sayre, showed. In June 1999, the U.S. Department of Labor upheld Sayre's complaint of continued unlawful harassment by Alyeska and a subcontractor. Sayre was working in a remote pump station and claimed she had been sacked for reporting safety compliance failures on the pipeline fire protection system. Her lawyers described Alyeska president Bob Malone's much trumpeted new "Open Business Environment"—an attempt to encourage internal reporting—as mere "smoke and mirrors." Jeannie Sayre was eventually reinstated.

Former inspection supervisor at the Valdez Marine Terminal, James Whitaker, pursued an unfair dismissal case against Alyeska. He also claims he was sacked because he spoke out. Alyeska maintains Whitaker was sacked for bringing a gun onto their property. He says this was a pretext to get rid of him after his outspoken criticisms of the operation at the marine terminal where he worked for eight years. Whitaker's open letter of complaints was included with the whistleblowers statements. He wrote: "I personally witnessed threats, intimidation and termination of employees throughout my career at the terminal (even after the promises to change were made to Congress)."

Whitaker said he had complained about the lack of enforcement of the legally binding Quality Assurance Program in relation to "qualification of inspection personnel, non-destructive testing, welding procedure approvals, vendor inspections, design change authorisations, record storage and retention." He also claimed he was "threatened by the project manager that if I did not get rid of one particular inspector, that my company would not be allowed on the (vapour control) project even though we were Alyeska's contracted third party inspection agency." Whitaker was in no doubt who knew what. "The Alyeska project manager was fully aware as the records were being altered, and did nothing. The individual that altered the records has since been promoted, while I have been terminated."

Alyeska, he wrote, had no desire to follow operating procedures. "It is time for the U.S. government at least to order a federal audit of records. . . . Alyeska will terminate an employee that earns $80,000 per year just to reduce headcount but then spend $80,000 at a time to televise propaganda commercials to the good people of Alaska making them believe that everything is OK." Such commercials, not surprisingly, did not tell Alaskans why BP was under criminal investigation by the U.S. Justice Department and the Environmental Protection Agency. The former imposed a $3 million fine in 1988 on one of BP's contractors whose employees had secretly dumped toxic waste at night on the North Slope over an eighteen-month period.

These revelations were initially made by a whistleblower back in 1995. The ongoing criminal investigation, however, also discovered falsification of dumping records and looked into whether BP was aware of the illegal operation, something the oil company had denied. (In February 2000 the federal court ordered BP to pay $6.5 million in civil penalties and $500,000 in criminal fines, to implement a new environmental management program, and also ordered five years of probation for late reporting of hazardous dumping down wells). Three senior employees of the contractor, Doyon Drilling, were fined $25,000 each and one received a twelve-month prison sentence. This particular whistleblower won his case against the contractor for intimidation including death threats from coworkers. Another former whistleblower expressed acute concern about these "rogue elements" in the Alaskan oil industry, who see critics as the enemy within and are willing to resort to violence and even attempted murder to silence them. He described an incident when the engine of a plane he had hired burned out because someone had sabotaged it with Ajax.

Many past whistleblowers, like safety specialist Doug Johnson who worked for an Alyeska oil spill response contractor, have also been subjected to smear campaigns. In his case, the contractor was responsible and made a settlement in 1998 after the Occupational Safety and Health Administration ruled that they had illegally retaliated against Johnson. He, too, had spoken out since 1994 about unsafe working conditions, falsified accident reports, inadequate training, and an oil spill response that did not meet safety standards.

SPYING

Under government pressure, Alyeska set up an Employees Concern Program (ECP) in 1995 for workers to internally report problems in an independent and confidential way. But two studies, one very critical by a government regulator in 1997, the other by consultants for Alyeska in January 1999, revealed a lack of trust in the ECP and a continuation of the "shoot-the-messenger culture." Alyeska's cynical commitment to the ECP was exposed in 1997 with the revelation that a company lawyer had ordered a covert probe to download from the ECP computer confidential files containing whistleblower names and allegations. Although not informed about this spying operation, president Bob Malone later apologized publicly. One of the new whistleblowers described the ECP as "a ploy to make it look like (Alyeska) is doing something for the regulator." Another of the group called it a "total scam," which reflects the increased sophistication of an embedded culture of intimidation.

It was no surprise, therefore, that like those before them, the July whistleblowers approached Chuck Hamel, an oil broker turned campaigner. His work since the mid-1980s as a conduit for troubled employees has led to three congressional investigations and cost the oil companies millions of dollars. He personally took an estimated $5 million from Alyeska as settlement for being the target in 1990 of another illegal spy operation authorized by senior management.

A private security company called Wackenhut, run by an ex-FBI agent, tried to discover Hamel's sources inside Alyeska. Affidavits from former Wackenhut agents exposed how they set up a bogus eco-friendly legal company, stole his mail and rubbish, and used electronic eavesdropping equipment. Congressman George Miller, who was being fed information by Hamel, was also targeted. Alyeska apologized, and Wackenhut has since won lucrative British government contracts operating private prisons and an immigration detention center.

ALYESKA RESPOND

Within hours of the whistleblowers' letter being published in the London *Guardian*, BP Amoco and Alyeska put out a holding statement: the integrity and safety of the pipeline was not imminently threatened, it said. As so often when confronted by allegations of impropriety, both companies announced an immediate internal investigation. But it rejected the call for an independent federal audit. The internal investigation was all that was on offer, journalists were told. But to take the sting out of the allegations an agreed line was spun in London and Anchorage: There was nothing new in the allegations, we knew about it and have been dealing with the issues for some time in cooperation with the local regulators.

While Alyeska and BP Amoco drafted a full response to each of the allegations, the whistleblowers were left pondering the company's initial response and trying to avoid what they described as a "witch hunt" within Alyeska. Congressman Miller expressed his immediate concern about the shoot-the-messenger culture in a letter to the federal Interior Department. "I want to know why Alyeska employees apparently continue to fear being sanctioned for signing their names to a letter raising concerns about the pipeline."

By the end of July that year, Alyeska had prepared a twenty-four-page response to the allegations called an "Issue Matrix." The overall conclusion was "we are safely operating the pipeline" and there are no imminent threats that need immediate corrective action. The Alyeska document said that the majority of the fifty-seven issues and incidents identified by the whistleblowers had already been identified internally. Twenty-four of these had now been "closed" following corrective action and thirteen have action plans in progress that Alyeska felt "will effectively address the issue." Another two action plans were in place the company claimed, but needed improvement or acceleration, while eighteen issues "require consideration and action plans to close." The serious allegations of senior management directing employees to circumvent the Quality Assurance Program, falsify inspection records, and allowing HIRD to exist, however, would be investigated, again internally, and "if substantiated, appropriate action taken."

The response matrix obscured the real admissions hidden in its fancy layout. Despite promises made during congressional hearings and the audit in 1993,

Alyeska had implicitly admitted that some of the same problems were still an issue. The company's response clearly admitted that *thirty-one* issues raised by the whistleblowers were currently, or would soon be, subject to action plans devised internally.

NO AUDIT

The whistleblowers say it is hard to avoid the conclusion that Alyeska's matrix response was designed to head off, at all cost, another devastating independent audit like the one in 1993. That audit was carried out by Owen Thero, a former U.S government-hired nuclear plant auditor. He was contracted by the federal Bureau of Land Management to consider the 1993 allegations. His subsequent report released to Congress showed there were many imminent threats to safety and the environment by the pipeline, which needed more than 4,900 corrective actions. Aware that Alyeska was trying to head off a repeat performance in 1999, the new whistleblowers asked a watchdog group called the "Project on Liberty and the Workplace" to commission Owen Thero to review the Alyeska matrix. Thero considered the 1999 allegations against the matrix and compared them with his 1993 audit report and 1994 corrective recommendations.

Thero's remit this time around was to "discern if the issues and concerns expressed in current allegations had been previously identified by (his) audit team, discussed with Alyeska, and therefore should have already been corrected." He did not consider the validity of the whistleblower allegations or Alyeska's response. But he did write "if the allegations are found valid, serious concerns would exist regarding the current safety/security of TAPS and its effect on the health and safety of the public and the environment/ecosystem." Thero was concerned about Alyeska's claim that the issues were not new and that they were dealing with them, because his 1994 recommendations required Alyeska be committed to "prompt" and "lasting" corrective action. This admission alone, he said, "would not support compliance with the TAPS Right of Way agreement or their own quality program."

Thero said that Alyeska's matrix response led to three major conclusions:

- Alyeska did not take prompt or effective corrective action in resolving the 1993 audit findings.
- Alyeska itself has validated several of the allegations raised by the whistleblowers.
- The dysfunctional Quality Assurance Program not only has existed at least since [the] 1993 audit, but also currently exists at TAPS.

The Joint Pipeline Office (JPO), a group of state and federal agencies criticized by the whistleblowers as an ineffectual government regulator, also wrote a report on the revelations letter. Unlike Thero, the JPO found there was no safety threat. It said its staff knew about most of the issues and Alyeska was currently working on or had resolved them. The JPO did, however, accept that "some issues identified in 1993 audits have recurred, some have resisted solution, and an active government enforcement posture remains necessary." It discussed the need for Alyeska to implement "an overall corrective action process." On the work culture within Alyeska, the JPO said that, since the 1993 Congressional hearings, Alyeska "has not completely resolved" the issues of corporate culture but that instances of harassment, intimidation, retaliation, and discrimination have been reduced. However, it importantly noted "the JPO has long believed that a driving cause of employee concerns is Alyeska's slow response in resolving the issues raised by its employees."

One such slow response can be seen in the handling of the allegation of falsified records at the Valdez Marine Terminal's TVRS. Alyeska admitted in its matrix that this issue was already identified in 1998 by themselves and the JPO, and that actions taken "have not been effective." Two days after the whistleblowers' letter was made public, Alyeska issued a corrective action report, months after the JPO had requested it. This failure to respond to the JPO until the whistle-blowers exposé in July 1999 demonstrated a cavalier attitude toward the regulator. In turn, the JPO's failure to enforce its own orders speaks volumes about the true regulatory framework operating in Alaska.

Nevertheless, the most surprising support for Alyeska came from the usually vociferous local citizen action group in Prince William Sound called the Regional Citizens Advisory Council (RCAC). The RCAC became a major player in the regulation of Alyeska after the Exxon Valdez spill and the resulting requirement of the Oil Pollution Act 1990 for citizen oversight. It is funded to the tune of $2 million a year by Alyeska but its contract specifically emphasizes its independence to review, comment, and monitor the company's oil spill response and prevention plans and protection of the environment.

The RCAC wrote a voluntary report for the Interior Department in August 1999. It said it had participated extensively in Alyeska's recent Management Review of the Tanker Vapor Recovery System and believed there was currently no safety risk of a catastrophic accident during tanker loading. The RCAC did ask the regulators, however, to seek a formal commitment from Alyeska in relation to the TVRS management review recommendations, which could be regarded as a veiled criticism of the company's failure to honor past promises.

RUSSIAN ROULETTE

Stan Stephens, who recently retired as president of the RCAC but remains a board member, does not share his colleagues' views about the TVRS. "There's no doubt there have been some major problems . . . There's no doubt that if the combination of events were to happen, it could cause a catastrophe," he said. "I think that's what RCAC has failed to put together."

Stephens said the new whistleblower allegations were correct. He believed the whole affair was the result of a continued "total lack of follow-up" of issues raised by employees. "I was quite taken back when JPO said (they) knew about these things, and were working on them," he said. "Well, they've known about them for a long time—why the heck haven't they done something? Why hasn't Alyeska done something if they've known about them?" Stephens was "sickened" by Alyeska's Matrix. "As far as I'm concerned, they are out of compliance with the Right of Way lease agreement. The JPO is the one that has failed there too. It has basically given them a go-ahead to not have to complete all the audit items, and given them extensions." Stephens also believed the JPO and Alyeska were covering their backs. "(They're) trying to fix the pipeline by public relations programs instead of digging in and getting it fixed." Although Stephens was a Malone supporter, he believes that the Alyeska president had "failed badly" to follow through on employee concerns. He said if Malone failed this time, he should go. "The only way (he is) going to change this, is to get rid of some top personnel—people who've been around a long time," he added.

Like the whistleblowers, Stephens believes a major independent audit is necessary. "And not by a government accountability office, but by the Attorney General's office in Washington DC," Stephens said. The call for an audit was also made in June 1997 by Richard Fineberg, an independent economist and former special adviser to the Alaskan governor on oil and gas policy, in an update of his September 1996 report called *Pipeline in Peril*. This report was commissioned by a local oil industry watchdog, the Alaska Forum for Environmental Responsibility, which was founded by marine scientist Stan Stephens, fisherwoman Riki Ott, and local government regulator Dan Lawn, with a financial settlement won by all three from Alyeska after being targeted by the Wackenhut spying operation in the early 1990s.

Fineberg's original 1996 report had concluded that the Alaskan environment was in danger because of Alyeska's plan to extend the lifetime of the twenty-two-year-old pipeline by thirty years, while carrying out cost-cutting measures. His 1997 update for the twentieth anniversary of the Trans Alaska Pipeline reminded Alyeska president Bob Malone that he had accepted the company would be held to a higher standard than other pipelines. TAPS was still a pipeline in peril he said, and there was a pressing need for an independent audit. Otherwise Alyeska would be playing "a game of Russian roulette with the environment."

Fineberg's overview of Alyeska's performance was devastating:

> Despite the signs of improvement noted throughout this report, the fact remains, this company has a wretched history. When the Exxon Valdez spill tested Alyeska's spill response capabilities in 1989, Alyeska failed to live up to its promises. In the aftermath of that episode, Alyeska replaced its president and said it was going to reorganize. Under a new president Alyeska launched an espionage campaign against its critics and a political campaign against its critics and a political campaign to limit its liabilities for tanker spill response.

In response to whistleblower criticism that brought congressional hearings and public criticism in 1993, Alyeska brought in another president and promised another reform effort. As tempting as it might be to herald Alyeska's 1997 effort as the dawn of a new era for the pipeline company, it should be remembered that during the same period that Alyeska has tried repeatedly to re-invent itself, major corporations, such as IBM and General Motors, have completely and successfully restructured themselves.

Fineberg still believes an independent audit is all the more pressing, but has little faith that the call will be heeded. "Many people have said they (Alyeska) would not have been able to pass an audit (and) that is why they do not want it." He says Washington should threaten to close down the pipeline unless all the measures and government regulations required to operate it safely are adopted. Again, he believes this is unlikely to happen. Chuck Hamel, the whistleblower conduit and Alyeska's nemesis, spoke with president Bob Malone. Hamel says he offered to cease his activities as a conduit if Malone would allow an independent audit of TAPS and Alyeska. Malone refused, he says.

GREENWASH

What is clear to the whistleblowers and Stan Stephens is that, despite Alyeska's continual efforts, Malone cannot fix the problems with public relations. The role of Billie Garde, a prominent whistleblower advocate now working for Alyeska, raises important issues about the current strategy by oil companies to engage their critics. Garde's consultancy company, Little Harbor, was contracted by Alyeska in 1998 to look at their "Open Business Environment"—the failed attempt to encourage internal reporting of problems. She was then being used to investigate one of the most serious of the July 1999 allegations, that senior executives directed employees to circumvent and falsify inspection reports.

The cooption of Garde by Alyeska can be seen in the broader context of the changing way oil companies are responding to their critics. They have tried to out-maneuver critics by adopting the language of the environmental move-ment, by "green-washing" their products and entering into dialogue with their opponents. This strategy is part of a wider attempt to exploit the NGO funding crisis and expose a rift between so called realists and militants. Even before the "realists" extract any commitment from the oil companies, these dialogues are already used in the company's glossy brochures made for schools and ethical pension fund managers.

The whistleblowers viewed with scepticism Billie Garde's alleged conversion to corporate public relations. They were also disappointed with the U.S. govern-ment's reaction to their letter, especially the Interior Department's statement that none of the problems on TAPS were significant enough to "pose an immediate threat to its integrity." They believe Alyeska has successfully "side-stepped" the call for an independent audit, and condemned the refusal by local regulators to accept that the combination of these issues *does* create an imminent threat to the pipeline and marine terminal. Without such an audit, the whistleblowers fear they will have to come out in the open and forego the protection that anonymity affords them in the current retaliatory climate. "If we did, we could just walk around and show where the bodies are," said one.

ENDNOTES

This is an extended and updated version of an article that appeared in the *Guardian* on July 12, 1999.

Information on the Group of Six whistleblowers can be found at: www.alaskagroupsix.org. See also Oilwatch Alaska at: home.gci.net/~oilwatch/.

BP's environmental record in Alaska is documented at: enviro2.blr.com/display.cfm/id/19536.

CHAPTER 6

Loaded Dice: Multinational Oil, Due Process, and the State

Matthias Beck and Charles Woolfson

In the year 2000, U.S. legal treatises were updated to account for a new landmark case. The update was listed under the rubric "malicious prosecution" and the main protagonist was Shell Oil Co. The case is technically known as *Leonardini v. Shell Co.* 216 Cal.App.3d 579 [1]. It involves the award of $197,000 in compensatory damages and fees and $5 million in punitive damages to a lawyer named Raymond Leonardini, who successfully sued Shell for actions taken against him in his capacity as representative of the California Pipe Trades Council.

Mr. Leonardini's story is unique in many respects, not least because of his success against Shell. After becoming a member of the California Bar, Mr. Leonardini worked for the California Department of Consumer Affairs, ultimately attaining a position as assistant cabinet secretary. Some years later, after starting his own private practice in Sacramento, Mr. Leonardini was retained by the California Pipe Trades Council. The council, an organization of plumbers and pipe fitters unions, soon became his principal client. This led Mr. Leonardini to become heavily involved in health and safety issues affecting plumbers and pipe fitters. When, during 1979 and 1980, the Commission on Housing and Community Development was considering the use of plastic piping for drinking water, laboratory tests were undertaken to investigate the health effects of polyvinyl chloride and chlorinated polyvinyl piping. Shell did not produce either of these materials, but rather was the sole U.S. producer of the raw material used for making polybutylene pipes. Polybutylene was not, at the time, subject to testing, because the ingredients, as declared by Shell, did not "ring an alarm." What Shell had not revealed was that polybutylene pipe systems used an additional potentially hazardous plastic as a coupler; or, as the presiding judges in the case noted:

> Shell's policy was that if the state did not discover any health problems with the system on its own, and did not specifically ask for that information, Shell would not volunteer it [1].

When, in 1980, California Assemblyman Lou Papan affected a temporary halt on the introduction of plastic pipes pending further testing, Shell told one of its representatives that "they have a battery of attorneys to handle people like that" and that "they'll turn it over to their legal department." Consecutively, Shell did send a letter to Assemblyman Papan threatening to take "appropriate legal action" if he did not stop from lumping polybutylene with other plastics.

Eventually, in December 1980, Mr. Leonardini, acting on behalf of his client the Pipe Trades Council, commissioned tests of polybutylene pipes. In one of the two pieces of pipe the laboratory detected the presence of a recently discovered carcinogen. The levels at which these toxins were found were later determined in tests paid for by Shell to reflect negligible "background" levels. In conjunction with the ongoing hearings, Mr. Leonardini also prepared a booklet entitled "Health Hazards Associated with Plastic Pipes: A Status Report," which was entered into the public record of the hearing. In addition to this, Mr. Leonardini gave about eighty copies of the booklet to the Pipe Trades Council.

When Shell subsequently opposed the drafting of an environmental impact report (EIR), the dispute escalated toward a nationwide controversy. In this context, Shell sent a letter to interested parties describing the controversy as a "big lie," paid for by the plumbers. Shell's main target, however, was not the public, but rather, Mr. Leonardini himself. According to testimony by disgruntled consultants, cited in the court opinion, Shell's managers felt that Mr. Leonardini:

> . . . was being too effectual at the hearings. And if he continued on the road that he was pursuing, he was going to wind up getting Polybutylene [into an] EIR. Successively, Shell's management felt "very enthusiastic" about doing whatever was necessary to see if they can eliminate [the plaintiff] and his tenaciousness from the hearing [1].

Following a failed attempt to "discuss" matters with the laboratory hired initially by the Pipe Trades Council, one of Shell's attorneys let it be known to the scientific adviser to the commission, Dr. Lappe, that it was ready to take action. In his testimony to the California Court of Appeals, Dr. Lappe recalled that the Shell attorney:

> . . . expressed some gratification about the way I was handling the issue at the time . . . however there are some boys in Houston—that was his phrase—who were playing hardball—and that was also his phrase—and that they are very concerned about people, specifically Mr. Leonardini, who are going on and describing [this in] greatly exaggerated terms. And that this was beginning to

hurt Shell economically to have these discussions and that something was going to have to be done to dampen or quiet these kinds of outspoken statements [1].

In August 1981, Shell eventually filed a complaint against Mr. Leonardini in the U.S. District Court for the Eastern District of California, alleging trade libel and seeking an injunction against the Pipe Trades Council and Mr. Leonardini further publishing their statements about polybutylene pipe. Following a year or more of legal wrangling, Shell eventually settled with the Pipe Trades Council but refused to honor Mr. Leonardini's request for a dismissal of its suit against him. In 1983, Mr. Leonardini then filed an action for malicious prosecution against Shell.

Reviewing the overwhelming evidence against Shell, a jury at the Superior Court of Sacramento County found for Mr Leonardini and awarded damages to him. Shell instantly moved for a new trial. Following further years of legal wrangling, the case was eventually heard by the California Court of Appeals for the Third District. In December 1989, the Appeals Court affirmed the verdict in full, amid Shell allegations that justice had tilted too far in favor of individual litigators acting on behalf of private interest groups.

Mr. Leonardini, to be sure, was among the lucky few who had the wits and resources to withstand the protracted pressure from Shell's "legal" machinery. His circumstances were exceptional in many ways. First, he is a highly qualified attorney with significant experience in trade litigation. Second, he could count, up to a point, on the support of a trades association that backed his criticisms of the oil giant. Last, and perhaps most important, Leonardini resided in one of the more progressive corners of the United States whose courts have often adopted an unexpectedly objective attitude toward big capital.

The annals of the legal battles fought by the oil companies, to be sure, are stacked with episodes in which the legal system has reinforced the power imbalances between big oil and community or employee interests. In October 2002, for instance, the 2nd Circuit U.S. Court of Appeals reaffirmed the dismissal of a claim of 55,000 Ecuadorians and Peruvians against Texaco for the environmental contamination of their homes and property while exploring and exploiting oil resources [2]. Again, this case was the outcome of a lengthy dispute in which the 2nd Circuit Court initially reversed a defense summary judgment in favor of the litigants on grounds of *forum non conveniens* [3]. The case was then reheard by the U.S. District Court for the Southern District of New York. This court again dismissed the case, this time on grounds that the possibility of the litigants pursuing their case in Ecuador overcame "the ordinarily strong presumption favoring [the] plaintiff's chosen forum." In blatant disregard for reality, the court argued that because the Ecuadorian Constitutional Court had ruled unconstitutional Ecuadorian Law 55, which had banned Ecuadorians from suing foreign oil companies for compensation, the Ecuadorians had adequate recourse to their own court in pursuing their claim.

The experiences of these Ecuadorians, like those of whistleblowers in the Alaskan Oil industry (described in Chapter 5 by Michael Gillard and his colleagues), are representative of the unrelenting dominance multinational oil companies exert when dealing with individual litigants. This dominance rests not only on the sheer ruthlessness of these companies in combination with their financial strength. It also rests on the complicity of legislatures and ultimately the courts, which in the United States, as elsewhere, all too often fail to support critical voices, whether they originate from developed countries or less developed ones.

Again, events in the Alaskan oil province help to illustrate that this bias is not restricted to the developing world. In the early 1990s, the courts of the state of Alaska were swamped with lawsuits arising from the conduct of oil multinationals. A large portion of litigation had arisen from the Exxon Valdez oil spill and its aftereffects, while a substantial number of suits involved oil workers who felt that they had been subjected to unfair treatment by their employers. One such worker was John Bozarth, a pilot for the Atlantic Richfield Company (ARCO). Mr. Bozarth had repeatedly complained about unsafe practices in ARCO's aviation department. Eventually, he was fired, according to company sources, not because of his complaints, but because he refused to participate in ARCO's new "random" drug-testing program. We do not know the reason for Mr. Bozarth's refusal; perhaps he was simply being stubborn, perhaps he had smoked marijuana and feared that a positive result would give ARCO a pretense to fire him for cause. What we do know is that Mr Bozarth's application for state unemployment was denied to him on account of his dismissal for "work-related misconduct." When he appealed to the Appeal Division of the Employment Security Division, the original refusal to provide benefits was upheld [4].

Mr. Bozarth thereafter brought his case before the Superior Court of the State of Alaska, in the Third Judicial District of Anchorage. His belief was that this court would thoroughly investigate his claim of retaliatory discharge. This was not to be. Relying on the doctrine of *collateral estoppel*, the Superior Court ruled that the issue of fact had been determined by a valid judgment and could therefore not be litigated again by the same parties. Adding insult to injury, ARCO, having won its case, moved for attorney's fees demanding the payment of $156,425 from Mr. Bozarth. The court found a "slight" overcharge and then determined that a reasonable fee for the services performed by ARCO's attorney's was $152,000. Deciding that Mr. Bozarth was liable to pay 50% of this amount, the court directed him to pay $76,000 to ARCO [5].

At this stage, perhaps believing that he had nothing to lose, Mr. Bozarth brought his claim before the Alaska Supreme Court, where it was heard by Chief Justice Rabinovitz and Justices Burke, Matthews, Compton, and Moore. In *Bozarth v. ARCO* (1992), the Alaska Supreme Court again found for ARCO [6]. Specifically, it stated that "there were no genuine issues of material facts, regarding Mr Bozarth's dismissal." As concerned the requirement for Mr. Bozarth to pay $76,000 to ARCO, the court concluded that "while the court's award of attorney's fees seems high, we are unable to say that the work performed by ARCO's attorney's was not necessary or appropriate, or that billing $152,000 for these services was unreasonable." Moreover, the court concluded that requiring 50 % of that amount to be paid by the plaintiff, "falls comfortably within the partially compensatory standard of Civil Rule 82," the rule governing the allocation of court costs.

It was at this stage that the case had taken its most interesting twist. While the Supreme Court denied all credibility to Mr. Bozarth's allegations that he had acted as a whistleblower, and that his dismissal may have had more to do with his complaints than his refusal to take a drug test, it had at the same time penalized him severely for having challenged his dismissal. Needless to say, this was welcome news for Alaska's multinational oil companies. They not only had a court ruling that took a critical view of the claims of whistleblowers, but also had the court use one of its civil rules—Civil Rule 82—to effectively penalize whistleblowers. Apart from far-reaching constitutional implications, the use of Civil Rule 82 raised serious questions about the incentive structure created for whistleblowers in Alaska, and, perhaps more important, its compatibility with other public policy goals. Specifically, if the state could not deny that the actions of whistleblowers could be beneficial to society, how could it impose the risk of what could amount to a huge financial fine on whistleblowers?

This problem did not go unnoticed among some of the Supreme Court judges. In fact, two of the five judges formally dissented with the majority's view of the adequacy of the fee award. Their statement represents an implicit acknowledgment of the special obstacles faced by individuals attempting to take Big Oil to court [7]:

> . . . trial courts must consider whether the award is so great that it imposes an intolerable burden on a losing litigant which, in effect, denies the litigant's right to access to the courts. The guidelines for making such a determination are not easy to express. Chief Justice Boochever in *Sloan* said that . . . "he was unable to delineate specific guidelines for a trial judge to follow in awarding attorney's fees." He then settled on the "admittedly arbitrary" figure of $2,500 as the maximum that I think could be awarded without unduly limiting access to the courts under the facts of this case [7].

While perceptive with regard to the potential injustices created by these practices, the judges' dissent hardly captured the full extent of the abuse of fee awards by the oil companies. By 1992, when the *Bozarth* case was heard, it had become common practice for oil multinationals to use the threat of high fee awards to deter and ultimately ruin employees and/or their families. As early as 1976, in *Sloan v. ARCO*, an Alaskan trial court had ordered the widow of a deceased construction worker to pay $10,750 to ARCO, when she lost a wrongful death case [8]. This judgment was overturned by the above-mentioned Chief Justice Boochever who awarded $2,500 instead, still a substantial sum for the widow of a construction worker to pay. In *Zeilinger v. Sohio Alaska Petroleum Co.* (1992), the plaintiff, a Sohio employee seeking redress for an alleged wrongful discharge, similarly was ordered to pay $80,470 to Sohio (which represented 40% of the claimed costs) [9]. On appeal, however, the Supreme Court was critical of Sohio's expense claims and reversed the original judgment as excessive. Indeed the following court statement indicates that the judges were well aware of the "high fee threat" strategy oil companies had come to use against their opponents:

> On its face, the claimed actual fees of $200,000 appear clearly excessive. The facts in the case were not particularly complex or unique, nor even subject to much dispute. The case did not involve questions of technical expertise, the legal issues weren't especially novel or original and the trial was relatively brief.

The plaintiff in *Van Huff v. Sohio Alaska Petroleum Co.* (1992) was less lucky [10]. In this wrongful discharge case, the Superior Court had ordered the plaintiff to pay $117,251 to his former employer, which represented 30% of the estimate Sohio gave of its attorney costs. On appeal, the Supreme Court was unwilling to engage in a downward adjustment of these costs, primarily because Van Huff had already sucesssfully achieved a reduction from 60% to 30% of costs in the superior courts.

Whether the award of fees of around $200 to $400 per hour to companies that maintain a large staff of salaried company attorneys is appropriate, is debatable. What is clear, however, is that the award of attorneys' fees, and the cost of legal proceedings had provided Big Oil with far-reaching capabilities to block individuals from access to justice in Alaska, as well as elsewhere in the United States.

In the United Kingdom, oil employees have faced significant obstacles to justice. In March 1992, in one of the worst offshore helicopter disasters, eleven men died, when a Bristow's Super Puma crashed in the North Sea off the Cormorant Alpha platform in atrocious weather. Evidence was to emerge that the men had been reluctant to take the helicopter flight that night but had eventually boarded under pressure. The relatives of the victims sought to pursue damages against Shell Expro (a partnership of Shell and Exxon), the platform operators.

Initially the relatives embarked on litigation against Bristow in the United Kingdom. Then they brought their suit against Shell and Exxon to the courts of Texas and Louisiana. Compensation was sought beyond that which, under the outmoded Warsaw convention on aviation accident compensation, restricts payment to those involved in a civil aircraft disaster to a sum in the region of £90,000. With the prospect of U.S. litigation, Shell sought and obtained interim interdicts in Scotland and injunctions in England against the bereaved families. This included some sixty-three individuals in all. The purpose of these restraining orders was to prevent the families from pursuing an award for higher levels of compensation in the American courts as against the courts of England and

Scotland. Violation of this court order, Shell warned, could have the result that families, which in this case also included young children, would be "subject to bodily imprisonment." Faced with such legal harassment, even case-hardened lawyers involved in the proceedings reeled in disbelief. Shell confirmed: "the action reflects the company's belief that the appropriate forum for a resolution of this matter is Scotland" [11]. Any reference to "imprisonment," said Shell, was "legal jargon."

Shell's attempt to block compensation cases in the U.S. courts proved not entirely successful, and the initial legal restraining orders sought in the Scottish High Court and south of the border were recalled [12]. Then, in late December 1994, a Texas district court judge in Brazoria County ruled that Exxon ultimately controlled the Shell–Esso joint venture operating installations like Cormorant Alpha and was therefore responsible for its aviation policy. Judge Neil Caldwell stated that Exxon could be held to conduct its business from the state of Texas, despite the company's attempt to avoid jurisdiction being granted. It "moved" its registered headquarters in the United States, among other legal maneuvers. In Judge Caldwell's view, there appeared to be [13, para. 53]:

> reasonable grounds to allege that the co-venturers SUKL/EEPUKL (Shell UK Ltd/Esso Exploration and Production UK Ltd.) appear to have been responsible for the crash of the G–TIGH because of their unrelenting push to reduce NPT (non-productive time) by way of reducing WOW (waiting on weather). By using the Super Puma G–TIGH (upgraded equipment) in storm conditions when WOW had previously caused NPT (non-productive time), the co-venturers (Shell/Esso) achieved their goal of reducing NPT and, not coincidentally, caused the death of eleven men and permanent disability of a remaining six.

The ruling opened a potential avenue for U.S.-level settlements to be awarded to the victims of the disaster, although further legal challenges from Shell/Esso continued. In April 1995, Shell/Esso and the relatives and survivors returned to the Court of Session in Edinburgh. The relatives asked for the interdict against them to be withdrawn, as they had been threatened that if the transfer went ahead, they would be summoned for breach of interdict. The companies also threatened to pursue a retaliatory £1 million expenses claim for costs incurred in defending the U.S. proceedings. U.S. attorneys acting for the deceased were described by Shell's QC as "dogs straining at the leash" [14]. The legal threats were justified as getting "the handlers to order the dogs to sit down" [15]. Shell did attempt, unsuccessfully as it turned out, to have the interdict preserved. An article in Shell's house magazine for employees by Richard Wiseman, head of Shell UK's Legal Division, put forward the company's position [16]:

> We are not fighting Texas jurisdiction to avoid paying huge damages as has been alleged by the media on several occasions. Shell UK is a British company with no operations outside the UK.

The ability of oil companies to persevere financially, through long and tedious court battles, is infinitely greater than that of individual plaintiffs. Judge Caldwell's initial determination of jurisdiction in favor of the latter could not distract from this crucial asymmetry. In the end, when faced with the imminent prospect of U.S. court proceedings going ahead, Shell proposed an out-of-court settlement, which was reached in early 1996, nearly four years after the disaster. The size of this settlement is undisclosed. While it is known that the families received substantially greater compensation than they would have obtained in the British courts, the imposition of "gagging clauses" left unanswered vital questions about corporate culpability.

Perhaps the most notable distortion of the issue of corporate culpability was to come in a case that became the longest and most expensive action ever pursued in the Scottish High Court system and indeed the longest trial in British legal history. This was heard before Lord Caplan over nearly three and a half years, during which 13 million words of evidence were recorded by a team of shorthand writers. The trial sought to recover £140m costs paid out by Occidental in settlements to contractors' personnel after the Piper Alpha disaster. Occidental, as the operators of the platform, had been roundly castigated for management failures in the initial inquiry into the disaster by Lord Cullen. The company now sought to recover these costs from the contracting companies themselves. Lord Caplan's judgment was delivered in six bound volumes amounting to nearly 1,500 pages. He identified individual named contractor company employees, one of whom was posthumously awarded a bravery medal for efforts to save his colleagues. These men were now publicly "blamed" for the operational safety failure that was held to be the immediate cause of the disaster. Lord Cullen had specifically avoided blaming the operatives in his earlier inquiry. Indeed evidence presented to Lord Cullen suggested systemic safety problems on Piper Alpha. It was also suggested that whistleblowers had been ignored and actively suppressed by Occidental's management, which feared potential litigation exposure [17]. At best, therefore, Lord Caplan's subsequent apportionment of blame to two deceased contractor workers reflects a formalism adopted by the legal profession that may have been appropriate to the analysis of what was essentially an insurance liability dispute. At worst, it was a judgment indicative of a legal bias, which allows judges to attribute major incidents to the human error of a specific workers, when in fact their real origin lies in corporate misconduct and gross negligence of a systemic and enduring nature.

Even where the evidence against multinational oil companies and their contractors has been insurmountable, they have been able to utilize the court system to their advantage, if only to reduce awards to employees. Again, an Alaskan case can serve as an example of the strategies employed by the oil companies and their contractors. In the case of *Norcon Inc. v. Kotowski* (1999) [18], the jury had found Norcon Inc. liable to Mary Kotowski for sexual harassment, intentional infliction of emotional distress, and negligent infliction of emotional distress. Due to the exceptional severity of these offenses, the jury awarded Ms. Kotowski a total sum of $3,780,604. This included $8,494 in lost earnings and $1,850 for emotional distress, with the remainder comprising punitive damages, a sum which appears by no means excessive, given the treatment Ms. Kotowski experienced at the hands of senior Norcon employees.

Ms. Kotowski was one of thousands of workers employed in 1989 in the clean-up operation following the Exxon Valdez spill in Prince William Sound. At the time Exxon had employed VECO Inc. to act as general contractor for the spill clean-up, which in turn employed its sister company Norcon as a subcontractor. Without going into the details of the dispute, which led to one of the lengthiest opinions published by the Alaska Supreme Court in recent years, it is worth noting that Ms. Kotowski's stream of mistreatments in the brief course of her employment included sexual harassment, physical intimidation, transfer, entrapment, arrest, and a four-hour interrogation by Norcon's security contractor. Much of this was triggered by a safety complaint regarding drinking on barges.

None of this deterred Norcon from appealing the judgment in a protracted litigation, which only came to a close as late as 1999. Finding that Norcon's denial of outrageous conduct had no merit, the Alaska Supreme Court focused on the appropriateness of the $3.7 million in punitive damages awarded to Ms. Kotowski. Discussing a number of Norcon's arguments, including profit figures submitted by that company, the court eventually came to the conclusion that the damage award was excessive, and that Norcon should be charged with damages of no more than a maximum $500,000 in order to avoid undue hardship to the company.

The court's willingness to override a jury decision in favor of a company, in itself, points to a biased view of company operations, especially when we consider the court's reluctance to reduce the fee awards to be paid by individuals to companies on the same grounds. It is worthwhile to examine some of the arguments that the court used to arrive at its decision.

Essentially, the court's argument for a reduction in damages followed two avenues. First, it was suggested that Norcon's conduct was not sufficiently damaging to justify a multimillion dollar award. This argument however, led the court into ambiguous territory:

> The sexual harassment to which Kotowski was subjected occurred on only two days. . . . It was thus of short duration. Although it was serious, frightening, and resulted in great emotional distress, it was not of disastrous proportions [19].

Not quite willing to go down the road of discounting a well proven and serious harassment incident, the court, however, felt that it could fully accept this argument in the second part of this paragraph. Here the issue of repeat offenses was introduced:

> However, given the evidence that the harassment of Kotowski was only one in a series of sexual harassment incidents, the seriousness of the conduct

for which Norcon is responsible is somewhat increased. Concerning the importance of the policy violated, there is a strong public policy against sexual harassment in the workplace [19].

Having explored and largely dismissed the "limited damages" argument, the *Kotowski* judgment next explored the appropriateness of the damages granted from an economic perspective. It was here that the judges found the major justification for their reduction of the punitive damages to almost one-eighth of the original amount awarded by the jury. Again, it is worth exploring the arguments of the court in some detail, if only to highlight the sublime disregard of reality employed in justifying this oil-friendly decision. The key to the court's acceptance of this reduction in damages was its perception of an inappropriate ratio between the damages awarded and the profits reported by Norcon:

> With respect to the wealth of the defendant, Norcon apparently had a pre-tax net profit of more than $19,000,000 in the 1990 fiscal year. This was doubtless related to the oil spill clean-up as profits were much less in the following years. The $3,700,000 award in this case would not necessarily bankrupt Norcon, but it is more than is necessary to drive home the message to Norcon that it should not tolerate sexual harassment and that it should take affirmative steps to guard against such conduct [19].

It is perhaps unnecessary to point out the numerous fallacies employed in this reasoning. First, sexual harassment was only one of the grounds for which the jury granted its damage award to Ms. Kotowski. Indeed, according to the relevant transcripts, aggressive conduct and intimidation against Ms. Kotowski commenced once she voiced complaints about safety violations. Second, it is difficult to follow the argument as to why a damage award of less than one-fifth of the profits (19%) of one year would be out of line with a public policy that seeks to severely penalize and ultimately eradicate the mistreatment of employees in the workplace. Perhaps even more astounding than the court's unwillingness to accept the need for serious deterrence is the sheer naiveté underlying its acceptance of Norcon's excessive damages argument. It is common knowledge that official reported profit statements often greatly underestimate actual profits, especially where companies are part of larger conglomerates in which there exists ample room for creative accounting. Given that Norcon knew about an outstanding damage award of $3.7 million it is not difficult to imagine that the company would have had a strong incentive to underreport profits. Limiting the investigation of profits to those made solely by Norcon, and not the mother companies, VECO and Exxon, moreover, was at least from the victim's perspective entirely arbitrary. It again indicates the court's acceptance of demands made by capital as compared to those of labor.

What our brief and eclectic review of oil litigation in the United States and United Kingdom has revealed is something that is not new to the literature. Oil multinationals are among the economically and politically most powerful companies in the world. As such, they are able to influence outcomes in all relevant levels of decision making, be it environmental or tax policies, court rulings, or infrastructure planning. Against this power, the feeble strength of any individual worker or campaigner is near meaningless. In her insightful analysis of the expansion of individual employment litigation in the United States, Katherine van Wetzel Stone concluded that "the enactment of numerous individual employment rights in the past decade has not compensated for what workers have lost in collective bargaining" [19]. She suggested that ". . . only when legal reforms restore the rights of unions to freely organise and collectively bargain over a broader set of issues will unions regain the strength to represent employee interests adequately both in collective bargaining and in the enforcement of other statutory rights."

Such a strengthening of unions is badly needed, especially in the oil industry where, worldwide, collective bargaining rights are being curtailed and individual employment rights are being violated. To keep the disproportionate power of oil multinationals in check requires the concerted, collaborative effort of organized labor, state regulators, with its inspectors, administrators, and so forth, and the judicial system. As yet, most advanced liberal democracies have failed to provide an adequate response to the overpowering position of multinational oil, with all its regional and supraregional implications. The implications of this are not merely academic. In most disasters we are aware of, be it those that involve the loss of life or environmental destruction, there was a whistleblower whose warnings of impending catastrophe were discounted or ignored, often to the severe detriment of that individual and ultimately his or her colleagues and their communities who have had to bear the costs of disaster. In the future, knowledge of the real costs of oil production will have to be a keystone to regulating the activities of Big Oil.

ENDNOTES

1. *Leonardini v. Shell Oil*, 216 Cal. App. 3d 547, 264 Cal Rptr. 883, Raymond J. Leonardini, Plaintiff and Respondent, v. Shell Oil Company, Defendant and Appellant, No. C000619 California Court of Appeals, Third District, December 12, 1989, Superior Court of Sacramento County, No. 310945, Lloyd Allan Phillips, Jr., Judge; see: www.casp.net/shell-1.html and following links.
2. *Gabriel Ashanga Jota, et al. v. Texaco Inc.*, Nos. 92-9102(L) [CON], 97-9108 [CON] 2d Cir.
3. Headline Legal News, *2d Circuit Affirms Dismissal of 55,000 Claims against Texaco* (2002); available at: www.lexisone.com/news/nlibrary/m1011803b.html.
4. *Bozarth v. Atlantic Richfield Oil Co.*, 833 P. 2d 2 (Alaska 1992); see: touchngo.com/sp/html/sp-3843.htm.
5. Alaska courts are at liberty to require losing plaintiffs to pay any %age of attorney costs to a successful defendant. Usually this amount is somewhere between 30% and 70% of the total cost of the defendant's attorney fees. However, during the 1970s, it was a

common practice of the Alaska Supreme court to impose only nominal fee awards where the defendant was not capable of larger payments.

6. *Arco Alaska, Inc. et al v. State of Alaska* (January 24, 1992), 824 P 2d 708; see: touchngo.com/sp/html/sp-3800.htm.
7. This partial dissent was authored by Justice Matthews, with whom Justice Compton concurred.
8. *Sloan v. Atlantic Richfield Oil Co.*, 552 P 2d 157 (Alaska 1976).
9. *S. Zeilinger v. Sohio AK Petroleum Co.* (1/3/92), 823 P 2d 653; see: touchngo.com/sp/html/sp-3794.htm.
10. *Van Huff v. Sohio Alaska Petroleum Co.*, 853 P 2d 1181 (Alaska 1992); see: touchngo.com/sp/html/sp-3857.htm.
11. *Scotsman*, April 11, 1994.
12. *Scotsman*, June 7, 1994
13. Judge N. Caldwell, Determination of 23d Judicial Court, Brazoria County, Texas, in the case of *Mr. and Mrs. Andrew Innes and children Scott Alexander Innes and Andrew David Innes et al., vs. Shell UK Exploration and Production Ltd. et al.*, December 23, 1994.
14. *Press and Journal*, December 29, 1994 (Aberdeen).
15. *Scotsman*, April 7, 1995.
16. *Expro Update*, May 1995, 7. For a full account of the proceedings see *Scots Law Times, Shell UK Exploration and Production Ltd v Innes 1995 Reports*, 807ff.
17. See C. Woolfson, M. Foster, and J. Beck, *Paying for the Piper: Capital and Labour in Britain's Offshore Oil Industry* (London and New York: Mansell, 1996), 244-249.
18. Norcon, Inc. v. Kotowski (2/19/99), 971 P 2d 158 at: www.touchngo.com/sp/html/sp-5085.htm.
19. K. Van Wetzel Stone, "The Feeble Strength of One: Why Individual Worker Rights Fail," *American Prospect Online* 4, no. 14, June 23, 1993; see: www.prospect.org/print/V4/14/stone-k.html.

AFTERWORD

Oil and Corporate Crime: The Russian Connection

Charles Woolfson

According to recent polls as many as three-quarters of Russian citizens believe that the results of privatization should be revised, fully or partially, and over half would not object to seeing the state prosecute business leaders. How are we to understand the contemporary popular desire for "class retribution" in Russia? What is the mass psychology that lies behind the poll results which may go some way toward understanding the complexities of the complicit relationship between criminalized Russian business and the state? What are outside observers to make of the "war against the oligarchs," evidenced in the arrest of Russian oil company, Yukos' most senior figure, Mikhail Khodorkovsky? Mr. Khodorkovsky, who is believed to be Russia's richest man, was seized by agents of the security police (FSB) in a dramatic airport raid in Novosibirsk and flown back to Moscow under armed guard to be charged with offences, including defrauding the state out of up to $10bn. At this time (August 2004), he remains in prison in Moscow awaiting trial and the survival of his oil empire in doubt.

In Russia today, the pervasive criminality of post-communist society, presents in unvarnished detail, a picture of corporate and organized crime. Its consequences are the almost limitless forms of degradation visited upon ordinary people in the transition to a market economy. One key to the poll results may be found in the crowded reproachful voices of the unwitting victims of the transition process; the cheated small savers of billion ruble rip-off investment banks and pyramid schemes, the everyday corruption which eats at the fabric of normal life, the massive erosion of state benefits for the needy and poor, the intimidation and humiliation of ordinary workers, on strike, more often than not, simply for unpaid wages. Viewed against a depressing and desperate picture of a ruined social and economic fabric, the balance sheet of losses and gains in the destruction of the Soviet economy, may begin to seem problematical, to say the least, to many ordinary Russians. Such views, increasingly reflected in the opinion polls, can no longer be dismissed as merely maverick, or the nostalgia of a generation which has failed to adapt to the exigencies of life under market forces. There is a pervasive understanding among the mass of the population that they are collective victims of a theft of historically unparalleled proportions.

Privatization was supposed to make workers "co-owners" but put 80% of Russian enterprises in private hands by 1996. Purloined state assets, initially were mainly the "blue chip" oil and chemical concerns. One of the most common strategies used to appropriate state assets was for the factory directors to take over a large share of the assets of their factories as payment for their contribution of "intellectual property." Another technique was for the director of a factory to consign the potentially most profitable parts of the enterprise to "daughter firms" controlled by his friends or relatives. These could in turn control the majority of the enterprise. A further means of stripping the assets of a factory was to rent out everything possible, with a small part of the rent specified in a formal agreement and the rest paid in cash to the director. But the circle of conspiracy does not end there. State enterprises were converted into joint stock companies, and the government normally retained a block of shares, while state officials frequently became directors. As a result, the boards of private enterprises—particularly those dealing with oil, gold, and diamonds—were frequently filled with powerful officials, sometimes on the level of deputy minister, who participated in the pillaging of the enterprise. Mikhail Khodorkovsky, as deputy minister of fuel and energy in the Yeltsin government, would seem to be a case in point. A former high ranking Moscow Komsomol official, Khodorkovsky became founder of the Menatep bank, using government connections to amass his vast wealth. The stripping of business assets, insider-dealing, the creation of "daughter firms," organized theft and nepotism has produced a largely criminalized entrepreneurial class.

At the same time as this explosion of corporate crime, there has been a parallel and interlinked explosion of *organized* crime. Indeed, it is sometimes difficult to distinguish between these phenomena. True, large-scale gangsterism was not new in Russia. Its contemporary roots predate the collapse of the Soviet system. They may be found, mostly in "unofficial privatizations" conducted by legalized co-operatives of the perestoika era of the 1980s, but stretch back to the 1970s, when the first clandestine factories were set up in the Soviet Union to produce goods for the black market. However, following the collapse of the Soviet system, in the first years of market "reform" in the early 1990s, organized crime received particular impetus, spurred by new opportunities accompanying the privatization process. Political reformers, led by Yegor Gaidar, as minister of finance, appear to have sanctioned the growth of such criminality as a means of speeding the transformation of the economy toward the market. In so doing, they may well have created a permanent legacy. Currently, one major shareholder in Yukos and former close associate of Khodorkovsky, Leonid Nevzlin, now living in self-imposed exile in Israel and with a personal fortune estimated at $2 billion, faces charges of fraud, tax evasion, and up to five counts of murder.

The physical seizures by rival gangs of factory managers and the untimely (or timely) removal of competitors, were not uncommon ways of settling business differences in the very recent past. Today, even a moderately successful enterprise, in addition to endless bribes to civic officials, has to operate in a business environment where administrative harassment is routine and the rule of law is uncertain. Judicially sanctioned theft in the form of "abusive takeovers" enables outside parties to act as corporate predators and acquire companies by submitting shareholder lists to court officials who, for a suitable price, alter them in the interests of the predator. However, those who took comfort in the notion that "wild capitalism" was simply a passing phase, akin to the growing pains of the new market economy, perhaps need to think again. While the fading trail of bodies left by routine extortion and gangsterism may have given the impression that things were beginning to move on, the public contract slaying outside his central Moscow office, in the summer of 2004, of the Russian editor of the US *Forbes* business magazine, seemingly for overzealous investigative journalism into the activities of the business elite, has provided pause for reconsideration.

While some leading U.S. exponents of free market dogma, like Jeffrey Sacks, appear to have partially recanted, those foreign advisors and their home-grown imitators who propounded the "necessary costs of transition" argument, as a justification for the catastrophic social and economic consequences of "shock therapy," may yet be called to account. Even the basic recipe for renewal, the comprehensive opening up of the economy to foreign investment as the spearhead of market forces, may be less of a panacea than was previously asserted. It is a little known fact that, for example, one of the largest foreign investors in the Russian economy is Cyprus—the reverse flow of those billions pillaged by private individuals in the process of privatization, so-called "return flight capital" movements. Such returning capital amounts to one third of the total FDI in the Russian economy, underscoring the very low level of incoming foreign investment. Currently 83% of investments in the Russian economy are in the form of international loans and trade credits (the fastest growing category). FDI in 2003 accounted for only about 17% of total investment, while portfolio investment (bonds, obligations, bills of exchange and similar monetary instruments, in addition to shares in enterprises) was less than 1%. Excluding oil investments and credit agreements, the volume of direct FDI in Russia (2003) is about $500 million, a trifling sum, even when compared to other transition economies.

The current "buoyancy" in the Russian economy is fueled by oil, while the international oil industry itself is no stranger to murky business environments.

Taking the longer view, Western oil conglomerates know that the eventual prize of access to substantial Russian oil reserves (the world's second largest crude oil exporter after Saudi Arabia), justifies the risks, moral and financial, of doing business in Russia. Even the recent return of BP to the Russian oil industry scene, in co-partnership with the Russian oil giant TNK, (BP having previously had its fingers severely burned in Russian oil ventures) is merely the exception that proves the rule. Talk by BP of improving the governance of Russian business by its new adventure is simply absurd.

While the first three Russian companies, (in mobile phones and the food industry), may have achieved full listing on the New York Stock Exchange, thereby satisfying U.S. accounting standards, informed observers speak optimistically of 50 years before the deeply criminalized character of Russian business undergoes significant change. Ironically, Russian oil companies which had been poised to seek listing, have had their applications delayed by U.S. accounting frauds, underlining neatly the global nature of corporate crime. These ongoing scandals (Enron, WorldCom, Tyco etc.) have resulted in the imposition of arguably more stringent U.S. rules regarding independent directors and stiffer disclosure requirements which Russian oil companies are currently unwilling or unable to meet. In Russia today, the idea of accountability in corporate governance hardly exists. The concept of an independent director with a duty to speak out concerning issues of corporate misdemeanor, is not only laughable, but personally inadvisable. As a result, at the very least, the ongoing dilemma for Western investors in Russia is routine complicity.

In this context, almost absurdly ironic, is the role of William Browder, the grandson of Earl Browder, who led the Communist Party of the United States. Earl Browder sought to dissolve the party in the 1940s and was eventually expelled for his "liquidationism." William Browder takes the legacy of his illustrious grandfather one step further. He is a venture capitalist in Moscow specializing in assisting Western investors, while at the same time promoting good corporate governance in the Russian business world. His supporters in this unlikely mission are probably even fewer than those who twice backed his grandfather's runs for the U.S. presidency. In fact, Browder or his associates are facing at least one lawsuit brought by a Russian company they own shares in. Whistleblowing may be institutionalized and legally supported in the United States and United Kingdom, but in Russia it is a different matter.

All this makes the current, if possibly temporary, "war on the oligarchs" difficult to comprehend. It certainly does not signal a stable business environment for foreign investment. Large-scale Western investments in the Russian economy are likely to remain rare, sectorally specific, as well as regionally skewed. Yet in a sense, all this is almost irrelevant to the prospects for cleaning out Russian business crime. Putin's "amnesty" on previous privatizations conducted under Yeltsin's rule, suggests the results of the privatization grab of the 1990s are unlikely to be reversed, even if there is some symbolic cutting down to size of political rivals from the business world, for electoral or other expedient reasons.

Criminality has comprehensively penetrated Russian business. A few contrite oligarchs may publicly apologize for previous excesses, some may seek sanctuary abroad, while others, like Khodorkovsky, appear to remain defiantly unrepentant. The IMF may threaten, and the EU may huff and puff about the need for "good corporate governance," but Russia today reveals the true criminogenic face of a capitalism which no codes of conduct can alter, and no judiciary can match. This is not a pathological variant of some "normal" state of economic being. It is the face of a perfectly viable economic system that requires neither rule of law, democracy, nor respect for individual rights to survive and prosper. It is an image that the West has created in its own likeness and it is colored, above all, by oil.

Selected Bibliography

Ada, I. "Let My People Go." *Norwegian Petroleum Diary*, no. 2 (2000): 27.

AFL-CIO (American Federation of Labor and Congress of Industrial Organizations). *A Tale of Two Nations: A Statistical Case for Free Collective Bargaining*. Washington, DC: AFL-CIO Department of Organization and Field Services, 1994.

Alberta Economic Development Authority. *Final Report: Joint Review Committee Right-to-Work Study*. November 1995.

Anderson, S., and J. Cavanagh. "Top 200—The Rise of Corporate Global Power." Washington, DC: Institute for Policy Studies, December 4, 2000.

Arab, P. "Sexual Harassment Ruled Workplace Safety Hazard." *Evening Telegram*, August 23, 1998: 9

Baird, M. "Hibernia Worker Still Awaiting Call." *Telegram*, December 6, 2001: A1.

Baird, M. "HMDC Appealing Board Order." *Telegram*, December 21, 2001: A1.

Bamberg, J. H. *British Petroleum and Global Oil, 1950-1975: The Challenge of Nationalism*. In *The History of British Petroleum*, Vol. 3. Cambridge: Cambridge University Press, 2001.

Barron, T. "Hibernia Loses Power." *Evening Telegram*, March 21, 1999: 2.

Beck, M., and C. Woolfson. "The Regulation of Health and Safety in Britain: From Old Labour to New Labour." *Industrial Relations Journal* 31, no. 1 (2000): 35-50.

M. Beck, J. Foster, H. Ryggvik; and C. Woolfson, eds. *Piper Alpha Ten Years After: Safety and Industrial Relations in the British and Norwegian Offshore Oil Industry*. Centre for Technology and Culture, University of Oslo, 1998.

Beeby, D. "Sea King Fleet Grounded." *Evening Telegram*, October 16, 1998: 1.

Beeby, D. "More Chopper Woes." *Evening Telegram*, November 27, 1998: 5.

Beeby, D. "Another Labrador Grounded Because of Engine Trouble." *Evening Telegram*, November 28, 1998: 5.

Bergesen, E. A., and P. Goyer, eds. *Human Rights and the Oil Industry*. Oxford: Intersentia, 2000.

"Piper Alpha 10 Years On." *Blowout: The OILC Magazine*, no. 55 (July/August 1998): 14-19.

"A New Era of Understanding!" *Blowout: The OILC Magazine*, no. 58 (October 1999): 9.

"Sold Down the River!" *Blowout: The OILC Magazine*, no. 61 (July 2000): 4-5.

"Ballots or Buy Out?" *Blowout: The OILC Magazine*, no. 60 (March 2000): 2-3.

"In, Out, In, Out, Shake It All About. . ." *Blowout: The OILC Magazine*, no. 62 (December 2001): 11.

Bonde, Petter Chr. "Risk Analysis in the Norwegian Sector—Views from a Senior Safety Delegate." Paper presented at the OFS/OILC Conference, Offshore Safety in a Cost Conscious Environment from British and Norwegian Perspectives. Proceedings of Conference, November 15-16, 1994, Stavanger, Norway.

Brody, D. *Workers in Industrial America*. New York: Oxford University Press, 1980.

Brown, W., S. Deakin, M. Hudson, and C. Pratten. "The Limits of Statutory Trade Union Recognition." *Industrial Relations Journal* 32, no. 3 (2001): 180-194.

Burgoyne Report Offshore Safety, Cmnd 7866. London: HMSO, 1980.

Cable News Network. "Major Oil Industry Accidents" (2001): www.cnn/com/2001/WORLD/americas /03/20/oil.accidents.

Canada-Newfoundland Atlantic Accord Implementation Act. Ottawa: Queen's Printer, 1986.

Canada, Department of Energy, Mines and Resources. Summary of Action Taken by the Government of Canada in Relation to the Recommendation of the Royal Commission on the Ocean Ranger Marine Disaster, April 1985.

Canada Department of Energy, Mines and Resources. Government of Canada Response to the Recommendations of the Royal Commission on the Ocean Ranger Marine Disaster, April 1986.

Canada, Royal Commission on the Ocean Ranger Marine Disaster (RCORMD). Report One: The Loss of the Semisubmersible Drill Rig Ocean Ranger and its Crew. Report Two: Safety Offshore Eastern Canada. 1984.

Canada-Newfoundland Offshore Petroleum Board (CNOPB). Annual Reports, 1986-2002.

Canadian Association of Petroleum Producers (CAPP). "Guide: Canadian East Coast Offshore Petroleum Industry, Training and Qualification." Calgary, February 2002.

Canadian Press. "Troubled Choppers Fly Again." *Evening Telegram*, January 15, 1999: 5.

Carey, M., and B. Kennedy. "Analysis of Human Failures During Evacuation, Escape and Rescue." Paper presented at the Human Factors in Emergency Response Offshore, 29-30 September 1993, Aberdeen.

Carr, E. *The Bolshevik Revolution 1917-1923*, Vol. 1. New York: Norton, 1950.

Carson, W. G. *The Other Price of Britain's Oil*. Oxford: Martin Robertson, 1982.

Central Intelligence Agency. *World Factbook 2002*. Washington, DC.

CEP (Communications, Energy and Paper Workers Union) "Union to Appeal Court Decision." Media release, July 17, 2000.

Clark, D., K. McCann, K. Morrice, and R. Taylor. "Work and Marriage in the Offshore Oil Industry." *International Journal of Social Economics* 12, no. 2 (1985): 36-47.

Clark, D., and Taylor. R. "Partings and Reunions: Marriage and Offshore in the British North Sea." In *Women, Work and Family in the British, Canadian and Norwegian Offshore Oilfields*, ed. J. Lewis et al., 112-139. London: Macmillan, 1988.

Collinson, D. L. "Shift-ing Lives: Work-home Pressures in the North Sea Oil Industry." *Canadian Review of Sociology and Anthropology* 35 (1998): 301-324.

Cooper, M. C. "Labour Relations Processes on Offshore Oil Production Platforms." Consultant paper prepared for Department of Environment and Labour, April 1997.

Cooper, M. C. Labour Relations Processes on Offshore Oil and Gas Fabrication and Construction Projects, report to the Government of Newfoundland and Labrador, St. John's. 2001.

Colquhoun, W. P., and J. Rutenfranz, eds. *Studies of Shiftwork*. London: Taylor and Francis, 1980.

CRINE Secretariat. *Cost Reduction Initiative for the New Era Report.* St. Paul's Press, November 1993.

Cullen, Hon. Lord. *The Public Inquiry into the Piper Alpha Disaster,* Vols. 1 and 2. London: HMSO, 1990.

Department of Energy, Mines and Resources Canada. Government of Canada Response to the Recommendations of the Royal Commission on the Ocean Ranger Marine Disaster. April 1986.

Department of Energy, Mines and Resources Canada. Summary of Action Taken by the Government of Canada in Relation to the Recommendations of the Royal Commission on the Ocean Ranger Marine Disaster. April 1985.

Drache, D., and M. Gertler. "The World Economy and the Nation-State: the New International Order." In *The Era of Global Competition: State Policy and Market Power,* ed. Drache and Gertler. Montreal: McGill-Queen's University Press, 1991: 3-25.

Drager, K .H., and J. Wiklund. "Advanced Computer Modelling for Solving Practical Problems in EER." Consultant paper, September 1993.

DTI (1998) Fairness at Work, CM, 3968. London: HMSO, 1998.

Dunsterville, L. *The Adventures of Dunsterforce.* London: Edward Arnold, 1920.

Engler, R. *The Politics of Oil: A Study of Private Power and Democratic Directions.* Chicago: University of Chicago Press, 1967.

Flanagan, C. "Terra Nova Engineering Jobs Still Not Relocated to Province." *Evening Telegram,* March 21, 1998: 25.

Flanagan, C. "Seismic Worker Spat Spills." *Evening Telegram,* June 6, 1998: 22.

Flanagan, C. "Ottawa Studying Safety Rules." *Evening Telegram,* October 7, 1998: 1.

Flanagan, C. "Production Halted After Alarm Sounds." *Evening Telegram,* March 3, 1999: 3.

Foster, J., and C. Woolfson, eds. *Workforce Involvement and Health and Safety Offshore: Power, Language and Information Technology.* Proceedings of International Conference. Glasgow: STUC, 1993.

Frynas, J. G. "Corporate and State Responses to Anti-oil Protests in the Niger Delta." *African Affairs* 100, no. 398 (January 2001): 27-54.

Gall, G., and S. McKay. "Facing 'Fairness at Work': Union Perception of Employer Opposition and Response to Union Recognition." *Industrial Relations Journal* 32, no. 2 (2001): 94-113.

Glasbeek, H. "The Corporate Social Responsibility Movement: The Latest in Maginot Lines to Save Capitalism." *Dalhousie Law Journal* 11(1988): 363-402.

Governments of Canada, Newfoundland and Labrador, and Nova Scotia. Proposed Amendments to the Accord Acts, to Incorporate an Offshore Occupational Health and Safety Regime. St. John's, November 1, 2002.

Grzetic, B., S. Shrimpton, and S. Skipton, S. WITT, *Women, Employment Equity and the Hibernia Construction Project: A Study of Women's Experiences on the Hibernia Construction Project, Mosquito Cove, Newfoundland.* St. John's, Report, June 1996.

Gunderson, M., and A. Ponak. *Union-Management Relations in Canada,* 3d ed. Don Mills: Addison-Wesley, 1995.

Harvie, C. *Fool's Gold: The Story of North Sea Oil.* London: Penguin, 1994.

Henanger, K. "Time and Toil Are Taking Their Toll." *Norwegian Petroleum Directorate,* no. 2 (2000): 18.

Hilliard, W. "Lawyers Battle City's Right to Fight Petroleum Board." *Evening Telegram*, September 1, 1998.

Hilliard, W. "Unionization Fails on Hibernia Platform." *Telegram*, March 31, 2001: 1.

HSC (Health and Safety Commission). The Role and Status of Approved Codes of Practice, HSC CD 85. London: HMSO, 1995.

HSE (Health and Safety Executive). Draft Offshore Installation (Safety Case) Regulations 199. London: HMSO, 1992.

HSE (Health and Safety Executive). A Guide to the Offshore Installations (Safety Case) Regulations 1992: Guidance on Regulations L30. London: HMSO, 1992.

HSE (Health and Safety Executive). Draft Offshore Installations (Prevention of Fire and Explosion, and Emergency Response) Regulations 199 and Approved Code of Practice. Consultative Document, London: HSE, 1993.

HSE (Health and Safety Executive). Prevention of Fire and Explosion, and Emergency Response on Offshore Installations." Offshore Installations (Prevention of Fire and Explosion, and Emergency Response) Regulations 1995 and Appended Code of Practice. HMSO, London, 1995.

HSE (Health and Safety Executive). An Interim Evaluation of the Offshore Installation (Safety Case) Regulations 1992. London: HMSO, 1995.

Hughes, H. HSE (Health and Safety Executive). Health and Safety in the Offshore Oil and Gas Industries, Proceedings of Conference, Aberdeen, April 6-7, 1992. Paper presented by H. Hughes "Towards a Goal-Setting Regime—Plans and Issues—the Operators' View."

Husky Energy. 2002: www.huskywhiterose.com.

International Labour Office—Occupational Safety and Health Branch. "Workers in Remote Areas: The Petroleum, Mining and Forestry Industries." Working Paper, 1995.

Kaufman, B.E., and M. Kleiner, eds. *Employee Representation: Alternatives and Future Directions*. Madison, WI: Industrial Relations Research Organization, 1993.

Kealey, G., and G. Long. *Labour and Hibernia: Conflict Resolution at Bull Arm, 1990-1992*. St. John's: ISER, 1993.

Kealey, G., and M. McBride. "Labour Relations at the Hibernia Project, 1990-1997." Draft Report, forthcoming.

Kerr, C. "The Impacts of Unions on the Level of Wages." In *Wages, Prices, Profits and Productivity*, ed. Charles A. Myers. New York: American Assembly, Columbia University, 1959.

Klein, B. 1984. "Contract Costs and Administered Prices: An Economic Theory of Rigid Wages." *American Economic Review* 74 (1984): 332.

Kochan, T., H. Katz, and R. McKersie. *The Transformation of American Industrial Relations*. New York: Basic Books, 1986.

Landolt, J. P., and C. Monaco. "Seasickness in Totally-Enclosed Motor-Propelled Survival Craft: Remedial Measures." *Aviation, Space and Environmental Medicine* (March 1992): 219-225.

LeBlanc, R. "A Tragedy in the Making?" *Express*, July 29, 1998: 17.

Lerner, S. W. *Breakaway Unions and the Small Trade Union*. London: Allen and Unwin, 1961.

MacDonald, M. "Hibernia First Unionized Offshore Oil Workers in North America." *Western Star*, October 11, 2001: 1.

McLoughlin, I., and S. Gourlay. *Enterprise Without Unions: Industrial Relations in the Non-Union Firm*. Buckingham: Open University Press, 1994.

McNeill, J. *Something New Under the Sun: An Environmental History of the Twentieth Century*. London: Penguin, 2000.

Mearns, K., and Flin, R. "Decision Making in Emergencies: A Psychological Analysis." Paper presented at the Human Factors in Emergency Response Offshore Conference, European Seminar, 1993.

Mitchell, B. R. *British Historical Statistics*. Cambridge: Cambridge University Press, 1962.

Monk, T. *Making Shiftwork Tolerable*. London: Taylor and Francis, 1992.

Moore, R., and P. Wyebrow, P. *Women in the North Sea Oil Industry*. Manchester: Equal Opportunities Commission, 1984.

Muttitt, G., and J. Marriott. *Some Common Concerns: Imagining BP's Azerbaijan-Georgia-Turkey Pipelines System*. London: PLATFORM, the Corner House, Friends of the Earth International, Campagna per la Riforma della Banca Mondiale, CEE Bankwatch Network & Kurdish Human Rights Project, 2002.

National Research Council, Canada. "The Offshore Escape, Evacuation and Rescue Database and Web Site: Standards Information Workshop." Escape, Evacuation and Rescue, www.nrc.ca/imd/eer/home_e.html, October 5, 2002.

Newfoundland, Canada-Newfoundland Atlantic Accord Implementation Newfoundland Act. St. John's, 1986.

Newfoundland and Labrador, Department of Labour. Submission on the Labour Relations Framework for Production at the Hibernia Offshore Oilfield. St. John's, 1997.

Nichols, T. *The Sociology of Industrial Injury*. London: Mansell, 1997.

Nishman, R. F. "Through the Portlights of the Ocean Ranger: Federalism, Energy and the American Development of the Canadian Eastern Offshore, 1955-1985." Masters thesis, Queen's University, 1991.

Norris, G. S. "The Employment Relations Act 1999 and Collective Labour Standards." *International Journal of Comparative Labour Law and Industrial Relations* 17, no. 1 (2001): 63-77.

Novitz. T. "International Promises and Domestic Pragmatism: To What Extent Will the Employment Relations Act 1999 Implement International Labour Standards Relating to Freedom of Association?" *Modern Law Review* 63, no. 3 (May 2000): 379-393.

OCA (Offshore Contractors Association). Partnership Agreement Between the Offshore Contractors' Association and the AEEU and GMB. 2000.

"Ocean Ranger Tragedy Raised Safety Issues." *Telegram*, February 16, 2002: B1.

OCIMF (Oil Companies International Marine Forum). *Results of a Survey into Lifeboat Safety*. London, July 1994

Offshore Design Associates Limited. Comparative Physical Model Study of Offshore Evacuation Systems. St. John's, March 1997.

OFS/OILC. *Offshore Safety in a Cost Conscious Environment from British and Norwegian Perspectives*. Proceedings of Conference, Stavanger, November 15-16, 1994.

OILC (Offshore Industry Liaison Committee). *Striking Out: New Directions for Offshore Workers and Their Unions*. Aberdeen: OILC, 1991.

OILC (Offshore Industry Liaison Committee). *OILC Submission to the European Commission Review Group for the Working Hours Directive*. Aberdeen: OILC, 1995.

Ontario Advisory Council on Occupational Health and Safety. *An Evaluation of Joint Health and Safety Committees in Ontario.* 1986.

Petrel Ocean Safety. *Escape and Evaluation Systems: Risk and Reliability.* London, March 1996.

Pike, W. J. "The Oil Price Crisis and Its Impact on Scotland's North Sea Development." *Scottish Economic and Social History* (1993): 13.

Porter, S. "Risky Business: Offshore Safety Standards Have Improved Since the Ocean Ranger Went Down, but There's Still room to Get Better." *Gulf News* 29, no. 6, February 11, 2001.

Punchard, E. *Piper Alpha: A Survivor's Story.* London: W.H. Allen, 1989.

Pyman, M. A. F., and P. R. Lyon. (1985) "Casualty Rates in Abandoning Ships at Sea." In The Royal Institution of Naval Architects, 329-332.

Reilly, B.; P. Paci; and P. Holl "Unions, Safety Committees and Workplace Injuries." *British Journal of Industrial Relations* 33, no. 2 (1995): 275-289.

Robens, Hon. Lord. *Safety and Health at Work, Report of the Committee 1970-72, Cmnd 5034.* London: HMSO, 1972.

Ross, M. *Extractive Sectors and the Poor.* Boston: Oxfam America, 2001.

Rowell, A. *The Exxon Valdez: A Case of Corporate Virtual Reality.* Amsterdam:. Greenpeace International, 1994.

Ryggvik, H. "Why Norway Was Different." In *Piper Alpha Ten Years After: Safety and Industrial Relations in the British and Norwegian Offshore Oil Industry*, ed. M. Beck; J. Foster; H. Ryggvik; and C. Woolfson, 57–105. Centre for Technology and Culture, University of Oslo, 1998.

Scott, J. C. *Domination and the Arts of Resistance: Hidden Transcripts.* New Haven and London: Yale University Press, 1990.

Shell International Petroleum Company. "Profits and Principles—Does There Have to Be a Choice?" *Shell Report.* London: Shell International, 1998.

Shell International Petroleum Company. *Shell Report*, 2002: www.shell.com.

Slaven, G., and R. Flin. "Selecting Managers for a Hazardous Environment: Offshore Petroleum Installations." *Personnel Review* 23, no. 5 (1994): 4-14.

Smith, J. "Hibernia Safety Measures Not up to North Sea Standards." *Evening Telegram*, June 15, 1997: 4.

Smith, P., and G. Morton. "New Labour's Reform of Britain's Employment Law: The Devil Is Not Only in the Detail But in the Values and Policy Too." *British Journal of Industrial Relations* 39, no. 1 (2001): 119-138.

Smith, S. *Allah's Mountains: Politics and War in the Russian Caucasus.* London and New York: IB Tauris, 1998.

Spaven, M., and C. Wright. "The Effectiveness of Offshore Safety Representatives and Safety Committees: A Response to Vulliamy." In STUC Proceedings of International Conference, Glasgow, 1993.

Spaven, M., H. Ras, A. Morrison, and C. Wright. *The Effectiveness of Offshore Safety Representatives and Safety Committees: A Report to the Health and Safety Executive.* Vol. 1: *Survey, Analysis, Conclusions and Recommendations.* Aberdeen: Offshore Study Group, 1993.

Speight, R. "Lifeboat Release Mechanisms—Part I." *Seaways* (August 1995): 12-14.

Speight, R. "Lifeboat Release Mechanisms—Part II." *Seaways* (September 1995): 16-21.

Speight, R. "Lifeboat Release Mechanisms—Part III." *Seaways* (October 1995): 7.

Spiller, P.T. "Politicians, Interest Groups and Regulators: A Multiple-Principals Agency Theory, or 'Let Them Be Bribed.'" *Law and Economics* 33 (1990): 65-101.

Stephens, P., and D. Lucas. "Modelling the Human Response in Emergency Escape." Consultant paper, September 1993.

Stones, I. *Rotational Shiftwork: A Summary of the Adverse Effects and Improvement Strategies*. Hamilton, ON: Canadian Centre for Occupational Health and Safety, 1987.

Sutherland, V.J., and C. Cooper. *Man and Accidents Offshore*. London: Eastern Press, 1986.

Terra Nova Alliance. Terra Nova Overview, 2000: www.terranovaproject.com/whatis/whais.htm.

Thom, A. "Managing Labour Under Extreme Risk: Collective Bargaining in the North Sea Oil Industry." Ph.D. dissertation, RGIT, Aberdeen, 1989.

Tombs, S. (1991) "Piper Alpha and the Cullen Inquiry—Beyond 'Distorted Communication?'" In *Offshore Safety and Reliability*, ed. R. F. Cox and M. H. Walter, 28-41. London and New York: Elsevier, 1991.

Tombs, D., and D. Whyte. "Capital Fights Back: Risk, Regulation and Profit in the UK Offshore Oil Industry." *Studies in Political Economy*, no. 57 (Autumn 1998): 73-101.

TUC (Trades Union Congress). *The Future of Workplace Safety Representatives: A TUC Health and Safety Report*. London: Congress House, 1995.

Tuohy, C., and M. Simard. *The Impact of Joint Health and Safety Committees in Ontario and Quebec*. Canadian Association for Administrators of Labour Law, 1993.

UKOOA (United Kingdom Offshore Operators Association). "UK Oil and Gas Industry Publishes First Report on Progress Towards Sustainability." News release, July 23, 2002. London: UKOOA

Veitch, B. "Newfoundland Offshore Regulatory Regime: Marine Evacuation Systems." Paper presented at the Institute for Marine Dynamics, National Research Council Canada, December 1998.

Walker, J. *Human Aspects of Shiftwork*. London: Institute of Personnel Management, 1978.

Waring, A. E. "Power and Culture—Their Implications for Safety Cases and EER." Paper presented at the Human Factors in Emergency Response Offshore Conference, European Seminar, 1993.

Westcott, C. "Oil Unions Look for Peace: Council Endorses Findings of Morgan Cooper Report." *Express*, March 21-27, 2001: 29.

Wheeler, D., H. Fabig, and R. Boele. "Paradoxes and Dilemmas for Stakeholder Responsive Firms in the Extractive Sector: Lessons from the Case of Shell and the Ogoni." *Journal of Business Ethics* 39 (September 3, 2002): 297-318.

Wildavsky, A. *Speaking Truth to Power: The Art and Craft of Policy Analysis*. Boston: Little, Brown, 1979.

Wood, S., and J. Godard. "The Statutory Recognition Procedure in the Employment Relations Bill: A Comparative Analysis." *British Journal of Industrial Relations* 37, no. 2 (June 1999): 203-229.

Wood, S., S. Moore, and P. Willman. "Third Time Lucky of Statutory Union Recognition in the UK?" *Industrial Relations Journal* 33, no. 3 (2002): 215-233.

Woolfson, C., and M. Beck. "Deregulation: The Contemporary Politics of 'Health and Safety.'" In *The Future of Labour Law*, ed. A . McColgan . London: Mansell, 1995:171-208.

Woolfson, C., M. Beck, and J. Foster. "Safety and Industrial Relations after Piper Alpha." In *Piper Alpha Ten Years After: Safety and Industrial Relations in the British and Norwegian Offshore Oil Industry*, ed. M. Beck; J. Foster; H. Ryggvik; and C. Woolfson, 1-56. Centre for Technology and Culture, University of Oslo, 1998.

Woolfson, C., J. Foster, and M. Beck. *Paying for the Piper: Capital and Labour in Britain's Offshore Oil Industry*. London and New York: Mansell, 1997.

World Bank. *Workers in an Integrating World. World Development Report*. Oxford: Oxford University Press, 1995.

The Westray Story: A Predictable Path to Disaster. Report of the Westray Mine Public Inquiry. Justice K. Peter Richard, Commissioner. Volumes 1 and 2, November 1997.

Yergin, D. *The Prize*. New York: Simon and Schuster, 1991.

About the Editors

Charles Woolfson is Marie Curie Chair, University of Latvia and Reader in Industrial Relations at the University of Glasgow, where he received his doctoral degree. His main areas of research have been in labor disputes, socio-legal studies of the regulation of health and safety, corporate social responsibility, and the offshore oil industry. He is a Member of the Glasgow Baltic Studies Unit. He has also held a Marie Curie Research Fellowship in Lithuania and a Visiting Fellowship at the Institute for Advanced Studies in the Humanities at the University of Edinburgh.

Matthias Beck is Research Professor of Risk Management at Glasgow Caledonian University and Director of the Cullen Centre for Risk and Governance (CRAG). He formerly lectured in economics at the St. Andrews and Glasgow Universities. In addition to economics, his main teaching has been in the field of research methods. Professor Beck has a doctorate from MIT and has conducted research in labor market studies, corporate governance, and quantitative sociology. He has co-authored numerous articles with Charles Woolfson on socio-legal and regulatory issues, and recently has published on the topics of financial governance and banking failures.

Contributors

JOHN FOSTER is Professor Emeritus, University of Paisley, Scotland, and was co-author with Charles Woolfson and Matthias Beck of the volume *Paying for the Piper* (Mansell: London, 1996). Foster is a leading activist and historian who has written extensively on working-class movements of the 19th and 20th centuries.

MICHAEL GILLARD is one of the U.K.'s leading investigative reporters who, together with his colleagues Melissa Jones and Andrew Rowell, has written on human rights abuses connected to the international oil industry for *The Guardian* newspaper, as well as provided TV documentary evidence of oil company links to paramilitary activity in Columbia.

SUSAN HART is an Associate Professor in Industrial Relations at Memorial University in St. John's, Newfoundland and Labrador, Canada. She teaches courses in industrial relations and qualitative research methodology. Her doctoral degree is from the University of Warwick, England, and her main areas of research have been comparative studies of regulatory regimes and worker involvement in safety and health in the offshore oil industry, and equality bargaining. She is currently working on two community-university research projects, o offshore employment and evaluation of safety management systems in the oil refining and mining industries.

JAMES MARRIOTT has been a core member of PLATFORM since its establishment. He is also a Trustee of renewable energy charity RENUE. In 1997 he was awarded the Environment Foundation Travelling Fellowship for his performance "Carbon Generations." He studied history at Cambridge University, and sculpture at Chelsea College of Art.

GREG MUTTITT is a researcher and analyst, specializing in the oil and gas industry. He has worked at PLATFORM since 2001, prior to which he was a founder and core member of the research group Corporate Watch. He has also worked for Greenpeace. He studied physics and philosophy at Oxford University.

Index